NO NEWS IS BAD NEWS

We work with leading authors to develop the
strongest educational materials in media studies,
bringing cutting-edge thinking and best learning
practice to a global market.

Under a range of well-known imprints, including
Longman, we craft high quality
print and electronic publications which help
readers to understand and apply their content,
whether studying or at work.

To find out more about the complete range of our
publishing please visit us on the World Wide Web at:
www.pearsoneduc.com

NO NEWS IS BAD NEWS:

Radio, Television and the Public

edited by

Michael Bromley

An imprint of **Pearson Education**

Harlow, England · London · New York · Reading, Massachusetts · San Francisco
Toronto · Don Mills, Ontario · Sydney · Tokyo · Singapore · Hong Kong · Seoul
Taipei · Cape Town · Madrid · Mexico City · Amsterdam · Munich · Paris · Milan

070.19 BRO

Pearson Education Limited
Edinburgh Gate
Harlow
Essex CM20 2JE
England

and Associated Companies throughout the world

Visit us on the World Wide Web at:
http://www.pearsoneduc.com

First published 2001

ISBN 0 582 41833 X

British Library Cataloguing-in-Publication Data
A catalogue record for this book is available from the British Library

Library of Congress Cataloging-in-Publication Data
No news is bad news: radio, television, and the public / edited by Michael
  Bromley.
       p.   cm.
    Includes bibliographical references and index.
    ISBN 0–582–41833–X (alk. paper)
    1. Broadcast journalism.   2. Television programs, Public service.
  3. Radio programs, Public service.   I. Bromley, Michael, 1947–
  PN4784.B75   N625   2001
  070.1'9—dc21   00–067390

10 9 8 7 6 5 4 3 2 1
05 04 03 02 01

Typeset by 35 in 10/11 pt Palatino
Printed and bound in Malaysia

Contents

Contributors

Diana Agosta is completing her PhD in Anthropology at the Graduate Center of the City University of New York; her dissertation explores how the post-war participatory community radios of El Salvador are expanding civil society and public space for the formerly marginalized majorities.

Warren Bareiss teaches mass communication courses at South Dakota State University, USA. He earned his doctorate in mass communication at Indiana University in 1996, and his dissertation was a participant observation study of a public/university radio station in New Mexico. Since earning his doctorate, Warren has published articles about public radio and telemedicine. As a researcher, Warren approaches communication from a cultural perspective, searching for patterns in the ways that people use communication technologies to inform their sense of personal and communal identity.

Michael Bromley (editor) is joint deputy director of the Tom Hopkinson Centre for Media Research at Cardiff University, Wales and a founder and co-editor of the journal *Journalism: Theory, Practice and Criticism*. He has published widely on journalism and the media, and with Hugh Stephenson edited *Sex, Lies and Democracy: The Press and the Public* (Longman 1998). He is a former journalist, and in 2000–1 was the Howard R. Marsh Visiting Professor of Journalism at the University of Michigan, Ann Arbor.

Simon Cottle is currently Professor of Media Communication at Bath Spa University College, England. He is the author of *TV News, Urban Conflict and the Inner City* (Leicester University Press 1993), *Ethnic Minorities and Television: Producers' Persepctives* (Avebury 1997) and he co-authored with Anders Hansen, Ralph Negrine and Chris Newbold, *Mass Communication Research Methods* (Macmillan 1998). Recently he has edited *Ethnic Minorities and the Media: Changing Cultural Boundaries* (Open University Press 2000) and is working on various research projects including media reporting of the racist killing of Stephen

Lawrence. Simon's research interests are generally concerned with media production, the sociology of news and the mediation of social conflicts.

Anne Dunn is Lecturer in Journalism at the School of Media and Communication at the University of Western Sydney, Australia. She was previously Senior Lecturer in Broadcasting at Charles Sturt University. She has worked in the print, television and radio media since 1972. Prior to joining CSU, she was Executive Producer of Radio Open Learning for the Australian Broadcasting Corporation (ABC). Altogether, she spent 13 years with ABC Radio and Television, in management, in policy and in broadcasting, including as a presenter, newsreader, journalist and producer. She is currently completing a PhD on ABC Radio news policies and practice.

Patricia Holland is a writer and researcher. She is the author of *What Is a Child?* (Virago 1992) and *The Television Handbook*, 2nd edn (Routledge 2000). She has contributed to many books on television, photography and popular media, and is currently working on the history of the current affairs programme *This Week* (1956–92) in association with Bournemouth University, England.

Brian McNair is Reader in Media Studies at the University of Stirling, and a member of the Stirling Media Research Institute. He is the author of several books and articles on journalism and public relations, including *Journalism and Democracy* (Routledge 2000), *News and Journalism in the UK*, 3rd edn (Routledge 1999), and *An Introduction to Political Communication*, 2nd edn (Routledge 1999).

Carol Nahra is an American freelance journalist based in London. She writes about documentaries for a number of publications, including *Dox* and *International Documentary*.

Tom O'Malley writes on media history and policy. His publications include *Closedown? The BBC and Government Broadcasting Policy 1979–92* (Pluto 1994); with M. Bromley (eds), *A Journalism Reader* (Routledge 1997) and, with Clive Soley, *Regulating the Press* (Pluto 2000). He is an editor of the journal, *Media History*, and is Principal Lecturer in Media Studies at the University of Glamorgan, Wales.

Heather Purdey is Director of the MA in International Journalism at City University, London. She has worked for more than 20 years as a journalist, mainly in local radio, and was director of training for GWR, one of the largest radio groups in Britain. In 1992 she founded the first broadcast journalism degree course in the UK.

Jo Tacchi is a Research Fellow in the Tom Hopkinson Centre for Media Research, Cardiff University, Wales. Her recent publications include 'Gender, fantasy and radio consumption: an ethnographic case study' in *On a Woman's Wavelength* (Routledge 1999) and 'The need for theory in the digital age' in *International Journal of Cultural Studies*.

Howard Tumber is Professor of Sociology and Dean of the School of Social and Human Sciences at City University, London. He is the editor of *News: A Reader* (Oxford University Press 1999) and *Media Power Professionals and Policies* (Routledge 2000), joint author of *Journalists at War* (Sage 1988) and *Reporting Crime* (Oxford University Press 1994) and author of *Television and the Riots* (1982). He is the joint founder and co-editor of the new journal *Journalism: Theory, Practice and Criticism.*

Graeme Turner is Professor of Cultural Studies and Director of the Centre for Critical and Cultural Studies at the University of Queensland, Brisbane, Australia. His most recent book (with Frances Bonner and P. David Marshall) is *Fame Games: The Production of Celebrity in Australia* (Cambridge University Press 2000).

Granville Williams teaches journalism and media policy at the University of Huddersfield, England. He edits *Free Press*, the bulletin of the Campaign for Press and Broadcasting Freedom, and is the author of *Britain's Media: How They Are Related* (1998).

Kevin Williams is Senior Lecturer in the School of Journalism, Media and Cultural Studies at Cardiff University, Wales. His most recent publication was *Get Me a Murder a Day! A History of Mass Communication in Britain* (Edward Arnold 1998).

Acknowledgements

Like any such project, this volume went through a lengthy period of gestation during which it enjoyed the support of many people. Although the collection had been planned beforehand, the occasion of the conference *Radiocracy* at Cardiff University in November 1999 was a fortuitous coincidence: at least six chapters published here owe something to this event. More than this, the conference provided an opportunity (alas still rare, at least in the United Kingdom) to explore and debate that area of broadcasting which is too often consigned to a position of assumed inferiority beside television. Academics and researchers in the broad communications field have been no less guilty of such discrimination, and the extent to which the *Radiocracy* experience contributed to ensuring that this volume more satisfactorily recognized radio in its definition of 'broadcasting' is tangible.

The *Radiocracy* conference was held under the auspices of the Tom Hopkinson Centre for Media Research (THC) at Cardiff University. The Centre, too, was supportive of this project, both by providing a continuing forum for research and debate, and through contributions by a number of its members to the collection. For most of the time that this volume was in preparation, John Hartley was the director of THC, but my personal indebtedness to him extends far beyond any institutional or formal relationship: specifically, in the current context, I am grateful to him for many continuing discussions around broadcasting, journalism and 'the popular'.

Bringing together an existing idea for a book with some of the relevant work associated with *Radiocracy* would not have been as possible without a close working relationship with my fellow deputy director of THC, Amanda Hopkinson, and Jo Tacchi (who is also a contributor to this volume), who were responsible for the organizational aspects of the conference, including the co-ordination of subsequent publishing ventures.

Under its current director, Terry Threadgold, the Centre continued to provide a supportive 'home' for this project. In addition, the Wales Media Forum, established by Ian Hargreaves, offered many opportunities to engage productively (and chiefly without the ritual antagonism which usually characterizes such meetings) with media practitioners, managers and policy makers, particularly in television.

I am also grateful to Hugh Stephenson, who as co-editor of *Sex, Lies and Democracy: The Press and the Public*, a volume to which this one is a kind of companion, helped develop the approach to bringing together practice and theory in the study of the contemporary 'press' (that is, those parts of the media in which journalism is the key aspect) which is continued with here.

As editor, I am acutely aware of how much I owe the contributors to this book. Each has been generous with their time, ideas and patience. All have enhanced my understandings of broadcasting and of communications and media processes. Most particularly, Tom O'Malley, Heather Purdey, Howard Tumber and Kevin Williams are colleagues, collaborators and friends, whose personal and intellectual support is not bounded by the extent of a single project, or the covers of a single book. Where appropriate, each contributor has acknowledged in their individual chapter any specific indebtedness they owe. All acknowledgements come with the usual rider that, as authors, we are ultimately responsible ourselves for what appears in print, and any errors of either commission or omission are not to be attributed to others.

Every one of us (but especially me as editor) is indebted to the Higher Education Division of Pearson Education in the UK, where the originally vague idea of publishing a successor volume to *Sex, Lies and Democracy* was actively pursued by Jane Powell, and subsequently taken on by Matthew Smith. Although undoubtedly many other people also contributed to this process, Paula Parish especially was a patient and painstaking editor.

Finally, Karen Hasin-Bromley rendered vital emergency aid when the task of managing the text electronically seemed likely to fall victim to computer viruses, corrupted disks and irrecoverable data; but that is by far the smaller part of the debt I owe her. Whatever boon to academic publishing digitalization may be, critical friendship remains immeasurably more valuable.

Michael Bromley
Ann Arbor, Michigan
November 2000

Publisher's acknowledgements

We are grateful to the following for permission to reproduce copyright material:

Independent Television News Limited for transcripted material from Channel 4 News Broadcast 1.12.99 and ITN News Broadcast 30.11.99 © Independent Television News Limited 1999, all rights reserved. These extracts are reproduced by kind permission of ITN, but their inclusion does not constitute or imply an endorsement by ITN of the views expressed by the author; Mirror Syndication International for the headline '. . . and Finally' from THE MIRROR 17.11.99; Telegraph Newspapers for the headline 'Students "misled" over jobs in the industry' in THE SUNDAY TELEGRAPH 4.2.96 © Telegraph Group Ltd 1996 and The Times Educational Supplement for an extract from the article 'Lured by media hype' in TIMES EDUCATIONAL SUPPLEMENT 2.2.00 © Times Supplements Limited.

Whilst every effort has been made to trace the owners of copyright material, in a few cases this has proved impossible and we take this opportunity to offer our apologies to any copyright holders whose rights we have unwittingly infringed.

Introduction

Michael Bromley

Much of the commonplace debate about broadcasting concerns ways, both broadly and narrowly conceived and implemented, of managing a complex set of inter-relationships and a highly nuanced interconnectedness between what is in and on television and radio, and how choices are made and by whom along the production–reception continuum. These cover a well-known range of options, from regulatory legal frameworks and more or less direct political control, through organizational and 'efficiency' imperatives, to the mobilization of professional criteria and public support and activism. In most cases, at the turn of the century, broadcasting is ordinarily perceived (generally far more than the press is) as a crucial articulator of democracy (however it is idealized and practised within both formal and informal political, social, economic and cultural contexts) and 'the popular' (in whatever ways it is conceptualized and expressed) to the extent that it is widely understood to be a precondition of 'popular democracy' as illustrated in Central and Eastern Europe in the late 1980s. Such thinking has given rise to beliefs in, on the one hand, the transformative necessity of broadcast conglomerates and programming whose reach and remit are global and whose flows are predominantly from North to South; and, on the other hand, the recuperative properties of community and individuated media in addressing diversity, social exclusion and the Fourth World everywhere (Buckley 1999).

This tenor of debate has become familiar in recent years in association with the processes of digitalization, and in particular the increasing universality of the Internet. It is difficult to argue, however, that the issues have arisen solely in these circumstances. The search for mechanisms for attaining normative conditions of the media, for managing an equilibrium between and among attributes such as 'popularity', 'independence', 'service' and 'responsibility', and a corresponding anxiety about them, long predates cyberspace. What has undoubtedly changed, and continues to alter, is the understood context of public–private divisions which stands at the centre of these considerations, and the implications this has for relationships of power. Is this – or was it ever – a dichotomous condition? The private, it is confidently asserted, *is* public (see Lumby 1999). The condition of Tony Blair's hair and the sexual practices of Bill Clinton have public meanings which transcend the reflex orthodoxies of the Fourth Estate (McNair 1999: 52; Williams and Della Carpini 2000). Where then do we locate the 'freedom' which is claimed by the media?

This kind of thinking would seem to suppose that the need to revisit concepts such as public service broadcasting is founded primarily in neither technological development, nor a changing broadcasting environment, however rapidly change may be occurring (Independent Television Commission 2000a: 1), but in more significant cultural and economic formations which themselves lead to, rather than are consequences of, these shifts. When the digital 'revolution' is hijacked from one perspective, plurality, diversity, public interest, social cohesion, 'vigorous democracy' and a civilizing mission may be reduced to mere brand values (Birt 1999).

Fundamental changes can be traced perhaps less in what constitutes the 'popular' than in the politics of the everyday – the supposed expression of 'market power' (see Snoddy 2000). When 'the market' provides, ideals such as public service broadcasting appear to be subverted (Independent Television Commission 2000b, 2000c); any constructed consensus – for example, over 'standards' – seems to fall apart (Barnett and Seymour 2000); a corporate moral economy superimposes itself, and projects once deemed essential are abandoned. In the United Kingdom, the 1997 Labour government, formed by a party founded in collectivism, champions media agglomeration, directly threatening the regional distinctiveness which has characterized the Independent Television Channel 3 service for 45 years and drawing broadcasting organisationally closer to the press (Independent Television Commission 2000d), while community broadcasting, a 'big idea' of the 1980s, receives virtually no support (Henwood 1994). As Granville Williams points out, this is in marked contrast to the position adopted by Labour as recently as 1992.

For at least a decade, these tendencies have been typed by many in terms of the dumbing-down and tabloidization of broadcasting (see Bromley 1998: 28–9). Such charges have a particular relevance to factual programming, and especially news, current affairs and news documentaries. This is not an uncontested view, of course. It is argued that, in many instances, broadcasting has not demonstrably abandoned its commitment to 'serious' content; that, contrarily, it has striven to make such topics more accessible to wider publics, and, in any event, those wider publics have interests which range beyond the scope of narrow agendas formed without reference to them half a century or more ago (Barnett and Seymour 2000; Hartley 1996; McNair 1999). The 'imagined audience', Patricia Holland argues, is now more subtley variegated. As a result, factual programming may be more 'messy' but as such it is also more authentic. The news, then, is less aggregrates of content arrived at professionally by its producers than it is a distinctive genre made as much by its reception. In one sense, 'the news' should be seen as a plural noun (as it is in many languages) – literally 'stories'; in another, it is the singular institution The News, in which individual programmes such as *The Nightly News* and *News at Ten* assume their place.

For most of the past 20 years the dominant ideological project has sought to establish the popularity of factual programming through a limited number of measures aggregated into the notions of 'competition' and 'choice'. Whatever the reliability of the method, its adoption, as Tom O'Malley makes clear, is constitutive of political decisions to (re)make policy. Competition as it affects broadcast news, current affairs and documentary has to be seen in the context of world trade agreements which promote ideas of abundance and consumerism, packaged to offer the prospects of a seemingly endless 'boom' (Pandya 1999). The chapters in this collection all testify in one way or another to this shared experience. They also indicate why factual programming in radio and television has a specific importance not borne by, say, the manufacture of chromed steel or the cultivation of bananas. It is where vast numbers of people most transparently and, therefore, consciously construct their key formal narratives. As radio and television have become more popular in one way (more sets bought and switched on for longer, and to the exclusion of different media), it is hardly surprising that they have become more popular in other ways, too. As their presence has been more and more played to, 'the people', Anne Dunn points out, feel emboldened to demand of broadcasting 'What have you done for us lately?'.

What also emerges from the contributions which follow is that broadcasting has so far demonstrated little of substance on which it has based its responses. For the most part, it has resorted to the knee-jerk. The changes in news and current affairs in Australia, described by Graeme Turner, represent what has become a standard pattern almost everywhere, and reflect a circumscribed interpretation of 'the popular'. Yet there appears to be little awareness in broadcasting of the paradox of resorting to greater standardization as a recognition of heterogeneity. It is no wonder, then, that the formulaic output of radio and television in some instances is regarded as less rather than more accessible and relevant: this may be as true in Wales as it is in El Salvador.

Notwithstanding the coincidence on a global scale of failures of imagination and concentrations of ownership, plus the evidence presented daily in programme schedules, there is still as yet considerable scope for the spirited domestication of broadcasting. Even within Western Europe, where liberalization and de-regulation have powerful patrons and one intergovernmental organization, the European Union, has expanding influence, Kevin Williams shows there is no real overarching uniformity. Broadcasting may flourish at the local, even community, level; may embrace participation, openness and interactivity, and help sustain a civil society founded in active critical citizenship. For most of the twentieth century this ideal was tied closely to the notion of public service broadcasting, exemplified, although by no means uniquely, by the BBC. As indicated already, much scholarly debate has been focused on the degree to which public service broadcasting has been instrumental in the formation of a Habermasian public sphere and is essential in this respect. Broadly speaking, there are three views: first, the pessimists conclude that the libertarian assault has fatally damaged the public service model and thereby diminished civil society; alternatively, optimists believe public service broadcasting has proved to be quite resilient and will continue to co-exist with more commercialized radio and television; and, finally, a group feels that the public service idea was itself flawed and that its demise, or at least diminution, actually contributes to the expansion of truly 'popular democracy'. All these perspectives are recognized in this volume.

It is indisputable, given the nature of journalism as an occupation, that 'intensifying commercial pressures', to use Carol Nahra's phrase, shape the journalism broadcast by radio and television. As the case of *News at Ten* examined by Howard Tumber demonstrates, this may be evident not only in content but also through styles of presentation, scheduling decisions, and statements of values, particularly in privileging crude popularity over prestige and a sense of professional duty. All the same, there are tendencies to overinvest television especially with utopian powers. Broadcasting has its limits: it may not always support the education hypotenuse of the public service triangle. The dangers then are, as Nahra points out, that broadcasting is stripped of its informational role, too; or, as Simon Cottle argues, that the information process is confined and diminished by news formats which are more closed than open and in which it is widely considered a form of professional heresy to relinquish editorial control. Even in the spaces supposedly specifically reserved for lay input, Jo Tacchi's research indicates, the agenda and rhetoric of producers prevail. The overall paradox is unsurprisingly reproduced in the training of broadcast journalists. A growing appreciation of the diversity of publics, Heather Purdey's investigations suggest, is challenging pre-existing 'professional' conformity, but not quite overturning it. The impression is of trainee radio journalists trapped in a maze of impressible and permeable ideals of public service, professionalism and corporate compliance. The old consensus may have been too cosy, but the morality which appears to be superseding it seems largely ungrounded.

That is not to say that the practices of highly developed late modern commercialism, which in broadcasting is increasingly dislocated from the publics it professes to serve, are necessarily either immoral or amoral. In the training of broadcast journalists in the UK, the public service ethos and in particular the impress of the BBC appear to have been so deeply ingrained that little or no sense of 'professionalism' arising independently out of journalism has hitherto been possible. The moment for that reform, Purdey argues, might now be upon us. Similarly, Brian McNair, while conscious of the 'tensions and dangers' resulting from the growth to pre-eminence of public (media) relations, is reluctant to join the swelling chorus of those who view 'spin' as a kind of dark art. Overly mediacentric analyses may exaggerate the efficacy of PR in determining power relations operating within closed groups, and underestimate the availability and utility of the techniques of this type of persuasive action to wider publics. PR, in other words, is a two-way street, and the ability to generate media interest has characterized the activities of many pressure groups and associations campaigning on media issues. Such organizations in both the USA and UK, Granville Williams demonstrates, have resorted to the panoply of PR techniques often condemned in other circumstances as superficial and underhand, including self-promotion, celebrity endorsement, direct public appeals and backroom lobbying. That they have had limited success may confirm McNair's belief that journalism is sufficiently resilient, when appropriate, to PR: campaigning on the media has always been a minority interest. On the other hand, Williams contests, the exponential strengthening of corporate power has further distorted the already uneven contest between media advocates and media lobbyists. Concerned citizens cannot muster the resources to compete with media moguls.

Not only how this imbalance may be corrected but whether there are grounds for doing so are central concerns of this book. Those who believe that commercialized diversity is an initial, if ultimately inadequate, expression of participatory citizenship have lately placed great store by the 'interactive, customisable, hypertextualized and multimedia' journalism (Dunn) of the converging digitalized media. Others look to the potential of the Internet in particular to circumvent the restrictions of conventional media. It can be argued that the utopian aspirations projected previously on different forms of analog media are now being transferred to cyberspace. Warren Bareiss provides a timely reminder of the complexities and incompleteness of the 'alternative model' of radio and television services existing in analog form. Viewed from the perspective of a national public service-commercial dominated mediascape (the typical Western European view), South Dakota appears richly endowed with 'alternative' radio and television stations. Yet there must also be some apprehension that 'community' services narrowcast in ways which are not in all respects immediately discernible from those of commercialized stations serving so-called niche markets and segmented audiences.

What distinguishes such 'alternatives' from the mainstream is their participatory mode. Diana Agosta makes clear that in what she identifies as an emergent civil society in El Salvador, effective participation is not confined to equalities of access, visibility and values but encompasses at its core the formation of a genuine partnership between the media and their publics. In many other circumstances the notion of such partnerships is curtailed or marginalized by a commercialism which has so far proved itself largely incapable of supporting the conditions in which they might develop (see Bertrand 2000). The extent to which this situation might be changed, with or without the intervention of new digital media forms, is perhaps the key issue.

References

Barnett, S. and Seymour, E. (2000) 'You cannot be serious', *Guardian Media* (10 July): 2–3.

Bertrand, C.J. (2000) *Media Ethics and Media Accountability Systems*, Transaction, London.

Birt, Sir J. (1999) *The Prize and the Price: The Social, Political and Cultural Consequences of the Digital Age*, The *New Statesman* Media Lecture (6 July), BBC, London.

Bromley, M. (1998) 'The "tabloiding" of Britain: "quality" newspapers in the 1990s', in Stephenson, H. & Bromley, M. (eds), *Sex, Lies and Democracy: The Press and the Public*, Addison Wesley Longman, Harlow: 25–38.

Buckley, S. (1999) 'Empowering communities', *Airflash – Community Media Review*, 66 (Autumn): 11–13.

Hartley, J. (1996) *Popular Reality: Journalism, Modernity, Popular Culture*, Arnold, London.

Henwood, J. (1994) 'Down your way?', *Spectrum* (Autumn): 10.

Independent Television Commission (2000a) *Bulletin*, 13, ITC, London.

Independent Television Commission (2000b) 'ITC calls for views on the future of public service broadcasting', ITC news release 45/00 (8 June), ITC, Cardiff.

Independent Television Commission (2000c) 'Consultation on public service broadcasting' (8 May), ITC, London.

Independent Television Commission (2000d) 'Consultation on regionalism in ITV' (7 June), ITC, London.

Lumby, C. (1999) *Gotcha! Life in a Tabloid World*, Allen and Unwin, St Leonards, NSW.

McNair, B. (1999) *Journalism and Democracy: An Evaluation of the Political Public Sphere*, Routledge, London.

Pandya, N. (1999) 'Digital media industry predicts boom', *Guardian*, Jobs and Money (23 January): 29.

Snoddy, R. (2000) 'A digital plot that's there to be lost', *The Times* 2 (7 July): 24.

Williams, B.A. & Della Carpini, M.A. (2000) 'Unchained reaction: the collapse of media gatekeeping and the Clinton–Lewinski scandal', *Journalism: Theory, Practice and Criticism*, 1,1: 61–85.

PART I

Public service and private interests

CHAPTER 1

Demise or renewal? The dilemma of public service television in western Europe

Kevin Williams

Broadcasting in western Europe has undergone considerable change since the late 1970s. Technological developments and the introduction of new regulatory mechanisms have ushered in a world of multi-channel, market driven television. This has brought about a re-adjustment of the structure, output and audience of television throughout the continent. This chapter examines these re-adjustments and documents the similarities and differences in the response to change in different parts of Europe. While there is a general crisis of public service broadcasting across western Europe with public funding for television being cut and the audience for public service television falling, variations exist. Comparison is made between Scandinavia, southern Europe and the major broadcasting systems of France and Germany. In Scandinavia the traditional public service model that shaped the development of western European broadcasting in the post war period has been most rigorously defended. In southern Europe, primarily Spain, Greece, Portugal and Italy, the new commercial order has advanced more quickly. Years of authoritarian government or clientalism have facilitated such advances but have also ensured in some cases the importance of news and political information at the centre of the media agenda. In France and Germany there has been a struggle between public service and commercialism which has produced certain compromises which are a feature of these television systems. However, all parts of Europe are having to confront pressures on news and current affairs which are being re-defined and re-packaged to respond to the developments that are taking place. The consequences of these changes in news and current affairs for the body politic are a matter of dispute.

Italian stalking horse

In 1976 Italy became the first European country to 'de-regulate' television. The state broadcaster Radio Audizioni Italiana (RAI) had held a monopoly of broadcasting from the end of the Second World War. De-regulation in Italy was as much a response to political factors as technological innovations such as satellite and cable which promised a multi-channel system. The stifling hand of the Christian Democrats, who had been the majority party in Italy since 1945, had brought forth calls in the 1970s for greater diversity on Italian television. Their defeat in the 1974 election provided the opportunity to do something about the situation. The resulting changes brought about a radical shift in the 'ecology' in Italian broadcasting. In its first phase de-regulation led to the setting up of hundreds of private television stations throughout the country – about 600 local television and more than 2500 radio stations were born (Mazzoleni 1997: 129). Lacking the public subsidy of the state broadcaster, RAI, and relying heavily on advertising revenue to fund their operations, the output of these stations was variable. Sartori (1996: 156) identifies three kinds of organizational types: independent stations, the 'pioneers of private television' who produced their own programming and sold their own advertising; the so called 'circuits' established by advertising sales agencies who began to incorporate television programmes and 'networks' who through merger and affiliation of channels centralized programming, advertising sales and management. The audience share of these early networks rose from 4 percent in 1977 to 24 percent in 1979. Their programming, however, has been described as a combination of 'artless idealism with naked profiteering'. It was not long before the television explosion encountered meltdown as local stations began to close. The end of the first phase of Italy's television experiment came when the 'big operators' began to buy up strings of local stations. The main beneficiary of this process was the TV entrepreneur, Silvio Berslusconi, who came to own three major national channels – Canale 5, Retequattro and Italia 1. The means by which most of private television was delivered into the hands of one man and one corporation, Berlusconi and Fininvest, has been attributed to 'a mixture of contradictory factors – managerial skill and lack of it, far-sightedness and obtuseness, active and passive political cronyism' (Sartori 1996: 158; see also Mazzoleni 1991).

The kind of programming Berlusconi's channels offered was organized around 'high advertising appeal', relying heavily on a schedule of quiz shows, 'sanitised nudity', bought in old US situation comedies and sport. Games and variety shows seemed to be on all the time. The most notorious was *Colpo Grosso* – put out by another private TV station – which had stripping housewives and as a main prize the chance to undress the show's dancers. Italian television pioneered the 'TV sex show' (see Blain and Cere 1995). Soap operas purchased from the United States and Latin America and dubbed into Italian also became part of the service. The invasion of foreign imports into Italy has been described as 'the most extraordinary collection of international programming stock ever seen in the history of television' (Sartori 1996: 160). The increase in foreign made material was a response to the need to produce programmes at the lowest possible cost and bought in soaps at the time were five times cheaper than producing the home made product. The new ecology of Italian broadcasting soon settled into the following pattern. RAI's share of the audience had fallen to around 45 percent, while Berlusconi's channels had risen to roughly the same amount. The remaining 10 percent or so was fought over by a myriad of local and regional stations including ones run by the Catholic Church, Italian political parties, trade unions and hard core porn interests. However, in order to survive, RAI had to drop part of its public service mission and become involved in a ratings battle. Sartori (1996: 156) details how a number of traditional programmes disappeared altogether from its schedule during these years which he labels the period of 'tactical degeneration'. First the Friday night drama series disappeared, then the slots for children's programmes were reduced and finally cultural offerings were relegated to later and later in the evening. To try and compete RAI had been driven 'downmarket', increasingly embracing the formats adopted by Berlusconi's channels. Criticism that it should concentrate on 'serious' programming was rejected as RAI argued that this would further diminish its audience. These changes were necessary according to RAI if it was to secure its future and the future of public service broadcasting.

The 1980s was an era of unremitting competition in Italian television. Mazzoleni (1997: 129) compares the period with the Wild West with 'unregulated competition, births and deaths of hundreds of broadcasting enterprises, rocketing programme costs and, above all, the consolidation of a private broadcasting industry, monopolised by a single trust'. In the end there was 'trench warfare involving two combatants – the RAI and Fininvest' (Sartori 1996: 160). During this period the amount of broadcast hours increased considerably – annual hours of television rose from around 6000 in 1976 to about 34,000 in 1986 (Wolf 1989: 53). However, advertising time on Italian television grew even more quickly. RAI in 1983 carried 40,000 advertising slots on its three channels which rose to 60,000 by 1987 while Fininvest channels had no fewer than 284,800 slots in that year (Wolf, ibid). RAI was operating on an income, two-thirds of which came from licence fees while one-third came from advertising (Henry 1989). This saturation of advertising meant that 'programmes, schedules, tones and even the appearance of on screen personnel were all determined by the need to satisfy the needs of advertisers' (Grundle 1997: 69). Demands were made for limits on advertising but it was in the area of programme quality that concerns became most pronounced. Informational programmes were virtually absent from Fininvest's channels, although prior to 1991 Berlusconi's channels were prevented from broadcasting live, which hampered their attempts to develop a news service (Grundle 1997: 63). However, the amount of time devoted to what was the centre of the public service schedule, news and current affairs, declined on RAI. Qualitatively, there were changes in the presentation of information programmes on RAI as more sensational, cine verite type formats of programmes such as 'Yellow Telephone', 'I Confess' and 'Public Prosecutor' replaced the more traditional and less spectacular news and current affairs output (Wolf 1989: 59). Public concerns at the more market oriented nature of RAI's news selection and presentation led to calls for a television journalism 'freer, more autonomous and more respectful of professional integrity' (Wolf 1989: 62). Only with such changes could the threats to journalistic standards and hence the national and civic culture be countered.

In these circumstances the government did nothing to put order back into the broadcasting sector. It was not until 1990 that a bill was passed to address the chaos. The Mammi law, however, only served in the eyes of critics as the 'legalization of the status quo' (Mazzoleni 1997: 129). While the law introduced new programming responsibilities and a number of measures to ensure transparency in the industry, it made no attempt to reform the system and left intact existing patterns of ownership (Sartori 1996: 159). Backed by what was then the 'biggest commercial TV network under single ownership outside the US', Berlusconi went into politics, establishing a political party, Forza Italia, which together with its partners won the Italian elections in 1994 and propelled Berlusconi to the Prime Minister's office (Hutton 1994). During his short stay in office Berlusconi wasted no time in trying to appoint new executives to RAI to ensure that the political bias of the organization went his way. By the 1990s RAI had split its service into three channels each supporting a particular political persuasion – RAI 1 remained in the hands of the Christian Democrats, RAI 2 was run by the Socialist party while the Communists controlled RAI 3. The result was an open civil war inside RAI with journalists passing votes of no confidence in their news directors and broadcaster pitted against broadcaster (Glover 1995). Berlusconi's departure from office and the loosening of his control over Fininvest has accompanied a convergence in the output of Italian television in the 1990s. While Fininvest channels have more 'fiction TV' than RAI, news and information have grown on commercial television; by 1995 this category of content accounted for 37 percent on RAI compared to 25 percent on Fininvest (McQuail 1998: 121). The amount of imported material had also declined on Fininvest.

Crisis of western European broadcasting

The Italian experience is seen as a good illustration of what is happening to broadcasting in western Europe. De-regulation brings about the growth of privately controlled television networks and the increased competition they present undermines public service broadcasting. The number of people who watch the public service channels is drastically reduced. In response, public service channels are forced to 'imitate commercial television in an effort to try and beat the competition' (Siune and Hulten 1998: 28). As a result, the traditional mixture of programmes catering for diverse audience tastes and interests that characterize public service television declines. Public service channels come to resemble more and more their commercial competitors. Serious programming devoted to information, education and culture disappears from the peak viewing hours – prime time – to be replaced by more entertainment oriented shows. The market driven imperatives of the new television lead to a lessening of the range of programme output and actually work to restrict choice for the viewer. While the amount of television broadcast expands, the variety of programmes on offer is reduced. The profit motive results in a relentless search to produce television at the lowest cost. In the case of western European broadcasting this means importing more cheap television programmes from the United States. The reliance on American and other foreign imports and the growth of low cost, entertainment driven programmes is seen as presenting a threat to national cultural identity and cultural standards (see Tunstall and Machin 1999). The impact of commercialization on the content of television is summed up in an official report in 1994 on the consequences for German television:

> ... we can observe a surplus of programmes, both in entertainment and information. The TV programme itself has become more sensational, more negative, focusing more on scandals and rituals in politics. Entertainment has increasingly focused on sex and violence, on simplistic stereotypes, more rapid editing as part of a slowly developing 'video-clip aesthetic', a new confusion of realities and television realities. (McQuail 1998: 119)

At the heart of western European broadcasting has been its 'delicate and often symbiotic relation to politics' (Brants and Siune 1998: 128). The new commercial order is changing the nature of politics and political communication. The maintenance of 'serious' programmes is seen as a particularly acute problem in the reporting of politics. The *raison d'être* of public service broadcasting is to provide a range and diversity of political coverage that enables the citizen to play his or her full part in the political process. News and current affairs were at the centre of the traditional public service schedule. Most commercial channels regard political coverage as marginal. As a result, the amount and quality of political information is falling. Competition is forcing public channels to scale back on politically informative news or push it to the margins of the schedule. The nature of political reporting on television is also changing. It concentrates more on the rituals and personalities of politics than the substance and issues (Brants and Siune 1998: 137–9). Investigative journalism is disappearing. There is also a change in the style and mode of the presentation of politics across the commercial and public channels which emphasizes immediacy and emotion at the expense of explanation and elucidation. Shorter, snappy and sensational items are more newsworthy. One writer has dubbed the new product as 'newszak' (Franklin 1997). The explosion of newszak and the changing nature of political reporting raise questions about the role of television in democracy. These developments are seen as favouring political parties and personalities that trade on the emotive and contributing to the degradation of public debate which accounts for the growing cynicism about politics, the rise of voter apathy and the decline of public participation in the political process. Blumler and Gurevitch (1995) have referred to this as the 'crisis of public communication'.

National variations

The generalized crisis suggested above points to the death of public service television in Europe as being imminent. For some it is already dead: in Tracey's words public service broadcasting is a 'corpse on leave' and any attempt to save it is more akin to 'the preservation of primeval bugs in amber than the continuation of any vibrant cultural species' (1998: 33). However, as Curran (1996) notes, the decline of public service broadcasting across western Europe has not been uniform. In some parts of the continent public service channels have been better able to resist the pressures from commercialization, in others public broadcasters have improved their performance to fight off the competition and elsewhere the public have rallied around public service to defend it. The picture of what is happening to public service television is varied and the reasons for this are found in a range of social, political and cultural factors.

It is important to point out that the concept of public service has been interpreted differently across western Europe. Whilst scholars (for example, Blumler 1992; Broadcasting Research Unit 1986) have striven to identify the common features of European public service broadcasting, national economies, cultures and politics have determined considerable variations in practice. As Brants and Siune (1992) state: 'public service broadcasting in Europe is relatively lacking in norms; in fact there is no uniformity even in the terminology used'. Three factors in particular have perhaps explained differences in public service broadcasting around western Europe – the ways in which the service is financed, the nature of the relationship between broadcasters and the state, and popular attitudes to and understanding of the public service mission to explain. Today, pure public service systems funded only by public subsidy, usually through a licence fee, do not exist (Humphreys 1996: 125). It was in the late 1980s that the handful of western European countries – Belgium, Denmark, Norway and Sweden – that supported public subsidy only systems began to run ads. There are still some channels such as the BBC in the United Kingdom, Norway's NRK and Sweden's SVT which are financed by a licence fee. However, most public service channels had for a long time been financed by a mixture of public and state subsidy and advertising revenue. Spanish state television, Television Espanola (TVE), had always raised the vast proportion of its revenue through advertising – in 1977, 94.1 percent of its financing came through advertising (Maxwell 1995: 27). Spanish television was exceptional in the extent to which advertising played a role in the financing of public broadcasting but advertising has been present in most European broadcasting systems. The revenue for German public service channels is raised through a mixture of advertising, which is limited to the hours between 6 and 8 pm and may not be shown within a programme, and a licence fee. France introduced commercials onto public television in 1968 and by 1977 it accounted for 25 percent of the revenue of the monopoly broadcaster, ORTF (Kuhn 1995: 131). Figures for 1979 show that in Greece advertising accounted for

29.2 percent of the revenue of the public broadcaster, while in Portugal 38 percent, Ireland, 48.9 percent and Holland, 25 percent (Maxwell, ibid). In Britain commercial broadcasting was introduced as early as 1955 with the launch of ITV (see Williams 1997). While BBC and ITV were kept separate in their sources of finance, British television audiences were introduced to advertising on their screens earlier than most other western Europeans. Some form of mixed revenue has been the reality for most west European broadcasters prior to the commercial deluge.

Politics has been central to the development of public service television in western Europe. Blumler (1992: 12) points out that public service broadcasting bodies are 'highly politicised organisations'. Not only has the state played a crucial role in the formation of these organizations but public service broadcasters have taken their responsibilities to the performance of the political process and maintenance of a healthy civic culture 'far more seriously' than their colleagues elsewhere in the media and in commercial systems in other parts of the world such as the United States (Blumler, ibid). However, the relationship between public service broadcasters and politics has varied across the continent. Kelly (1983) identified three different forms which bring television and politics together. There are *formally autonomous systems* in which arrangements have been established to separate decision making from the government of the day. Such arrangements exist in Britain, Ireland and Sweden. *Politics in broadcasting systems* ensure that the governing bodies of broadcasting organizations have representatives from all the countries major political parties as well as other social groups and movements associated with them as in Germany, Denmark, the Netherlands and Belgium. Finally there are what Kelly terms *politics over broadcasting systems* in which the government and other organs of the state can intervene directly in the day to day decisions of broadcasters such as in Greece, Italy and France. Countries in which public service broadcasters have been able to maintain some independence from the state or which have been able to ensure some degree of equality of representation in their coverage of politics have, by and large, been better able to defend the ideals of public service. What some have labelled 'savage de-regulation' (see Traquina 1995) has been more apparent where public perceptions of the state and its intervention in broadcasting have been most negative.

Finally there is the matter of public and political support for the ideals and objectives of public service broadcasting. Western European countries which are more culturally homogeneous and have experienced a long period of political consensus in the post war years have been better able to provide more sturdy foundations for public service broadcasting. The social democratic welfare states of northern Europe contrast noticeably with the more politically and ideologically riven polities of southern Europe. Serving the nation, building a national culture and maintaining balance and objectivity in news and political reporting is more straightforward in a climate of cultural homogeneity and political consensus. Popular support for the process of public enlightenment is another important factor. Social democracy in Scandinavia emphasized the importance of education as well as the role of radio and television in serving as the 'social cement' during periods of change (Sondergaard 1996: 12). Dahlgren (2000) relates how the Social Democratic Party's implementation in Sweden of the 'folkheim' – the people's home – with its emphasis on economic and social security and opportunity for all citizens, shaped the structure and output of the media. In such circumstances mass commercial culture was seen as 'vulgar, if not downright threatening to an enlightened democracy' (Sondergaard 1996: 11). Thus it is not surprising that in response to the efforts of the Norwegian Broadcasting Corporation (NRK) to adapt to the new competitive environment in the mid-1980s there was a 'public outcry at what was seen as a trivialisation of television output' (Syvertsen 1991: 105).

Based on these factors it is possible to suggest that what is happening to public service broadcasting in western Europe is far more varied and complex than the picture of an impeding process of eclipse painted by some commentators. To examine these variations in more detail, comparison is made between what has happened in Scandinavian countries and the countries of southern Europe and between two of the 'big players' amongst western European media systems, France and Germany. The comparison will in particular focus on the fate of news and current affairs and the nature of political reporting.

Northern exposures

Scandinavia has been exposed to the forces of the new commercial broadcasting order as much as elsewhere in western Europe. Up until the late 1980s the Nordic countries had maintained their public service broadcasting monopoly with only minor adjustments (see Bondebjerg and Bono 1996). The case of Denmark is typical (see Bondebjerg 1996; Sondergaard 1996; Petersen and Siune 1997; Holm 1998). One institution – Danmarks Radio (DR) – had a monopoly on radio and television broadcasting until 1983 with a single television channel which broadcast six hours every day and 50 percent of the programmes were news and culture. The monopoly was broken when local broadcasting began on an experimental basis in 1983, leading in 1988 to the creation of a second channel, TV 2, which carried both national and regional television. TV 2 has been described as a 'reaction to the challenge from foreign channels broadcast to Denmark via satellite and . . . cable' (Petersen and Siune 1997: 36). This channel was from the outset funded by advertising and the licence fee. By the beginning of the new millennium, both the amount of television and television viewing had increased in Denmark. The two terrestrial channels, DR and TV 2, have been joined by TV 3, a wholly commercial channel broadcast by satellite from London to all of Scandinavia and exempt from national laws and by DR 2, a satellite channel set up by the public service broadcaster to reach the younger and better educated segments of the population. Since 1997 local television in

Denmark has been allowed to network and is now called TV Denmark and in effect behaves like a third terrestrial channel. It is a commercial channel. Cable penetration is high in Denmark (around 60 percent), which allows Danes access to many foreign TV channels. Thus from one single channel 12 years ago, the Danish viewer is today presented with a variety of channels.

The result is that the Danish public spends more time watching television, with double the amount of channels on offer than there were a decade ago. Danish channels are watched much more than foreign channels. DR is watched by around 25 percent of the audience, TV 2 about 35 percent while the remaining 40 percent is split between the other channels (Tufte 1999: 86). The growth of commercial practices has had an impact on programme content. Fictional programmes grew rapidly in the early 1990s and for a fully commercial operation such as TV 3 this category accounts for more than 80 percent of the output of the channel. But such programming also increased on the other channels – nearly 50 percent of TV 2 and 30 percent of DR were devoted to entertainment and fictional programming in the mid 1990s. News programmes, however, have also increased. Petersen and Siune (1997: 45) describe Danes as 'news freaks'. In 1996 one third of the population watched the main news on TV 2 while nearly 50 percent the main bulletin later on DR. By 2000 the amount of news in prime time on both channels had increased, rising on TV 2 from 17.7 percent of the output in 1995 to 22.3 percent in 2000, and on DR from 19.4 percent to 26.9 percent (*Jyllands Posten*, 15 February, 2000).[1] News has become more central to the programming policy of both channels as the entertainment content declined – for example, series (mainly soaps) fell from 21.5 percent in 1991 to 3.9 percent on DR and 15.2 percent to 3.6 percent on TV 2.

The growing amount of news on Danish television has been accompanied by a debate about the nature of news programming. A recent study of Danish TV news found that TV newscasts are today more likely to contain shorter items and more feature material (Hjarvard 1999). The increased sensationalism of news reporting, with more focus on conflict and scandal, on crime, 'soft news', and news presentation in terms of style and angles has been identified by other researchers as a change in Danish news (cited in Brants and Siune 1998: 138). The Media Committee – set up by the government in 1994 to monitor the state of the Danish media – identified politically relevant information on TV news as having become 'sporadic and incoherent' (Holm 1998). However, the nature of change in news has been disputed. Graham Holm (1999) identifies how Danish television news has resisted the introduction of techniques associated with American commercial television news. She talks about the deep rooted traditions of Danish society laying down powerful cultural boundaries which 'protect Danish TV journalism from outside influence, boundaries so powerful that penetration is a slow process'. The refusal of news reporters to 'sign off' is but one of a many examples of resistance to changes in style, content and presentation. Despite this slow rate of change some journalists argue that 'television as a medium is just now coming of age in Denmark' (Graham Holm

1999). They argue that Danish television in the public service era was simply 'radio with pictures'. Bondebjerg (1996: 51) refers to the 'ideology of objectivity which made it difficult to produce investigative and in-depth journalistic programmes'. He welcomes the growth of 'more personal and controversial forms of documentary' since the 1980s. In 1988 DR – followed a year later by TV 2 – established a documentary group whose only function was to develop documentaries. The result has been, despite recent cuts in DR's documentary group, high ratings, international recognition and documentaries being a 'powerful element in modern Danish television culture' (Bondebjerg 1996: 54). The two main features developed in these documentaries have been the first person participant observation and investigative reporting. The decline of government intervention and the loosening of party affiliations in broadcasting appears to have provided an impetus to the development of a more independent, personal and critical journalism.

The situation in Denmark is reflected to a greater or lesser extent in other northern European broadcasting systems. The shift in the schedules as a result of commercialization and de-regulation has been gradual. The emphasis is still on news and current affairs which have adapted to the new realities of the market on their own terms and in accordance with what Danish audiences want and within the parameters of Danish society and its traditions. Similar developments are observable in Norway (see Syvertsen 1992) and Sweden (see Djerf-Pierre 2000). There is evidence to show that trends in northern Europe support a divergence rather than convergence in the content of television. Research indicates that across the Nordic region news, current affairs, documentary and domestic fiction have increased on public service television (McQuail 1998; Siune and Hulten 1999). It is also the case that public service criteria have been incorporated into the new commercial channels in Scandinavia, in particular in relation to the diversity and quality of programming policy commitments. While television in northern Europe has had to change in response to the pressures of commercialization and de-regulation, this change is characterized as a 'modernization' of the concept of public service rather than its demise.

Due South

The ethos of public service has never been as deeply ensconced in southern Europe as it has been in the Nordic nations. The sharp decline of the public broadcaster is a noticeable feature of this part of Europe. Within the very first year of their operation, 1989, two private entertainment channels, Mega Channel and Antenna TV, dominated Greek television (Papathanassopoulos 1997). The public channels saw a steady erosion of their audience, dropping from 61.6 percent of viewers in 1989 to 7.9 percent by 1995 and by 1997 their cumulative debt was reported as 45 million drachmas. Similar experiences are found in Spain and Portugal. RTVE in Spain built up huge debts which were covered by the government as its audience plummeted from 76.6 percent of the television viewing market in 1990 to 34 percent by 1997 (Lopez *et al.* 1999: 353). In Portugal the two channels of public broadcaster, Radiotelevisao Portuguesa (RTP), had fallen to just over 39 percent of the audience by 1996 (Rui Cadima and Braumann 1999).

The demise of the public broadcaster in southern Europe has been accompanied by a shift in the nature of programming. The rise in the number of television hours has seen the growth of cheap and cheerful programming. Traquina (1995) has shown how soaps and quiz shows came to dominate the main public service channel, RPT 1, in Portugal following the introduction of commercial television. He found that in 1993 entertainment programmes (films, soaps and game shows) were more prevalent in prime time on the main public service channel than on the two main commercial channels. The three genres took up 68 percent of prime time programming on RTP 1. The output of Greek television has also seen an increase of game shows, soap operas and films. This has led critics to describe private channels as 'glorified versions of tabloid newspapers' (Papathanassopoulos 1997: 362). The slow and sluggish response of the public television channels to such fare was one of the main reasons behind their decline. In Spain the arrival of private television channels produced a 'serious shortage of programmes' which threw the industry into a 'state of great uncertainty' (Vilches 1996). By 1995 fiction, films and TV drama accounted for 43 percent of the total output of Spanish television. The influx of American and foreign programming has been a noticeable feature of the situation in all of these countries. For example, of all the films shown on Spanish television in 1994, 58 percent were American (de Mateo 1997: 205). However, the unrestricted competition in the television market in these countries has led to a spiralling upwards of the cost of programmes and programme making which has hampered the development of the service. There are too many stations and channels for the relatively small domestic advertising market. In Portugal, to ease this situation, the government in 1997 decided to remove advertising from the second public channel and reduce its amount on RTP 1. The insufficiency of advertising revenue to cover the financial needs of operators has resulted in the rising cost of bought in programmes as channels compete for their purchase. The result is that for much of the period since de-regulation the general state of the television business in southern Europe – with some exceptions – has been very precarious. Both private and public channels have made considerable losses and the production of 'quality' programmes, that is, high cost productions, has suffered.

The fate of public television in southern Europe is intimately tied to a history of excessive direct state control over the media. In all three countries discussed above, broadcasting was regarded as an arm of the state until the mid-1970s. Public service was compromised by politicians using television as an instrument of propaganda and political interest. The under-development of civil society ensured that policy makers focused on what was politically expedient. Papathanassopoulos (1997: 365) argues that in Greece the de-regulation was a 'knee jerk reaction to the politics of the time and to electoral speculation rather than a response to the needs of the industry'. Syngellakis (1997) explains how the chaotic system of de-regulated television was introduced in response to the internal electoral needs of the socialist government of the day and the pressures being exerted on Greece to adjust rapidly to the norms of democracy in order to ensure its membership of the European Community. A similar situation was found in Portugal and Spain as media interests and owners made their deals with politicians who had been steeped in the tradition of the state intervening directly in the business of television (see Bustamente 1989; Traquina 1995). The use of television as an 'instrument' outlived the authoritarian military regimes. In Greece, for example, director generals of the public service broadcaster, ERT, changed on average every 12 months well into the 1990s (Papathanassopoulos 1997: 364). De-regulation and privatization was fuelled by the desire to remove the shackles of dictatorship and the need to democratize. However, the tradition of a strong centralized state ensured that changes in the structure of television were slow to develop. When they did the discredited public service broadcasters found it difficult to maintain the loyalty of their viewers.

The de-regulation of television in southern Europe has thus coincided with freeing it from the dead hand of direct state intervention. Starved of non governmental news for so long has meant that there exists a considerable popular demand for news and information programmes. News is central to the output of both private and public stations. In Greece one of the advantages of de-regulation is that 'contemporary TV news is faster, less boring and, at least, the newscasters are what they are supposed to be – not readers of the government's announcements as they were in the past' (Papathanassopoulos 1997: 361). Private channels, in particular, have responded to the public demand for news. In Portugal the private channels from the very early days carried a considerable amount of information programming in prime time, more than their public service competitor (Traquina 1995: 231–2). News has also featured in Spain with both the public and the newly autonomous regional television channels devoting a significant part of their output to the genre (see Lopez *et al.* 1999) while Syngellakis (1997) states that 'Greek television programming is dominated by news and information'. The growth of entertainment on television in most of southern Europe has been accompanied by that of news and information. However, the lack of an investigative tradition of journalism has retarded the development of a critical television journalism that challenges the entrenched power of the established political parties.

Franco-German differences

At the heart of Europe the clash between 'northern' and 'southern' responses to de-regulation and commercialization has been encapsulated by the changes in the broadcasting systems in Germany and France.

Two of the 'big three' players in western European broadcasting have taken different paths in adapting to the new broadcasting order. In both countries broadcasting was a public monopoly until the mid 1980s. The break up of the public service monopoly took a different form in each. Following the introduction of competition in the early 1980s, France embarked on a radical change when the Chirac government in 1986 initiated the transfer of TF1, the leading public service channel, into private hands. The channel was sold to a consortium headed by the Bouygues construction company. One of the consequences of this development was the eventual demise in 1992 of La Cinq, one of the commercial channels introduced by the Socialist government in 1985. Thus not only did the channels that remained in the public sector, Antenne 2 and FR 3, suffer but also some of the early commercial operators. Humphreys (1996: 233) highlights the lessons of the French experience for 'headstrong free marketeers and privatisers': more channels compete for limited advertising revenue which increases competition for programmes and media stars that drives up costs and eventually squeezes profit margins which result in bankruptcy. The search for cheaper programmes is part of this scenario and France, through the process of de-regulation it adopted, put considerable pressure on its indigenous production base. The decline of French sourced production came at a time when the French government was leading European efforts to resist the flow of American material into the continent. The success of Canal Plus, a pay for programmes channel, which up to 1997 was received in 6 million French households, attests to viewers perceptions of the content of terrestrial television in France.

The situation in Germany saw the integrity of public service television maintained. The decision of the Federal Constitutional Court in 1981 to end the public monopoly paved the way for the growth of commercial channels from 1984 onwards. After some initial problems the new commercial channels started to slowly gain ground and from 1992 the public service channels had lost their position as market leaders (Hickethier 1996: 113–14). With viewing figures declining, its limited share of advertising revenue falling and government refusing to raise the licence fee, German public service broadcasting went into crisis in the mid 1990s. This gave rise to a national debate in which calls were made for the discontinuation of the main channel, ARD (Hickethier 1996: 115). By the late 1990s Germany had six main TV channels, three public and three commercial, sharing almost equally 80 percent of the total audience (Tunstall and Machin 1999: 198). However, there is no evidence that the content of the public service channels has come to mirror that of the commercial stations. There is much more news and information on the former: ARD and ZDF, the two leading public channels on a 24-hour basis broadcast 40 percent and 44 percent information programmes compared to 14 percent for the two leading commercial channels (McQuail 1998: 122). Public service has consolidated its position without copying the formats of commercial television. Hickethier (1996: 117) argues that public television was able to strengthen its position by adopting a two fold strategy: the expansion of serial making and the augmentation of news. More up to the minute reporting, the introduction of news specials and more in depth coverage of world events were emphasized. The amount of news remained stable on public service television between 1985 and 1995, at about 18 percent, while on the commercial channels its presence in prime time has dropped considerably, to between 4 and 5 percent (McQuail 1998: 122). While the style and mode of presentation of news on both services has become similar there is evidence to show that in recent years news output on the commercial channels have come to resemble that of the public broadcasters. There has been a decline of 'human interest' stories on RTL and SAT 1, the leading private channels, and both commercial and public broadcasters have increased the number of political stories on the news (McQuail 1998: 122). Pfetsch (1996) found in her study of German television in the early 1990s that the amount of political information on both services had increased. She concluded that 'private channels caught up with public channels regarding the contents of political information while the public channels caught up with the commercial channels in their presentation formats' (1996: 446). For Hickethier (1996: 118) what has happened with news and political reporting on German television is one aspect of how commercial broadcasting is being influenced by the public service model.

The differences between the situation in France and German can be attributed to a range of factors. However, the relationship between politicians and policy makers and the media was important. Partisan political control dominated the development of French television. De Gaulle used to govern by television; an astute media performer he ensured that his opponents were denied access to airtime as well as packing all the key position in broadcasting with his closest allies. Nothing much has changed since his departure from the scene. Successive presidents of both the left and right have used television to pursue their own advantage. The decisions of the 1980s to introduce commercial television and privatize TF1 were the product of short term political opportunism. Mitterrand's decision to allow two private channels was determined by his concerns about losing the 1986 legislative elections. Placing these channels in the hands of his supporters he hoped to fend off defeat. As Kuhn (1995: 175) notes, the legacy of governments pursuing their own political interest has been 'to the detriment of the implementation of the public service ethos'. In Germany the establishment of broadcasting was underwritten by the efforts to use the media as an instrument of democracy. The lessons of the Third Reich taught post war German governments that broadcasting should be secured 'against capture by either the state or sectional interests' (quoted in Negrine 1998: 226). The political re-education programme in Germany enhanced popular support for broadcasting encouraging social diversity and established regulatory structures to ensure that this goal was enforced. This firmly cemented public service broadcasting into foundations of political, administrative and public support which has enabled the model to exert its influence over the development of commercial television in Germany.

Public service and new technology

The original rationale for public service broadcasting in western Europe was the scarcity of frequencies. Regulation was necessary to ensure that the confusion and chaos of airwaves wrought by competing radio signals in America was avoided. Monopoly was seen as 'natural' in such circumstances (Negrine 1998: 228). The arrival of the new media technologies of cable and satellite in the late 1970s brought to an end the problems of scarcity. Terrestrial television in a national context was swept aside by the capacity to deliver more signals across national boundaries. Today we are on the verge of another great technological leap forward into the era of digital television and the Internet. Digital television with the capacity to deliver more TV pictures via satellite, cable or terrestrial transmission will increase the number of channels available for viewers. The Internet holds the possibility of not only changing the way in which television and other media is delivered but also how viewers interact with what they see and hear. These developments further threaten to undermine public service broadcasting.

However, the threat varies across western Europe. Kleinsteuber (1998) draws attention to the different rates at which new media technology is penetrating the continent. Some countries have high cable and satellite penetration – Scandinavia, Germany and the Benelux countries. Belgium is nearly totally cabled. Other countries such as Italy, Portugal and Greece have no significant cable take-up. There are a group of nations such as Britain, France and Spain who have only recently come to cable and satellite. The degree of penetration has implications for development of digital television. So has the ability and willingness of viewers to pay for their television services. Digital television can be free and some public service broadcasters are experimenting with such a digital service – for example, Germany and Italy. But in addition to payments for the relevant apparatus to receive the service, it is likely that many of the channels will be offered by subscription. In certain parts of western Europe viewers have shown themselves to be reluctant to pay for their television. Pay TV struggles where the range of 'free television' is wide. In Germany and Italy, for example, such services have met with limited success while in Britain and France with a limited number of channels pay TV channels such as Canal Plus and BSkyB have been very successful. Thus the market for the take up of new digital services is highly fragmented. Crucial to the growth of digital television will be a small number of large media corporations. Only these companies will be able and willing to take on the risks, while the public service channels and the new telecom companies will lag behind (Kleinsteuber 1998: 72). In the future these operations are likely to strengthen their hold over the western Europe television market with the possible consequence of further weakening the public service model.

There is still much dispute about the potential of the new digital technology. Interactivity will, if you believe all the hype, allow viewers to choose their own programme schedule (De Bens and Mazzoleni 1998). This is something that worries not only programme makers but also advertisers. Whether more than a small elite of viewers will take advantage of such applications remains a matter of doubt. What is certain is that in a new digital world more programmes will be needed to fill up the increased space on our television sets. This raises the spectre of yet more American programmes on European television. But it also perhaps reinforces another trend in western Europe broadcasting, namely the growth of regional and local television. Local television channels are rapidly increasing across Europe (de Moragas Spa *et al.* 1999). In some countries, locality has been the basis for the development of the television system since 1945, for example Germany, while in others it is only a recent arrival on the scene, for example, the establishment of Sianel Pedwar Cymru (S4C) in the United Kingdom. However, regional and local television is a feature in most western European broadcasting systems. In Spain, for example, it is not possible simply to talk in terms of public and private television while the 'autonomic' regional channels command nearly 17 percent of Spanish viewers (Lopez *et al.* 1999: 353). These channels are a mish mash of private, community and public services but with a strong commitment to local news and information. The 'digital revolution' is likely to increase their presence. The relationship between de-regulation and decentralization is problematic but the growth of small scale local television services can be seen as a addition to the development of democracy in western Europe.

What a difference policy makers make

The effects of de-regulation are being felt all over western Europe as rules and regulation concerning the delivery of television are being swept aside and new commercial television channels and new commercial forces are coming on stream. National responses to these changes, as we have seen, differ. How broadcasting systems adapt to the new conditions depends on a series of domestic factors, including the strength of national cultures, the financial regimes for funding broadcasting, popular attitudes to information, education and entertainment and above all the relationship between broadcasting and the state. At the centre of these changes is the fate of public service television delivering a diversity of programming, including a commitment to news and information necessary for the operation of the political process. This fate rests not only in the hands of the viewers but is also crucially determined by the attitudes of policy makers. In countries where policy makers have had an understanding of and commitment to public service and the political will to support it, de-regulation has been accompanied by specific obligations on programme content and quality. Hence in countries such as Germany and Denmark we are more appropriately talking about re-regulation and the public service commitment has survived albeit in a different form. In other countries where no obligations have been placed on public or private broadcasters to broadcast particular kinds of programmes or meet quota requirements for domestic production then public service has withered.

Note

1 These figures are based on prime time viewing (6pm–11pm) for 18–23 January for respective years.

References

Blain, N. & Cere, R. (1995) 'Dangerous television: the TV a luce rossi phenomenon', *Media Culture and Society*.

Blumler, J. (ed.) (1992) *Television and the Public Interest*, Sage, London.

Blumler, J. & Gurevitch, M. (1995) *Crisis of Public Communication*, Routledge, London.

Bondebjerg, I. (1996) 'Modern Danish television – after the monopoly era', in Bondebjerg, I. & Bono, F. (eds), *Television in Scandinavia: History, Politics and Aesthetics*, University of Luton Press, Luton.

Bondebjerg, I. & Bono, F. (eds) (1996) *Television in Scandinavia: History, Politics and Aesthetics*, University of Luton Press, Luton.

Brants, K. & Siune, K. (1992) 'Public broadcasting in a state of flux', in Siune, K. & Truetzschler, W. (eds), *Dynamics of Media Politics*, Sage, London.

Brants, K. & Siune, K. (1998) 'Politicisation in decline?', in McQuail, D. & Siune, K. (eds), *Media Policy: Convergence, Concentration and Commerce*, Sage, London.

Broadcasting Research Unit (1986) *The Public Service Idea in British Broadcasting*, BRU, London.

Bustamente, E. (1989) 'TV and public service in Spain: a difficult encounter', *Media, Culture and Society*, 11: 67–87.

Curran, J. (1996) 'Reform of public service broadcasting', *The Public Janvost?*, Vol. 3, No. 3.

Dahlgren, P. (2000) 'Media and power in transition in Sweden', in Curran, J. & Park, Myung-Jin (eds), *De-Westernizing Media Studies*, Routledge, London.

De Bens, E. & Mazzoleni, G. (1998) 'The media in the age of digital communication', in McQuail, D. & Siune, K. (eds), *Media Policy: Convergence, Concentration and Commerce*, Sage, London.

De Mateo, R. (1997) 'Spain', in Ostergaard, B. (ed.), *The Media in Western Europe*, Sage, London.

Djerf-Pierre, M. (2000) 'Squaring the circle: public service and commercial news on Swedish television 1956–99', *Journalism Studies*, Vol. 1, No. 2: 239–60.

Franklin, B. (1997) *Newszak and News Media*, Edward Arnold, London.

Glover, J. (1995) 'Factions and fiction', *Guardian*, 27 February.

Graham Holm, N. (1999) *American Influence on Danish Journalism*, Center for Journalistik og Efteruddannelse, Danmarks Journalisthojskole http://www.cfe.dk/vidbase.nsf/Nye+nyheder.

Grundle, S. (1997) 'Television in Italy', in Cornford, J. & Rollet, B. (eds), *Television in Europe*, Intellect, Exeter.

Henry, G. (1989) 'Public convenience: European broadcasters want to present a unified front against deregulation', *The Listener*, 6 April.

Holm, Hans Henrik (1998) 'Journalism education in Denmark: the challenges of the market and politics', Danmarks Journalisthojskole.

Hickethier, K. (1996) 'The media in Germany', in Weymouth, A. & Lamizet, B. (eds), *Markets and Myths: Forces for Change in the European Media*, Longman, London.

Hjarvard, S. (1999) *TV-nyheder i konkurrence*, Samfundslitteratur, Copenhagen.

Humphreys, P. (1996) *Mass Media and Media Policy in Western Europe*, Manchester University Press, Manchester.

Hutton, W. (1994) 'Moguls on the podium', *Guardian*, 30 March.

Kelly, M. (1983) 'Influences on broadcasting policies for election coverage', in Blumler, J. with A.D. Fox, *Communicating to Voters: Television in the First European Parliamentary Elections*, Sage, London.

Kleinsteuber, H. (1998) 'The digital future', in McQuail, D. & Siune, K. (eds), *Media Policy: Convergence, Concentration and Commerce*, Sage, London.

Kuhn, R. (1995) *The Media in France*, Routledge, London.

Lopez, B., Risquete, J. & Castello, E. (1999) 'Spain's consolidation of the *autonomic* system in the multichannel era', in Moragas Spa, M. Garitaonandia, C. and Lopez, B. (eds), *Television on Your Doorstep*, University of Luton Press, Luton.

Maxwell, R. (1995) *The Spectacle of Democracy: Spanish Television, Nationalism and Political Transition*, University of Minnesota Press, London.

Mazzoleni, G. (1991) 'Media moguls in Italy', in Tunstall, J. & Palmer, M. (eds), *Media Moguls*, Routledge, London.

Mazzoleni, G. (1997) 'Italy', in Ostergaard, B. (ed.), *The Media in Western Europe*, Sage, London.

McQuail, D. (1998) 'Commercialization and beyond', in McQuail, D. & Siune, K. (eds), *Media Policy: Convergence, Concentration and Commerce*, Sage, London.

De Moragas Spa, M., Garitaonandia, C. & Lopez, B. (eds) (1999) *Television on Your Doorstep*, University of Luton Press, Luton.

Negrine, R. (1998) 'Models of media institutions: media institutions in Europe', in Briggs, A. & Cobley, P. (eds), *The Media: An Introduction*, Longman, London.

Papathanassopoulos, S. (1997) 'The politics and the effects of the deregulation of Greek television', *European Journal of Communication*, Vol. 12(3): 351–68.

Petersen, V. & Siune, K. (1997) 'Denmark', in Euromedia Research Group, *The Media in Western Europe*, Sage, London.

Pfetsch, B. (1996) 'Convergence through privatisation? Changing media environments and televised politics in Germany', *European Journal of Communication*, 11(4): 427–51.

Rui Cadima, F. & Braumann, P. (1999) 'Portugal: analysis and perspective of regional television', in De Moragas Spa, M., Garitaonandia, C. & Lopez, B. (eds), *Television on Your Doorstep*, University of Luton Press, Luton.

Sartori, C. (1996) 'The media in Italy', in Weymouth, A. & Lamizet, B. (eds), *Markets and Myths: Forces for change in the European Media*, Longman, London.

Siune, K. & Hulten, O. (1998) 'Does public service broadcasting have a future?', in McQuail, D. & Siune, K. (eds), *Media Policy: Convergence, Concentration and Commerce*, Sage, London.

Sondergaard, H. (1996) 'Fundamentals in the history of Danish television', in Bondebjerg, I. & Bono, F. (eds), *Television in Scandinavia: History, Politics and Aesthetics*, University of Luton Press, Luton.

Syngellakis, A. (1997) 'Television in Greece', in Cornford, J. & Rollet, B. (eds), *Television in Europe*, Intellect, Exeter.

Syvertsen, T. (1991) 'Public television in crisis: critiques compared in Norway and Britain', *Media, Culture & Society*, 6: 95–114.

Syvertsen, T. (1992) 'Serving the public: public television in Norway in a new media age', *Media, Culture & Society*, 14: 229–44.

Tracey, M. (1998) *The Decline and Fall of Public Service Broadcasting*, Oxford University Press, Oxford.

Traquina, N. (1995) 'Portuguese television: the politics of savage deregulation', *Media Culture & Society*, 17: 223–38.

Tufte, T. (1999) 'Denmark: new legislation, last minute rescue?', in De Moragas Spa, M., Garitaonandia, C. & Lopez, B. (eds), *Television on Your Doorstep*, University of Luton Press, Luton.

Tunstall, J. & Machin, D. (1999) *The Anglo American Media Connection*, Oxford University Press, Oxford.

Vilches, L. (1996) 'The media in Spain', in Weymouth, T. & Lamizet, B. (eds), *Markets and Myths: Forces for Change in the European Media*, Longman, London.

Williams, K. (1997) *Get Me a Murder a Day!: A History of Mass Communication in Britain*, Arnold, London.

Wolf, M. (1989) 'Italy: from deregulation to a new equilibrium', in Nowell-Smith, G. (ed.), *The European Experience*, BFI, London.

CHAPTER 2

The decline of public service broadcasting in the UK 1979–2000

Tom O'Malley

> There comes a time when one should recognise that the game is up, at least in any way which we would recognise, and that the objective circumstances within which the institutions of public service broadcasting find themselves, not just in Britain, but everywhere, are antithetical to the basic principles and will continue to be so into any foreseeable future. (Tracey 1998: xiv)

> In the long term, the diffusion of new communications technology threatens to disperse the TV audience and, consequently, to fragment the forum of societal debate established through public service television . . . However, the imminent demise of traditional public service regimes is greatly exaggerated. (Curran 1996: 108)

There is no doubt that broadcasting in the United Kingdom underwent massive change in the last quarter of the twentieth century (O'Malley 1994; Goodwin 1998). There is less agreement, amongst writers on the subject, about what the significance of these changes were for the idea of public service broadcasting as the organizing principle of policy for broadcasting. Was the game up for public service broadcasting by the end of the twentieth century or, were predictions about the demise of public service broadcasting in some sense exaggerations? This chapter tends towards the former rather than the latter view, and argues that a renewal of public service principles in broadcasting and mass communications in the UK presupposes a major shift away from the market driven framework adopted since 1979.[1] In this context, broadcasting is understood as the delivery of radio and TV programming by terrestrial, satellite or cable technology

A retrospective view of mass communications in the UK during the twentieth century would include the observation that the emergence of public service broadcasting was, in part, a consequence of the perception among political elites that the new medium of broadcasting was, potentially, politically dangerous and needed to be controlled. As time went on, public service broadcasting evolved into a complex social institution (Scannell 1990), insulated to a large degree from direct market pressures, within a context, especially after 1945, of growing demands for greater accountability of the media to the public (O'Malley 1998).

Running parallel with this process, and exemplified most acutely in the United States of America (McChesney 1993) was a tendency for the media to become more and more commercially driven. Nicholas Garnham has argued that since the mid-nineteenth century in the UK, there has been a tendency 'by which commodity exchange invades wider and wider areas of social life and the private sphere expands at the expense of the public' (Garnham 1990: 121). In the UK, broadcasting from the moment it was established in 1922 was continually under this kind of pressure; most dramatically from pirate radio in the 1930s and 1960s and again from the consequences of the arrival of commercial television (1954) and commercial radio (1972) (Crissell 1997). Nonetheless, the impact of commercial pressures was severely modified in the UK system where, up until the early 1980s, all broadcasters, be they funded by licence fee or advertisements, were required to act as public service broadcasters.

From 1979 onwards, in the UK and Europe, political decisions were taken which began to dismantle the structures that had insulated broadcasting from the market, at the same time as other areas of publicly controlled industry were being subjected to similar changes. These changes in UK broadcasting policy were, arguably, indicative of a much longer term shift in the way policy elites viewed the role of the relationship between the market and the state. Any hostility or suspicion about the role of market forces in broadcasting which underpinned policy-making up to the end of the 1970s had, by the turn of the century, dissipated and been replaced by a positive attitude to these forces.

In order to grasp the nature and significance of this change in attitude to public service broadcasting, this chapter outlines, briefly, the scope of the changes which have occurred in UK broadcasting since 1979. The more optimistic assessments of these changes are then reviewed in the light of the way in which official definitions of public service broadcasting and the purposes of broadcasting have changed since 1979. In this context, official definitions refers to statements about public service broadcasting found in government sponsored inquiries, Green and White policy papers, and in the positions taken by both senior figures in the broadcasting industry and politicians.

Changes

The period after 1979 witnessed major changes in the amount of broadcast media available to the UK public. From the early 1980s onwards, but in particular after the publication of the Peacock report on the financing of the BBC, (*Report of the Committee on the Financing of the BBC* 1986) the Conservative governments of Margaret Thatcher (1979–90) and her successor, John Major (1990–97) pursued a dual strategy. This involved changing the BBC by squeezing its finances and altering its management, and encouraging more market forces in broadcasting by allowing the rapid expansion of commercially funded cable, satellite and digital services. The main legislative tools for these changes were the Broadcasting Acts of 1990 and 1996 (O'Malley 1994; Goodwin 1998).

In 1981 in the UK there were three national TV channels (BBC1, BBC2 and the regionally based ITV network), four national BBC radio stations (Radios 1, 2, 3, and 4) and 40 local radio stations, about half of which were run by the BBC, the other half by businesses regulated by the Independent Broadcasting Authority (IBA). Ten years later, in 1991, a fourth national TV channel, Channel 4 was on the air, plus the Welsh channel, S4C. A fifth national BBC radio station (Radio 5) had been added, and there was also one national commercial channel. There were 160 local radio stations, 75 percent of which were commercial, and 70 licensed cable and satellite channels (Department of National Heritage 1992: 9). By 1995 about 5 million homes in the UK had satellite dishes (Crissell 1997: 241). Commercial radio station licences had increased from 143 in 1992 to 205 in 1997 (Radio Authority 1998: 11). By 1998 the commercial television and satellite sector had grown further. In addition to the ITV regional stations, Channels 4 and S4C, a new station with partial national coverage, Channel 5, had been added. There were 5 digital terrestrial licences in operation and 201 satellite television services under licence from the Independent Television Commission (Independent Television Commission 1999a: 104).

A short overview of the effect of these changes on the share of total audiences gained by each channel gives some indication of the impact of the expansion of the 1990s on the system. In 1980 the share of viewing held by stations in the UK was: BBC1 39 percent, BBC2 12 percent and ITV 49 percent (Goodwin 1998: 155–6). By 1989, after the arrival of Channel 4 the shares were: BBC1 37 percent, BBC2 10 percent, ITV 44 percent and Channel 4 9 percent (Saatchi and Saatchi 1990: 70). So, by the end of the 1980s audience shares were not dramatically different to ten years previously. It was during the 1990s that the effect of increased competition was felt on the audience share of the BBC and ITV. Between 1992 and 1998 BBC1's share fell from 34 to 30 percent and ITV's from 42 to 32 percent. BBC2 and Channel 4's share rose from 10 to 11 percent and from 9 to 10 percent respectively, and the new Channel 5 had achieved 4 percent. More significantly, in the same period, cable and satellite's share of viewing rose from 4 to 13 percent. Between them the two new areas of commercial competition in the 1990s, Channel 5 and the new cable and satellite services, had taken a massive 17 percent of audience share in just six years, from BBC1 and ITV, with the main impact being felt by ITV (Department for Culture, Media and Sport 1999: 44).

The impact on ITV's share in homes, which also took the commercial channel Sky's digital services, in other words where ITV faced head on competition, appeared even more dramatic. Data covering the week to 7 November 1999 indicated that 'ITV's audience share has fallen from a national average of 32 percent to under 23 percent in households taking Sky digital services. ITV's share in multi-channel homes last year [i.e. 1998] before the launch of digital TV, was some 26.3 percent' (Barrie 1999). Allowing for the fact that the figures quoted here provide only a very broad outline of the impact of channel expansion on audience share, it is evident that the 1990s saw an accelerating redistribution of audience share away from the channels which had been in place in 1979. The implications of this change for the revenues of ITV were such that it became much more concerned to schedule material that competed directly with its commercial rivals and, in turn, more competitive scheduling had become of increasing importance to both the BBC and ITV (Ellis 2000). In addition, the BBC's main source of revenue, the licence fee, came under fresh political scrutiny in the late 1990s (Culture, Media and Sport Committee 1999). One survey, funded by a manufacturer of digital TV equipment, discovered that by 1999, 65 percent of respondents were unhappy with the value for money of the TV licence fee (Pace Micro Technology 2000). There was an increasing sense of uncertainty about the future of the BBC and the licence fee by the end of the century.

What kind of change?

The changes which took place after 1979 were interpreted variously during the 1990s. One perspective tended to stress the significance of the shift and to raise questions about the future of public service broadcasting. In 1994 Richard Collins noted that during the 1980s, at a European level, competition increased within national markets and European regulation 'eroded the basis on which national broadcasting and audio-visual policies' were made (Collins 1994: 162). The strategies pursued by public service broadcasters in Europe when faced with the challenges of more commercial competition were criticized by Achille and Miege as, in general, being 'particularly damaging because they have distanced themselves from their public service mission' with 'the pursuit of audiences taking priority over the search for quality or originality' (Achille and Miege 1994: 41). Peter Humphreys has noted that although Europe in the 1980s and 1990s saw the creation of new, or re-regulated structures governing broadcasting, which often contained commitments to public service ideals, 'Formal re-regulation may cloak far-reaching changes in the culture of regulation, in the values underpinning its interpretations, and generally in its relationship to the new marketised realities' (Humphreys 1996: 194).

In the UK context one perspective on the changes of the 1980s and 1990s was that 'the foundations of public service broadcasting were seriously undermined' and that 'the public service broadcasting system in the UK was mortally wounded in the 1980s' (O'Malley 1994: xiv). Colin Shaw, who had had a long career in broadcasting regulation, attacked the legislative bedrock of these changes, the Broadcasting Act 1990, as 'directed principally but by no means exclusively, at the commercial sector' and argued that it was 'threatening to make a mockery of the meaning of the word choice' (Shaw 1993: 1).

Others, whilst recognizing the far-reaching nature of the changes, have stressed the difficulties of making judgements about the long term implications of the changes. Nicholas Garnham has noted how the changes at the BBC after 1986, which were designed to make it more market orientated, raise the question of 'Whether the policies the BBC has itself adopted to achieve this end are or are not a creeping commercialisation and a prelude to privatisation is a matter of continuing debate' (Garnham 1998: 216–17). The official historians of the ITV system during the 1980s also reserved judgement. They argued that whilst the 1990 Broadcasting Act changed 'fundamentally the control and the economics of commercial broadcasting in Britain' the full consequences of the changes would not be felt for 'some time' and that 'It is impossible to judge whether the much vaunted "golden age" of television passed during the period covered by this book' (Bonner with Ashton 1998: 6, 479).

Another more optimistic assessment of the changes in Europe and the UK has stressed the continuity of institutions, values and practices between the 1970s and the 1990s, whilst at the same time not denying the importance of the changes. The high political drama of the early to mid-1980s in the UK led to genuine fears that the BBC and public service broadcasting might be destined for a swift demise. By the early 1990s, however, as the political temperature cooled, so a more optimistic appraisal gained currency. Writing in 1992, Jeremy Tunstall argued that the 'Thatcher government attempts at radical breaks with the past were largely failures' and that even if under her direction 'commercialism received the main emphasis, various conceptions of "public service" remained central'. Even the linchpin policy instrument, the Broadcasting Act 1990, made changes which were 'much more modest than some Conservative government rhetoric of the mid-1980s implied' (Tunstall 1992: 241–2, 247). Barnett and Curry, whilst recognizing that in the mid-1990s the survival of the BBC was not a foregone conclusion, still felt that in spite of a series of 'defensive engagements fought out in Whitehall and White City, in which the BBC's form has been pummelled almost out of shape . . . [it] appears, so far, to have survived with its core intact' (Barnett and Curry 1994: 263).

The BBC's 'survival' according to *The Independent* newspaper was down to its Director General John Birt; it was 'a tribute to the political skills of Mr. Birt in convincing ministers of the merits inherent in his reforms' (Anon 1994). Like Tunstall, James Curran detected 'exaggeration' in predictions about the demise of public service broadcasting (Curran 1996: 108). Jean Seaton drew attention to the importance of recognizing that, in effect, the BBC survived the turmoil of the 1980s:

> Birt and his team managed to steer the Corporation through the greatest challenge of its existence. By the mid-1990s the BBC felt as if it were slightly grimly, on a course it understood. It is a story which may show how flexible British establishment institutions can be. The BBC remained a national and international institution; it had not, in the end, been fatally politically compromised. (Curran and Seaton 1997: 234–235)

Peter Goodwin stressed the 'real and substantial changes' in UK TV in the mid-1990s compared to 20 years earlier, but also emphasized the 'significant continuity', for 'alongside these changes, battered but by no means bowed, the old duopoly still survived' (Goodwin 1998: 162). Others have stressed how 'a number of state regulatory structures and arrangements have been for the most part perpetuated or safeguarded in the UK compared to France' (Regourd 1999: 29) and that in Europe as a whole 'Public service broadcasting has remained far more resilient to the challenge of market forces, and it is important not to exaggerate the penetration of national markets, by international media companies' (Ward 1999: 835).

This latter body of relatively optimistic commentary on the changes stresses institutional survival (of the BBC, ITV and the regulatory structures) and the continuance of a strong public service element in the UK and other European systems. Viewed in the light of the turmoil of the UK broadcasting policy in the 1980s and 1990s these judgements have a great deal of truth in them. Viewed, however, in the longer term, and in the light of an examination of what has happened to official discourse about the social ends of broadcasting, they need some modification. There occurred a major decline in the status of public service broadcasting as the organising principle in official discourse about broadcasting policy in the UK after 1979, such that by the year 2000 UK policy makers were no longer committed to public service ideals. In spite of the survival of institutions with public service labels attached to them, the drift of policy thinking was unequivocally towards substituting commercial for public service ideas as the organizing principle of policy thinking. This in part explains the changes in legislation which created the increase in channels and competition described above. It also provides evidence which tends to support the more pessimistic view that, as far as the UK was concerned the 'game' for public service was up by the year 2000 (Tracey 1998: xiv).

From Crawford to Annan

Radio and television broadcasting in the UK were regarded by policy makers as public services, from the foundation of the British Broadcasting Company in 1922, through to the creation of commercial TV in 1954 and commercial radio in 1972. The idea and practice of public service changed over time and was subjected to almost constant public critique. Nonetheless, the idea that all broadcasters should be fully committed to public service ideals survived the shift from an advertising free, licence fee funded system to one, after 1954, which rested on both forms of funding. Scannell has pointed out that the 'terms under which commercial broadcasting was established by government made it part of the public service system from the beginning . . . it was an extension of public service broadcasting not an alternative' (Scannell 1990: 17–18). Anthony Smith has also stressed that until the early 1990s commercial TV 'had functioned as part of a public service system' (Smith 1993: 7).

In 1960 the Pilkington Committee articulated this sense of all broadcasting having public service goals, a perspective which went back to the 1920s:

> What is significant is this: that a control which derives from the need to ensure the orderly use of scarce frequencies – and is thus technical in its

purpose – is applied here for reasons which are essentially social . . . For broadcasting is, by common consent, of profound social significance; it is an end to which the operational and technical aspects are the means. And inevitably the considerations which have shaped the exercise by successive governments of their control of broadcasting have been, above all, social considerations.

The Committee linked this perception backwards to the views of the Crawford Committee on broadcasting in 1926 and commented on the mixed licence fee and advertising funded system in operation since 1954 thus:

The British Broadcasting Corporation and the Independent Television Authority have been formally charged with the duty of using this, the most influential medium of communication, as a means of disseminating information, education and entertainment. (*Report of the Committee on Broadcasting* 1960: paras 20–2, 1055)

From its earliest days, then, UK broadcasting was understood by policy makers to be of profound social significance and was therefore structured to ensure that all broadcasters had wide ranging obligations to disseminate 'information, education and entertainment'.

The next major inquiry into broadcasting after Pilkington was chaired by Lord Annan between 1974 and 1977. This Committee sat in the context of widening post-war demands for greater accountability in the press (O'Malley 1998) and the development of a vociferous debate about the social purposes of broadcasting (Committee on the Future of Broadcasting 1977: para.2.28). Since the Pilkington Committee, voices from many quarters had been raised demanding a more inclusive, accountable form of public service broadcasting (Smith 1976; Heller 1978; Garnham 1980). Annan's report tried to balance an appreciation of this changed atmosphere with a strong preference for institutional, political and regulatory continuity. The Committee endorsed the status-quo, but with some important exceptions. In order to meet the demand for a more pluralistic form of public service broadcasting Annan suggested a fourth channel designed to 'encourage productions which say something new', but, crucially, it 'should not be allowed to develop into another competitive channel or one which is predominately ITV2'. It also recommended a new Open Broadcasting Authority which 'should not have the same obligations of programming as those of the BBC and the IBA, but should operate more as a publisher of programme material . . . In general, the Authority should have the maximum freedom which Parliament is prepared to allow' (*Report of the Committee on the Future of Broadcasting* 1977: pages 482–3).

These two proposals were designed to extend the range of the public service broadcasting. The criticisms levelled at the Annan report, not least of all because of the paucity of its economic analysis, were many (Heller 1978; Garnham 1980; Curran and Seaton 1997). Nonetheless, Annan's recommendations were predicated on the assumption that public service broadcasting principles should both develop and apply across an expanded system. This, in retrospect, became the fundamental difference between pre- and post-1979 definitions of public service broadcasting.

After Annan

The pressure brought to bear on the whole system of public service broadcasting by the Conservative governments of Margaret Thatcher was acute and, in the context of the attack on the BBC, dramatic. Where broadcasting policy was concerned, informed observers were acutely aware of what the long term implications were for ITV and the BBC of introducing more commercial competition into the system. The economist Martin Cave argued in July 1985, whilst the Peacock Committee was collecting evidence and the BBC was widely perceived to be under severe threat, that it was the whole of public service broadcasting that was in peril:

> But the major question is whether the whole concept of public service broadcasting can survive the changes now in process or contemplated . . . With unrestricted entry into broadcasting and an extension of advertising to the BBC, the most likely outcome is that the pattern of British broadcasting will generally approximate to that of the USA, with an oligopolistic advertiser financed sector for mass audiences, minority interest programming financed by charges, and a third sector financed by public or private subsidy. It remains to be seen whether this is an improvement over the present situation. (Cave 1985: 34–5)

The Committee on Financing the BBC, chaired by Alan Peacock, rejected the immediate introduction of advertising onto the BBC because it wanted a smooth transition towards a system driven by market forces. The Committee thought that putting advertising on the BBC would destabilize the system by undermining ITV in the medium term and would not help in achieving a transition towards the Committee's ultimate goal. This goal consisted of a broadcasting system giving consumers the right to 'exercise their preferences for programming through the mechanism of pay-per-view and subscription. Within this context, the Committee argued:

> The best operational definition of public service is simply any major modification of purely commercial provision resulting from public policy. Defined in this way the scope of public service will vary with the state of broadcasting. If a full broadcasting market is eventually achieved, in which viewers and listeners can express preferences directly, the main role of public service could turn out to be the collective provision . . . of programmes which viewers and listeners are willing to support in their capacity of taxpayers and voters, but not directly as consumers. These would include programmes of a more demanding kind with a high content of knowledge, culture, education and experiment (including entertainment). (*Report of the Committee on the Financing of the BBC* 1986: para. 580)

There was understandable relief felt by defenders of the BBC at the way Peacock took the heat out of the debate about the Corporation's immediate political survival, but the long term implications of the policy direction advocated by Peacock were to prove much more significant. The perspective developed on public service broadcasting in Peacock became the orthodoxy of politicians and policy makers during the 1990s. Policy makers drove the older holistic conception to the margins, leaving Pilkington and Annan behind, and articulated public service as only a part, albeit an important part, of an expanded commercially-driven system. The Conservative governments of the late 1980s put the BBC on the political and economic defensive, restructuring management and imposing real cuts in licence fee income. They then turned their attention to gradually implementing the scenario sketched out by Peacock, one of introducing more commercial forces into the system (O'Malley 1994).

The 1988 White Paper on broadcasting policy in its phraseology began to focus on the BBC, rather than the BBC and ITV, as being the mainstay of public service broadcasting: 'The BBC will continue as the cornerstone of public service broadcasting'. Channel 4 and S4C were seen as participants in the public service mission, but the old ITV system was subtly pushed partly out of the public service ring. ITV was now seen as merely having 'positive programming obligations but also greater freedom to match its programming to market conditions'; these obligations were not going to be 'as extensive as those now governing ITV'. As well as a lighter form of regulation, ITV was to lose its obligation to show educational programmes. The proposal for a new commercial TV channel, Channel 5, included the idea that it should not have any obligation to transmit regional or educational programmes. Future satellite services were to have only consumer protection obligations, but no obligation to show news and current affairs, a diverse programme service, regional or educational programming.

In essence the White Paper proposed a new structure for broadcasting based on Peacock's vision. It divided the previously unified public service broadcasting system into three: the BBC, S4C and Channel 4 were full public service broadcasters, ITV and Channel 5 were to be partial public service broadcasters and the rest, the new services, were to be outside the public service system. The rhetoric of 'light touch regulation', the BBC as a 'cornerstone' of public service broadcasting, and the need for 'consumer protection' were the most visible expressions of this sea change in official discourse about broadcasting (*Broadcasting in the 90s* 1988: 1–2, 7, 33). The details of the Broadcasting Act 1990 were broadly in line with the White Paper. Commercial radio had a whole raft of regulations lifted and a new light touch regulator, the Radio Authority, was created; the Independent Television Commission (ITC) replaced the old IBA, and the three way split between different types of broadcasters developed in the White Paper was enshrined in law.

There is no doubt that the BBC survived the 1990 Act as did the idea of a regulated commercial sector and, given these facts it is easy to see why many people writing in the early part of the 1990s saw the Act as essentially a compromise, in the British tradition of gradualist change, in broadcasting policy (Tunstall 1992). But the Act enshrined in law a radically new conception of policy, one which, whilst including the continuation of some form of public service in broadcasting, articulated its presence as marginal to a system in which commercial competition was to be the mechanism for driving expansion. The wider social purposes of broadcasting enshrined in the principles and practices of the system up to 1990 were replaced by a view which placed commercial goals at the centre of policy. This was apparent at the time. Damien Green, writing for the Conservative think tank, the Centre for Policy Studies, recognized that the new directions in which broadcasting was going would eventually make the funding of public service broadcasting through the licence fee indefensible (Green 1991).

By 1992 the Conservative government of John Major was significantly less hostile towards the BBC than its immediate predecessors but, in its statements on broadcasting, articulated the new thinking more sharply than in the 1988 White Paper:

> From 1993, only the BBC and Channel 4 will continue to be required to broadcast programmes as public services, although other channels and services will continue to have some public service obligations . . . Some public service objectives may be shared, to some extent, by other broadcasters. However, there may be a number of objectives which, taken together, are uniquely suitable for a public service broadcasting organisation, which like the BBC is operating throughout the world. (Department of National Heritage 1992: 14–15)

The whole public service tradition, as conceived in government before 1979, had therefore unravelled at the level of strategic thinking. Public service broadcasting was, as one official in the Broadcasting Policy Division of the Department of National Heritage put it, largely the remit of the BBC, which by July 1994 was being described routinely as 'the major public service broadcaster' (Olliviere 1994). It had given way to a system where positive requirements for all broadcasters were a thing of the past. By the end of the 1990s it was clear that:

> The 1990 Broadcasting Act marked a decisive shift towards the commercial broadcasters. Even though there are still positive programming requirements, there was a shift in focus from 'positive regulation' designed to achieve public service objectives, to 'negative regulation' designed simply to ensure that minimum standards of taste and decency were met. (Koboldt et al. 1999: 49)

Labour and public service broadcasting

This was the legislative expression of the change in the way policy makers understood the social purposes of broadcasting; if there were to be desirable social ends achieved through the positive regulation of broadcasters, these ends would only be met by manipulating one segment of the system. Underlying this was the idea that as broadcasting was increasingly a commercial activity, then the government had no role in trying to impose obligations on private business over and above those that were strictly necessary to ensure conformity with competition policy and laws such as those covering defamation, libel, indecency, etc. The extent of this shift can be further illustrated by the fact that the British Labour Party (in opposition from 1979 to 1997) changed its position on media policy in the 1990s. In 1991 it was openly critical of the 'Tory party's distaste for public service broadcasting' and was 'particularly concerned about the cross-ownership of newspapers and television' (Labour Party 1991: 31–2).

By the mid-1990s its position had shifted towards accepting the definition of public service broadcasting which had developed under the Conservatives, and this shift was marked in the rhetoric of key spokespeople such as Mo Mowlam MP, Shadow National Heritage Secretary who, writing in 1994, made it clear that the Labour party was now keen to be seen as a convert to the new commercial assumptions underpinning policy:

> Our future proposals will be designed to implement our principles. They will take into account the need to ensure high employment standards for skilled employees, to create an even-handed and competitive environment to encourage UK companies to grow and compete in Europe . . . What is needed above all is a new competition policy and a rationalised regulatory structure to meet the challenges of a new market place. (Mowlam 1994: 17; see Goodwin 1994 and 1998)

After Labour came to power in 1997 this kind of language dominated its official statements about policy. In a key policy statement on information technology, Labour made it clear it had adopted the Conservative policy principle of differential regulation for broadcast services:

> New services should not simply fall through the net, nor should traditional broadcasters be handicapped by regulation based on distinctions which no longer apply. (Department of Trade and Industry 1998a: 24–5)

Within this context, public service was only one perspective which would be there to provide 'universal access to a range of information, education and entertainment services and acting as a benchmark of quality' (ibid).

In July 1998, in a much fuller statement, the retreat from public service broadcasting as a central tenet of policy was even more pronounced. Public service broadcasters were now defined as providers of 'a service which is not solely determined by commercial considerations', thereby implying that their other activities were in some significant sense understood as being determined by commercial considerations. In addition the statement raised the question of relieving existing terrestrial broadcasters of positive programming requirements:

> As new services develop, it is necessary to consider what, if any, programming requirements should apply to them, and whether the constraints which

the existing provisions place on the competitive position of terrestrial broadcasters remain necessary to achieve public interest objectives.

In this passage, the idea that programming requirements could act as
positive stimuli to higher quality services all round was replaced by the
idea that they were 'constraints'. In addition, the passage equated programme requirements, and by implication public service broadcasting,
with the idea of public interest objectives. This phraseology hinted at
the idea that there might be public interest objectives in broadcasting
which could be achieved without regulation. Where positive programming requirements were to remain 'they should be set at a level and
delivered in a way which minimises market distortion and allows providers as far as possible to compete on equal terms'. The whole drift of
Labour government language, in line with Peacock's vision, was one of
regulatory minimalism.

Insofar as public service broadcasting was built on the idea that regulation was the instrument needed to achieve a strong, socially desirable
set of broadcasting and cultural outcomes, it was clear that by 1998 the
Labour government had abandoned this assumption. For Labour regulation was now an impediment: 'Regulation should be the minimum
necessary to achieve clearly defined policy objectives. The presumption
that broadcasting and communications should be regulated should therefore in general be reversed' (Department of Trade and Industry 1998b:
paras 2.5, 3.19, 3.26, 4.40; see also, ibid, 1999 paras 1.1, 1.2, 3.7 and
Campaign for Press and Broadcasting Freedom 1998).

The Labour Secretary of State for Culture, Media and Sport, Chris
Smith, repeated the idea that public service broadcasting was in effect the
main preserve of the BBC: 'The BBC is our premier public service broadcaster and I was delighted to read a week ago of the comments made by
Mr. Alan Yentob . . . that the BBC's pre-eminent task is to act as a benchmark of quality in the broadcasting environment' (*House of Commons,
Hansard Debates* 1999). By 1999 the ITC, whose predecessor the IBA had
had powers to promote high standards, was now using the language of
minimalist regulation. It asserted that it had 'given ITV more scheduling flexibility in the increasingly competitive television market place'.

As part of this process the ITC had, in April 1999, allowed the ITV
companies to remove the national news programme *News at Ten* from
peak time schedules, so that the network could challenge its cable
and satellite rivals for audience share across the whole evening (Independent Television Commission 1999b). The ITV companies claimed
that the competitive situation meant that a million people a week were
switching off *News at Ten*. The companies also let it be known that they
equated demands from politicians for the reinstatement of the programme with political interference (Gibson 1999; Robins 1999). Given
the Labour government's attitude to regulation, the ITV companies
were indeed acting within the spirit, if not the letter, of the new regulatory framework when they took their decision to drop one of the most
important news programmes of the previous three decades from their
peak time schedules.

The new climate had by then been thoroughly integrated into the thinking of the BBC. In July 1999 Sir John Birt, the Director General, in a keynote speech described as 'likely to be my last major opportunity to speak as Director-General of the BBC', registered the shifts that had taken place in thinking about broadcasting at senior levels of the broadcasting establishment. He stressed that the BBC 'must remain a publicly funded body with public purposes', thereby implying that the organization was not in essence a public service broadcaster, but a broadcaster for which public purposes sat alongside other purposes. This echoed the language of broadcasters having public interest objectives, which by then was being used by the government (Birt 1999). Birt was expressing the reality of the new policy environment at the end of the century. The competitive forces willingly fostered by policy makers in the 1980s and 1990s had undermined the very idea that public service was at the centre of broadcasting policy. By defining the BBC as a broadcaster with 'public purposes' Birt was both acknowledging this and arguably hinting that, in the future, the BBC would have other non-public purposes.

Birt's approach was correct. Public service broadcasting was not the way to describe either the whole system or significant parts of it. Indeed, by the end of 1999 there emerged evidence that over the 1980s and 1990s not only had the concept of public service broadcasting declined as the central organizing principle of broadcasting policy, but that, with the changes in economics and industrial structure, the programming on UK TV had shifted, from being characteristically wide ranging, challenging and diverse across all channels, to something much narrower:

> There has been a significant decline over the last twenty years in foreign affairs coverage, which is now wholly confined to BBC2. Commercial television has effectively vacated political and economic current affairs, which is now covered almost exclusively by the BBC . . . The number of hours devoted to single plays has dropped by half over the last twenty years while the time given to soap operas has multiplied by five . . . The drive for ratings in peaktime has greatly increased over the last ten years, and appears to be almost as dominant on the BBC and Channel 4 as ITV. Especially on ITV, ratings targets or guarantees increasingly dictated programming decisions. (Barnett and Seymour 1999: 5)

As one commentator put it in January 2000:

> In the short term, the most pressing concern is to attempt to resolve what, if any, public service obligations Britain's commercial channels should carry as they compete with dozens of other choices . . . The related issue of redefining the BBC's remit is unlikely to be resolved until after the current charter expires in 2006. (Clarke 2000)

The decline of public service broadcasting

It would be wrong to argue that organizations with the label public service attached to them did not survive in the UK into the 1980s and

1990s. To do so would be an exaggeration. In spite of the secular decline in audience share, the increased competitive environment and the pressure all of this has put on programming, the BBC in particular, and elements within the ITV system, have worked energetically to sustain the wider social purposes of broadcasting encapsulated in the idea of public service broadcasting, and with a degree of short term success.

The longer perspective developed in this chapter, however, points in a different direction. Whilst in the 1960s and 1970s policy debate assumed that the wider social importance of broadcasting dictated that all new services should conform to public service ideals and thereby to promote high standards and limit the detrimental impact of commercial forces on programming, by 2000 this assumption had disappeared from the statements made by senior broadcasters and the government.

Conservative and Labour politicians and senior figures in the industry assumed that commercial forces should dominate all broadcasting services with public service broadcasting or, as it was becoming increasingly defined, broadcasting with public purposes or public interest objectives as a kind of benchmark for quality on the margins of the system. This perspective was no longer an extrapolation from the directions implicit in the Peacock report (O'Malley 1994) but a view which was rooted in the kinds of changes since the 1980s in official discourse about broadcasting which have been discussed in this chapter. The more optimistic views outlined earlier, accurate as they were in many respects, need to be modified in the light of an appreciation of the nature and significance of the shift discussed here. In the sense outlined in this chapter, public service broadcasting did decline after 1979 as the organizing concept of UK broadcasting. Its decline, less apparent in the early 1990s, was by the turn of the new century an established fact of UK government policy.

What, however, did all of this imply? Firstly, Garnham's view that commodity exchange has been taking over wider and wider areas of social life, seems borne out by the evidence presented here. Commodity exchange had become the very essence of policy thinking in broadcasting by the end of the twentieth century (Garnham 1990: 121). Secondly, public service broadcasting in the conception dominant in the mid-1970s allowed a great deal of space for public demands for change and accountability to have legitimacy. The removal of the idea that public service was what broadcasting was about undermined the legitimacy of public demands for change and accountability, if only because the drift of policy was to redefine the industry as essentially an arena of private commercial transactions subject to the minimum of public regulation. Thirdly, the implications of this shift for democratic culture in the UK need to be more frequently and widely debated. There became, by the end of the century, a need for a reassertion of the public's rights over mass communications, in order to promote universal access to cultural goods. The trend by the year 2000 was to allow the nature of communications to be defined by private companies, whose perspective on politics and cultural issues would always be narrower than that of a publicly accountable system.

These changes occurred because of wider changes in the political culture of UK policy-making elites. The Conservative and Labour party leaderships became converted to various versions of a neo-liberal market orientated agenda (O'Malley 1994; Goodwin 1998). Change in broadcasting policy will therefore come about in the context of wider challenges to the dominance of market orientated thinking in political culture. Nonetheless, there is room for public argument about how to change the situation. This would involve asserting the need for all mass audience forms of broadcasting (terrestrial or otherwise) to carry a range of public service obligations; using the tax system to build and sustain strong public service organizations and to fund diversity of production; limiting cross media ownership; and building on the insights of the 1970s and 1980s to assert the need for new forms of democratic accountability in all forms of mass communications. Where these changes would involve alterations to established European Union or multi-lateral trade agreements which privilege free markets in mass communication, UK governments could assert a much more pro-active line in seeking change to those and work with other governments who seek similar outcomes globally.

As Robert McChesney has argued, when the balance of political forces suggest change is a long way off there persists a need 'to maintain a historical perspective on the present and the future, and reassert the optimism that is necessary for meaningful human existence' (McChesney 1993: 270). Public service broadcasting did decline in the UK after 1979 and with it declined the scope for democratic control over mass communications. The lesson of this development must be that political action is necessary to reassert the rights of the public over a form of communication, which during the twentieth century proved so central to the political and cultural life of the UK.

Note

1 The idea that changes in the technology of delivery (i.e. from terrestrial to satellite transmission) implies that public service principles should not apply to all major broadcasting services is in essence a political decision and is implicitly rejected in this chapter.

References

Achille, Y. & Miege, B. (1994) 'The limits to the adoption strategies of European public service television', *Media, Culture and Society*, 16: 31–46.

Anon (1994) 'The public and the private BBC', *Independent*, 7 July.

Barnett, S. & Curry, A. (1994) *The Battle for the BBC*, Aurum, London.

Barnett, S. & Seymour, E. (1999) '*A Shrinking Iceberg Travelling South . . .*': *Changing Trends in British Television: A Case Study of Drama and Current Affairs*, Campaign For Quality Television, London.

Barrie, C. (1999) 'Digital hits ITV and BBC audience ratings', *Guardian*, 18 November.

Birt, J. (1999) *The Prize and the Price. The Social Political and Cultural Consequences of the Digital Age*, New Statesman Media Lecture, BBC, London.

Bonner, P. with Ashton, L. (1998) *Independent Television in Britain. Vol 5. ITV and IBA 1981–92. The Old Relationship Changes*, Macmillan, London.

Broadcasting in the 90s: Competition, Choice and Quality (1988) Cm 517, HMSO, London.

Campaign for Press and Broadcasting Freedom (1998) *Putting People First: The Campaign For Press and Broadcasting Freedom's Response to Regulating Communications: Approaching Convergence in the Information Age* [Cmnd 4022, HMSO, July], CPBF, London.

Cave, M. (1985) 'Financing British Broadcasting', *Lloyds Bank Review*, No. 157: 25–35.

Clarke, S. (2000) 'Rights and responsibilities', *Broadcast*, 14 January.

Collins, R. (1994) *Broadcasting and Audio-Visual Policy in the European Single Market*, John Libbey, London.

Curran, J. (1996) 'Mass Media and Democracy Revisited', in Curran, J. & Gurevitch, M. (eds), *Mass Media and Society*, 2nd edn, Arnold, London: 81–119.

Curran, J. & Seaton, J. (1997) *Power without Responsibility*, 5th edn, Routledge, London.

Crissell, A. (1997) *An Introductory History of Broadcasting*, Routledge, London.

Culture, Media and Sport Committee (1999) *The Funding of the BBC. Minutes of Evidence. 7 December 1999*, HMSO, London.

Department for Culture, Media and Sport (1999) *The Future Funding of the BBC*, Department for Culture, Media and Sport, London.

Department of National Heritage (1992) *The Future of the BBC. A Consultation Document*, Cm 2098, HMSO, London.

Department of Trade and Industry (1998a) *Our Information Age. The Government's vision*, URN/677, Department of Trade and Industry, London.

Department of Trade and Industry (1998b) *Regulating Communications: Approaching Convergence in the Information Age*, Cmnd 4022, HMSO, London.

Department of Trade and Industry (1999) *Regulating Communications: The Way Ahead. Results of the Consultation on the Convergence Green Paper*, Department of Trade and Industry, London.

Ellis, J. (2000) 'Scheduling: the last creative act in television', *Media, Culture and Society*, 22: 25–38.

Fairchild, C. (1999) 'Deterritorializing radio: deregulation and the continuing triumph of the corporatist perspective in the USA', *Media, Culture and Society*, 21: 549–61.

Garnham, N. (1980) *Structures of Television*, rev. edn, BFI Publishing, London.

Garnham, N. (1990) 'Public service versus the market', in Garnham, N. (ed.), *Capitalism and Communication: Global Culture and the Economics of the Information Age*, Sage, London: 115–35.

Garnham, N. (1998) 'Media policy', in Briggs, A. & Cobley, P. (eds), *The Media: An Introduction*, Longman, London: 210–23.

Gibson, J. (1999) 'ITV chief rejects demands for return of News at Ten', *Guardian*, 18 November.

Goodwin, P. (1994) 'Labouring under a misapprehension', *Broadcast*, 8 July.

Goodwin, P. (1998) *Television under the Tories. Broadcasting Policy 1979– 1997*, BFI Publishing, London.

Green, D. (1991) *A Better Public Service Broadcasting in the 90s*, Centre For Policy Studies, London.

Heller, C. (1978) *Broadcasting and Accountability*, BFI Publishing, London.

House of Commons, Hansard Debates (1999) House of Commons, London, 29 March: col. 716.

Humphreys, P. (1996) *Mass Media and Media Policy in Western Europe*, Manchester University Press, Manchester.

Independent Television Commission (1999a) *Annual Report and Accounts 1998*, Independent Television Commission, London.

Independent Television Commission (1999b) *Bulletin*, No. 10, November, Independent Television Commission, London.

Koboldt, C., Hogg, S. & Robinson, B. (1999) 'The implications of funding broadcasting output', in Graham, A., Koboldt, C., Hogg, S., Robinson, B., Curries, D., Siner, M., Mather, G., Le Grand, J., New, B., and Corfield, I. *Public Purposes in Broadcasting. Funding the BBC*, University of Luton Press, Luton: 47–71.

Labour Party (1991) *Arts and Media. Our Cultural Future*, Labour Party, London.

McChesney, R. (1993) *Telecommunications, Mass Media and Democracy. The Battle for Control of U.S. Broadcasting, 1928–1935*, Oxford University Press, Oxford.

Mowlam, M. (1994) 'Party Principles', in *Spectrum*, Summer, Independent Television Commission, London: 17.

Ollivierre, S. (1994) Letter to T. O'Malley, Department of National Heritage, 15 July.

O'Malley, T. (1994) *Closedown? The BBC and Government Broadcasting Policy 1979–92*, Pluto, London.

O'Malley, T. (1998) 'Demanding accountability: the press, the Royal Commissions and the pressure for reform, 1945–77', in Stephenson, H. & Bromley, M. (eds), *Sex, Lies and Democracy*, Addison Wesley Longman, Harlow: 84–96.

Pace Micro Technology (1999) *The Pace Report 2000: Executive Summary*, Kinross & Render Marketing and Public Relations Press Release, London.

Radio Authority (1998) *Annual Report and Financial Statements for the Year Ended 32 December 1997*, Radio Authority, London.

Regourd, S. (1999) 'Two Conflicting Notions of Audiovisual Liberalisation', in Scrivens, M. and Lecomte, M. (eds), *Broadcasting in Contemporary France and Britain*, Berghahn Books, New York, Oxford: 29–45.

Report of the Committee on Broadcasting 1960, Cmnd 1753, HMSO, London.

Report of the Committee on the Future of Broadcasting (1977) Cmnd 6753, HMSO, London.

Report of the Committee on the Financing of the BBC (1986) Cmnd 9824, HMSO, London.

Robins, J. (1999) 'ITV breached rules over move of News at Ten', *Independent*, 13 November.

Saatchi & Saatchi (1990) *Television in Europe to the Year 2000*, Saatchi and Saatchi, London.

Scannell, P. (1990) 'Public service broadcasting: the history of a concept', in Goodwin, A. and Whannel, G. (eds), *Understanding Television*, Routledge, London: 11–29.

Shaw, C. (1993) 'Introduction', in Shaw, C. (ed.), *Rethinking Governance and Accountability*, BFI Publishing, London: 1–3.

Smith, A. (1976) *The Shadow in the Cave*, Quartet, London.

Smith, A. (1993) 'The future of public service broadcasting', in Stevenson, W. (ed.), *All Our Futures*, BFI Publishing, London: 4–11.

Tracey, M. (1998) *The Decline and Fall of Public Service Broadcasting*, Oxford University Press, Oxford.

Tunstall, J. (1992) 'The United Kingdom', in Euromedia Research Group, *The Media in Western Europe. The Euromedia Handbook*, Sage, London: 238–255.

Ward, D. (1999) 'Book Review', *Media, Culture and Society*, 21: 834–5.

CHAPTER 3

Sold out: Recent shifts in television news and current affairs in Australia

Graeme Turner

The commercial and regulatory context within which television news and current affairs operates in Australia has undergone marked changes over the last decade or so, and this has been reflected in significant shifts in format and content. A widening of deregulatory policy across the media in general; the official recognition of what were previously *de facto* national commercial television networks; changes in ownership of all the commercial networks; the introduction of pay television; political attacks on the news and current affairs performance of public broadcasting; an increase in the intensity of competition between different media forms for advertising revenue; and a declining audience base for television news and current affairs programming, have all posed new problems and challenges.

The consequences of specific programming formats have not been positive. We have seen a number of attempts to redefine news and current affairs in order to attract younger audiences or to revitalize traditional standards of 'quality' journalism. More typically, though, we have seen the market leaders adopting an increasingly tabloid and entertainment-based format, moving away from the daily news agenda in an attempt to arrest the decline in total audience numbers. As a result, the news diet for Australian television viewers has changed significantly, and the legitimacy of any form of public service remit for news and current affairs programming has been seriously undermined.

The Australian context for television news and current affairs

Australian television is a mixed system, comprised of two publicly funded national networks, three national commercial networks servicing the metropolitan areas, several groups of regional stations affiliated with one or other of the national networks, and a pay television sector dominated by two major metropolitan providers. The public networks are the Australian Broadcasting Corporation (ABC), which has a residually Reithian charter modelled on the BBC (one nationally networked channel on TV, and a national radio network); and the Special Broadcasting Service (SBS) which operates one TV channel and a radio network broadcasting a culturally diverse range of programmes including a significant proportion in languages other than English. SBS also supplies a World Movies Channel to the pay television providers. The ABC and SBS are funded directly by the Federal government and thus, while they are responsible to the Parliament, they are vulnerable to the funding (and thus the political) priorities of the government of the day. As the primary (and chronologically the first) 'national' network, the ABC is not allowed to take advertising or sponsorship of any kind, but SBS is.

The commercial networks – Nine, Seven, and Ten (named after the channel number allocated on the original standard TV set) – are centralized around the state capital cities and their national schedules employ very little regional variation. While they are licensed by government (and only three licences per capital city market are issued), the commercial networks are under minimal independent regulatory pressure to observe any of the public interest requirements which are both explicit and implicit in their licences. Up until the late 1980s, regular public renewal hearings were held for each licensee in each capital city. While, admittedly, these were ritual events which were unlikely to cancel a licence (although they did insert special conditions where licensees were held to be at fault), these hearings did at least require licensees to demonstrate how they had fulfilled the promises made at their previous licence hearing. At the same time, the hearings offered the opportunity for community groups and individuals to make formal submissions about the quality of the service provided. Around 25–30 percent of the Australian audience watches the market leader, the Nine Network; a slightly smaller proportion watches the chief competitor, the Seven Network. Ten averages less than 20 percent of the mass audience and the ABC and SBS average under 10 percent most of the time. Pay television was introduced in the mid-1990s through a combination of satellite and cable methods of delivery. It has a penetration rate of around 17 percent of the market in terms of the number of subscribers, but only picks up around 4 per cent of the viewers at the moment (this figure is a total of sets in use across 20–30 pay-TV channels).

Ownership of the Australian media is highly concentrated. Despite the existence of 'cross-media' regulations which restrict the ability of media proprietors to, for instance, operate a television channel in a metropolitan market where they also operate a newspaper, and despite the existence of foreign ownership laws which should have required Rupert Murdoch to divest himself of his 67 percent share of the Australian newspaper market when he became an American citizen, the owners of the commercial free-to-air networks all have controlling interests in other media companies. Kerry Packer, proprietor of the Nine Network, for instance, also owns Australian Consolidated Press, the largest publisher of magazine titles in Australia. The Seven Network has been affiliated at various points in its history with the two dominant newspaper groups in Australia, Fairfax and News Limited, as well as with the pay provider Optus. The Canadian television broadcaster, CanWest, controls the Ten Network. Similarly, with pay-TV, the free-to-air commercial networks, Nine and Seven, hold significant financial interests in both the providers – Foxtel and Optus – as well as supplying programming such as news and sports services.

In the deliberations which resulted in television's introduction to Australia in 1956, the provision of television news and, a little later, current affairs underpinned the political judgement that on balance television represented a social good. News has always been the flagship for channel promotion, and news presenters have played a significant role in representing the identity of individual channels and, more recently, networks. News programmes have consistently rated in the top ten most popular programmes over the years. Viewer loyalties to current affairs programmes may have fluctuated since their introduction in 1967 but they are still among the top rating performers for both the commercial sector and for the ABC. Nevertheless, in terms of total audience numbers rather than ratings percentages, television news and current affairs is now in decline.

The first successful current affairs programme, *This Day Tonight* (*TDT*), was launched by the ABC in 1967 and ran for 11 years – topping the ratings for its timeslot most of that time. In 1971, it spawned a competitor, *A Current Affair*, which has run almost continuously since – although it has swapped networks and modified formats on occasions. Early current affairs established its market position by taking on big political issues and by investigative forms of journalism. *TDT*, in particular, was known for this and for the quality of its journalists: its alumni have dominated Australian television journalism ever since. As we shall see, however, while current affairs still operates as one of the flagship formats for the commercial and public sectors, this is no longer related to its interrogation of political issues or its use of investigative reporting. To understand why this is so, we need to review some aspects of the regulatory and political environment which developed during the mid-1980s – aspects which were influenced by the neo-liberal, rationalizing, commercial imperatives that could be found in one form or another in most western media markets but which have had especially clear consequences for Australian audiences.

Deregulation, politics and the public interest

The second half of the 1980s saw a convulsive restructuring of Australian broadcasting. The expansion of the FM band in radio, with the government's consequent auctioning of FM licences to AM band licensees, transformed radio from a predominantly local or regional medium into a nationally networked medium (Bennett *et al.* 1993). In television, although government policy had hitherto explicitly precluded the establishment of national commercial television networks (in deference to, among other things, the importance of maintaining a degree of localism), there had been a *de facto* metropolitan network which linked channels 9, 7 and 10 with their respective affiliates in Sydney and Melbourne – and with slightly looser connections to partners in other capital cities. This arrangement was the subject of intense political pressure during the late 1980s. Over the period 1986–8, commercial television stopped being 'a licence to print money' and became instead a highly risky commercial enterprise. The organizations which controlled channels 9, 7 and 10 in most of the capital cities were sold twice over this period, in each case finding themselves (temporarily) in the hands of a proprietor with no previous experience in the media who drove them further into debt or asset-stripped them to support other enterprises. (Two of those pro- prietors, Alan Bond and Christopher Skase, were eventually charged with white collar crimes.) As a result, within two years all commercial metropolitan television companies were in debt, one was in the hands of a receiver, and the viability of the industry was in doubt.

The government response to the political pressures this situation gen- erated was to release the regulatory ties in a number of ways. These included the relaxation of a range of licence provisions which protected various forms of public interest and accountability, but the most import- ant strategy was to finally legitimize the establishment of formal net- works as a means of allowing the broadcasters access to the commercial benefits of rationalizing their operations on a national basis. As a result, the networks were installed as the primary structural feature of com- mercial broadcasting in Australia and their commercial and political power increased as a consequence. Importantly, this decision implied that the government regarded the commercial viability of these organ- izations as of greater importance than liberal-democratic assumptions about the broadcasters' public service responsibility to the local, re- gional and national community. From the government's point of view, it turned out pretty well. By the beginning of the 1990s, the networks had returned to the hands of experienced media proprietors and were operating at a profit.

Over this period, other regulatory strategies which exercised some oversight on the broadcasters' commercial activities, such as the public licence hearings, also disappeared. With them went the Australian Broad- casting Tribunal, the regulatory authority which had shown exemplary courage in pursuing proprietors regarded as operating against the pub- lic interest (Alan Bond, for one). In 1992, a regime of self-regulation was formalized through a new Broadcasting Services Act which established the largely toothless Australian Broadcasting Authority as the protector of the public interest.

The public sector, of course, did not have to deal with these kinds of commercial pressures; their problems were political. As has been the case throughout the western world recently, political commitment to the principle of public broadcasting has declined. In Australia, given some changes in programming I will talk more about later, the ABC was virtually the only sector of the electronic media where political reporting was both extensive and critical. Governments of all political persuasions resented the kind of interrogation they received from the ABC – on radio and television. As a result, the ABC was harassed by continual accusations of political bias. The charter of the ABC is sufficiently ambiguous to provide ample opportunities for those who wanted to interpret it in such a way as to accuse the national broadcaster of failing to effectively perform the full range of services Parliament required. With few supporters of the ABC in Parliament, funding cuts were frequent and deep, justified by rationalist economic policy and the invocation of 'user-pays' mantras. SBS was forced to take advertising as a way of supplementing a budget so small that it makes virtually any kind of in-house production almost impossible, but even this has not made a substantial difference to the scale of their operation.

At one point, in 1996, there was a sustained and organized political campaign, aimed at influencing the findings of a government review of the performance of the ABC. The Mansfield Review, preceded by draconian budget cuts, was explicitly asked to consider whether (amongst other things) the ABC needed to provide news and current affairs services if they simply duplicated what the commercial sector provided. In response to this challenge, the ABC commissioned research which demonstrated that, amongst other things, the ABC was the only provider of current affairs in radio and was the most effective provider of information-based (rather than entertainment-based) current affairs on television. The research also revealed significant differences between the prevailing news values on commercial and ABC television news – the high proportion of crime stories as against political stories, for instance, on commercial networks (Turner 1996). The Mansfield Review tapped into a surprisingly deep well of popular support: 11,000 submissions from the general public came to its office, overwhelmingly in favour of supporting the national broadcaster in its current (or expanded) form. As a result of the defence presented by the ABC and of the level of popular support expressed, the foreshadowed withdrawal of funding for its news and current affairs services did not eventuate.

This is a familiar story, and there have been many such threats in the past. While it did not have the intended effect on this occasion, the Mansfield Review of the ABC did introduce a number of changes within the national broadcaster that have affected its ability to compete with the commercial networks in the provision of news and current affairs. This brings us to the issue of the consequences of these political interventions for the nature of news and current affairs television in Australia through the 1990s.

News and current affairs programming through the 1990s

The establishment of the national commercial networks produced significant changes within the Australian television industry. More advertising had to be sought from national rather than local or regional advertisers if the network was to benefit from a centralized structure.

Unfortunately, this was also true of the newly rationalised commercial radio industry; it too, had to reduce its dependence on local advertising and compete with television for the national advertising dollar. The market became intensely competitive in a very short period of time, as television networks pursued the audience ratings that would give them an edge in the struggle for advertising revenue. Added to the mix in the latter half of the 1990s was the introduction of pay television. Although pay-TV began without advertisements, within a year of its arrival advertising had begun to appear on the two main pay networks.

Within such a climate, the strategic importance of news and current affairs programmes – the network flagships charged with the responsibility of capturing the audience at the beginning of prime time and delivering them to the 7.00pm programmes – could only increase. Accordingly, the importance of audience ratings to these programmes also increased. The commercial scrutiny consequently directed onto the specific news values, the choice and treatment of stories, and the generic formats being used, was intense. Not only did it affect the level of competition between networks but also between individual programmes within networks (*A Current Affair*, for instance, competed vigorously for stories against its Nine Network stable mate, *Sixty Minutes*).

In response to such pressures, the third placed Ten Network dropped out of current affairs altogether and moved its flagship news bulletin out of the conventional timeslot of 6.00pm to 5.00pm, effectively abandoning the competition for the mass audience to the more successful networks and restructuring its programming schedule around a niche demographic – young people from 18–39. Seven and Nine, however, have remained locked in head-to-head competition, matching each other with mirror-image formats for their news (at 6.00pm) and their nightly current affairs programme (at 6.30pm). Given the similarities in format (and often the same repertoire of stories), competition between the network news and current affairs programmes concentrated on such differentiating factors as the audience appeal of those in front of the camera and the promotability of the night's key stories as exclusive, entertaining and visually exciting. Competition for exclusive stories encouraged the kinds of arrangements usually referred to as chequebook journalism (paying subjects for exclusive rights to their stories); the need to provide entertaining stories encouraged the sensational, the conflictual, and the visually spectacular; and the need to present everything coming up on the screen as new and exciting encouraged a particularly hyperbolic mode of self-presentation.

The key to these changes is probably the emphasis on exclusivity. This emphasis encouraged principles of selection which placed a high priority on the promotability of the story – not only in terms of its intrinsic news values but also in terms of how easily it could be promoted through short teasers in advance (often days in advance) of the story being screened. (Stories on breast implants, for example, offered this potential where politics did not.) The importance of exclusivity also intensified competition for the most high profile stories; gaining exclusive rights not only provided newsworthy content for the programme, it also locked out the competition. The result was that many important stories would only be covered by the network with the exclusive rights to the key individuals in those stories, as any other strategy resulted in publicizing a rival network's property. Not only does this have an effect on the range of viewpoints offered on a story and the independence with which the journalist can treat it but it also structurally incorporated, more fully than ever before, the role of personal agents and publicists into the processes of news gathering, story selection and the transformation into programming.

The move towards the entertaining and the sensational was a move towards what is usually thought of as a tabloid format: hidden camera stories, conflictual interviews (or what in America is called 'attack' journalism), foot-in-the-door or car park confrontations, a preponderance of stories on weight loss, miracle cures for back pain, or cosmetic surgery, and a shift towards consumer affairs and away from politics. More important for my purposes here than the taste-based critique usually addressed towards tabloidization (Hartley 1996, Franklin 1998, Langer 1998, Lumby 1999), however, is the fact that this constitutes a retreat from the news agenda of the day.

The original brief of current affairs programming in Australia and elsewhere was to provide background to and analysis of the news of the day. Rather than simply running its own agenda, it took on a complementary relation to the news. Given that the news in Australia does not customarily include much analysis or comment, this complementary function is an important one. It has been largely abandoned in the search for higher ratings. *A Current Affair* now devotes an average of 30 percent of its programme every night to material which is not on the news agenda and which is generated, in-house and in advance, for its entertainment value.

Over at the ABC, funding cuts limited the resources available to follow stories and sustained political criticism produced an excessively cautious treatment of some issues and a hypersensitivity to accusations of biased or unbalanced coverage. At the same time as the network was being asked to be more relevant and to pursue ratings, it was being starved of the funds required to produce quality news and current affairs programming. Consequently, news and current affairs made increasing use of talking heads rather than filmed stories; the specialized television reporter gave way to a radio and television reporter providing the same content to both media; and the treatment of politics was routinely produced as a debate between contending parties, scrupulously regulated for equal time and rarely challenged with the results of independent investigative reporting. Increasingly, the ABC has employed tactics usually identified with tabloid formats – such as the use of reconstructions in crime stories, for instance, or faux interviews with foreign correspondents (taped hours before with another interviewer, and performed identically by different news readers across the country). This has not necessarily been in order to move down market; rather it may be a response to the difficulty of providing interesting material without the resources to fund continuing investigations or even, in some cases, to provide a camera crew or an outside broadcast van. Political stories are still covered. However, they are covered by way of an interview between the programme's presenter and a journalist – often reporting second hand on reports from others, and with very little film or actuality footage in support.

The story so far, then, is not a happy one. There are other stories, however, which reveal the existence of competing if not entirely countervailing forces – even within the context I have been outlining. The Ten Network's move to provide an alternative timeslot for news in the early evening has been successful; the audiences for this timeslot have grown 25 percent since it was introduced. Always the most downmarket, magazine styled, news service, there has not been any appreciable change in its content or approach but it does extend the reach of news programming across the schedule. News and current affairs formats have mutated in other ways on the Ten Network. Successes have included the late evening talk show, *The Panel*, and what started off as a copy of the UK's *Have I Got News For You* but is now a unique mixture of game show, news and variety, *Good News Week*. It is being seriously suggested that young audiences derive more news from these hybrid formats than from the traditional news format.[1]

Such possibilities have motivated sporadic attempts to produce a current affairs format which will appeal to the young. The market leader, *A Current Affair*, has a core demographic among the over 50s, and it has become a commonplace of media planning to recognize the large scale evacuation of young consumers from the news audience. Attempts to address that shift in Australia have included the ABC's *Attitude* and the Seven Network's *The Times*. Both of these programmes adopted a new mode of address and changed the look of their programmes in order to attract a younger audience. Gone were the authoritative, quasi-objective and serious reporters. In their place were the cheeky, opinionated and lively reporters of *The Times* or, with *Attitude*, no visible reporter at all as the subjects of stories were allowed direct access to the camera and the viewer – unmediated by noddies or even the inclusion of the interviewer's questions. The look of these shows resembled the visually busy, multidimensional layout of the popular fashion or music magazine, or of contemporary computer screens. Cutting rhythms were closer to the speed of an MTV clip than those of conventional news, and standard rules of composition and editing were routinely transgressed so that *Attitude*, for one, took on rather an avant-garde look. The sources used for interviews tended to be the individual at risk – the youth who attempted suicide – rather than the institutional or authority figure conventionally charged with explaining their behaviour – the doctor or social researcher. *Attitude*, in particular, had an ethnographic rather than a journalistic modality; it gathered its stories for us to observe and withheld anything which might look like the programme's judgement or comment.

Both programmes offered genuine alternatives to the dominant models of news and current affairs currently being screened, and aimed seriously at a young audience. Unfortunately, neither of them survived. In both cases, the time required to build a loyal audience was not provided as they were moved around the schedule nervously in search of the ratings. *Attitude* survived for three series, *The Times* for two, so they were creditable failures in commercial terms. They had their critics – even among the desired demographic: *Attitude* was seen as being a little too worthy for its own good, while *The Times* could occasionally fall into a patronizing discourse that identified its producers as adults trying to be 'one of the kids'. Nevertheless, they remain useful reminders that there can be alternative forms of current affairs and suggest what they could look like.

A second development occurred in late-night news programming which, until the mid-1980s, simply did not exist in Australia. This situation changed with Seven's networking of a cult success from Sydney, *Clive Robertson's Newsworld*, in 1987. Robertson was a former radio host who presented a one hour news programme at 10.30pm which could have come straight out of the movie, *Network*. Robertson was the antithesis of the conventional newsreader. He commented acerbically on the stories he ran, as well as on how they had been edited or compiled; he refused to read sports results when he had no time for the particular sport involved; and he pulled faces when the names of certain politicians featured in stories he read (Ronald Reagan, or then Australian Prime Minister Bob Hawke). Most significantly, he was permanently depressed – by the content of what he read, by the triviality of what he was asked to read, by the prospect that there could be people whose lives were so impoverished they might stay up late to watch him. Perversely, the format was a runaway hit, increasing the total audience for the timeslot and provoking a series of copies on the rival networks. One such alternative employed an extremely successful variety show host, whose career had hitherto been built on comedy, to present the news. Initially the host, Graham Kennedy, read the news himself but this was so disconcerting (and, for some viewers, offensive) that he eventually handed this task over to a conventional network news reader. This left Kennedy and his sidekick free to use the news as a platform for talk and comedy. The logic of this format lead to the eventual incorporation of a live audience in the studio – for a news programme! The third competitor was a more conventional late-night talk show, modelled on David Letterman but including two segments of news updates to attract what had become a late night news audience.

By 1994 these programmes had disappeared in favour of a conventional half hour news report at 10.30pm on all networks, with the ABC incorporating a debate-styled current affairs programme in its half hour. Seven eventually dropped out of this competition. It is significant, and not a little ironic, that this ratings battle over transgressive news formats has resulted in the growth of the conventional news audience at this time of night and an extension in the provision of news services to the Australian audience. The point of this brief survey is not simply to privilege one form of programming over another. I accept the defences mounted of, for instance, examples of tabloidization such as Ricki Lake's talk show and the increasing news interest in the private lives of celebrities (Shattuc 1997). Changes to the news diet, reorientations of what constitutes important information for the public domain, need to be understood as shifts in cultural discourses rather than simply deplored or applauded. It is perfectly possible to agree with the argument that what counts as news these days has fundamentally changed in favour of a more democratic counterdiscourse to an overly institutional and masculine news agenda. Nevertheless, and notwithstanding the complexity of the shifts in programming I have been describing in the Australian context, I want to make some critical comments about what I consider to be among the negative consequences of these shifts for Australian audiences.

The consequences for news and current affairs in Australia

For a start, it is worth stating that there definitely has been a change in news values. A content analysis conducted across radio and television in 1996 (Turner 1996) found that politics no longer dominated the news. Crime stories were the leading category, across the public and commercial sectors alike. When compared with figures generated a decade or so earlier, there was a substantial growth in two areas where coverage had been barely existent before. Once there had been no sport section in the evening news; now it can account for as much as 30 percent. And celebrity stories, while not there in numbers, had become routine components of the news diet, performing a leavening function in an agenda dominated by bad news. Further, there was now a local celebrity industry which thrived on feeding this material to the media, and this is reflected in the number of local celebrity stories finding their way into news and current affairs programming (Bonner et al. 1999).

These shifts may well represent the democratized and suburbanized public sphere implicit in John Hartley's discussions of popular journalism. But they do not only represent that. The privileging of the lively, the visual, and the domestic does not necessarily require the complete withdrawal of investigative resources, say, from current affairs coverage of politics. This is, though, what has happened as the networks seek the ratings they require for these flagship programmes. As a result, the commercial interests of producers and proprietors, not the silenced voices of the suburbs, are prevailing over the public interest in information. Nowhere was this clearer than in the recent public debate over Australia becoming a republic, a debate that was fought by way of slogans and celebrity endorsement rather than a substantial supply of information to the public. Once the primary interest is ratings, a story on the republic had to be a debate between two high-profile Australians (or more) rather than a careful, informed and independent comparison of the competing cases. What is lost here was once thought fundamental to current affairs: the provision of background, informed comment and analysis, and a deeper understanding of the issues involved in the news stories of the day. Whatever else may have improved in this area, that seems rather a lot to give away.

Whose interests are being served by popular journalism, when those of the public are not? Of course, the answer is commercial interests, but we can be more specific than that. Reviewing changes in the conduct of television journalism in Australia over the last decade, we would have to say that, overwhelmingly, they reflect the need to serve the interests of the individual programme. The heightened commercial power of the high profile presenter; the representation of journalism as a spectacle of performance through aggressive interviews, street confrontations and other forms of attack; the competition for exclusivity: all point to a situation where the obligations of public service have given way to the imperative of building the market position and brand name of the pro-gramme. In Australia, where the responsibilities for redress and correc-tion are left almost entirely to the media outlet concerned, this has had very bad consequences for those who want to complain about media misrepresentation, or those who want a correction or apology. It is simply not in the interests of any television news outlet to respond to such complaints unless they come from powerful people. As a result, concern about the behaviour of television journalists in Australia has grown to the point where we now have a satiric series, *Frontline*, devoted solely to producing thinly fictionalized versions of real media industry events which display media professionals as rapacious and irresponsible. Ironically, perhaps fortunately, this frantic pursuit of ratings success and programme profile has not won over the Australian audience. While the late evening slot has grown steadily in audience numbers over the last ten years, news and current affairs audiences have shrunk in all other time slots. In fact, the total television audience in the capital cities has shrunk. This has to some extent masked what is a major and poten-tially catastrophic decline in network news and current affairs audi-ences. Because the total number of sets in use during the timeslot of 6–7pm have shrunk by around 6 percent and because the ratings are usually expressed as a percentage of the sets in use, it has not been readily apparent that total audience numbers have dropped. However, journalist Jon Casimir has documented an average decline of 10 percent for the commercial news and current affairs audience in Sydney over the period 1991–8 (*Sydney Morning Herald* 1998). While the audiences for most programmes have declined, it is the ratings leaders – those who have most enthusiastically hitched their star to the new agenda for television journalism – who have lost most. The Nine Network's *A Current Affair* has dropped 29 percent while its news has dropped 23 percent. This suggests, for a start, that the sprint down market has not worked and thus the case for what were always questionable news values is no longer even commercially plausible. Casimir also suggests that, given the particularly deep erosion of the youth and young adult audience, they may be permanently lost to television news. They have simply found other sources, and the future of the industry has been gambled away.

Reporting on this history, I have two, perhaps contradictory, re-sponses. One is roughly that which is outlined in an earlier article where I warn against an automatic assent to what John Langer calls the 'lament' for popular journalism: the tendency for generalized taste-based critiques, which are often expressed as an ethical diagnosis of the broad cultural trend towards tabloidisation, to divert us from specific, case-related critiques of journalism practice (Turner 1999). While this position does endorse the more optimistic accounts usually identified with the work of John Hartley, and while it does reject the moralizing censoriousness which builds up around the tabloidization critique of talk shows, reality TV and the like, it also insists upon the necessity of dealing with the specific historical effects of specific performance in the news media. This brings me to the second response, which is to acknowledge that the interests of Australian consumers in this specific case, their current levels of access to information and analysis of issues of public significance, have not been well served by the developments reviewed above. Not only has the news diet lost some key 'food groups' but the regulation of the quality of even this restricted diet has been neglected. Government policy frameworks have been modified so as to provide two clear opportunities for the commercial networks over the period surveyed. The legitimizing of the networks and the withdrawal of a regime of independent regulation have deliberately cleared away obstacles to a thoroughly commercial operation. In what constitutes a substantial ideological shift, government has decided that commercial imperatives are the most important consideration in setting the media policy environment for the future. This has been fundamentally damaging – and not only in terms of its immediate effects. The capacity to correct the situation at some time in the future has been significantly reduced because of the institutionalized downgrading of an important principle as constitutive of the relationship between government and the media in Australia: that is, that broadcasters operating a scarce public resource for private commercial gain still bear public responsibilities for which they can be held to account. These responsibilities include not only the provision of entertainment but also the provision of public information and points of view, while preserving citizens' entitlement to access and redress. In Australia, these entitlements have been sold out in order to ensure the commercial networks of their continuing profitability, and the price paid has been the dismantling of the public's implication in government systems of media regulation.

Note

1 The ethnographic research of Jason Sternberg at the Queensland University of Technology, so far unpublished, is encouraging such conclusions.

References

Bennett, T., Frith, S., Grossberg, L., Shepherd, J. & Turner, G. (eds) (1993) 'Who killed the radio star?: The death of teen radio in Australia', *Rock and Popular Music: Politics, Policies and Institutions*, Routledge, London.

Bonner, F., Farley, R., Marshall, D. & Turner, G. (1999) 'Celebrity and the media', *Australian Journal of Communication*, 26:1.

Franklin, B. (1998) *Newszak and News Media*, Edward Arnold, London.

Hartley, J. (1996) *Popular Reality: Journalism, Modernity, Popular Culture*, Edward Arnold, London.

Langer, J. (1998) *Tabloid Television: Popular Journalism and the 'Other News'*, Routledge, London.

Lumby, C. (1999) *Gotcha! Life in a Tabloid World*, Allen and Unwin, Sidney, NSW.

Shattuc, J. (1997) *The Talking Cure: TV Talkshows and Women*, Routledge, New York.

Sydney Morning Herald (1998) *The Guide*, 'The Big Turn off', 22–8 June: 4–5.

Turner, G. (1996) 'Maintaining the news', *Culture and Policy*, 7:3.

Turner, G. (1999) 'Tabloidisation, journalism and the possibility of critique', *International Journal of Cultural Studies*, 2:1 (April).

PART II

Production of journalism genres

CHAPTER 4

Television news and citizenship: Packaging the public sphere

Simon Cottle

How the play of strategic and definitional power meets up with the professionally crafted forms of journalism demands serious thought and sustained enquiry. This is so because the forms of journalism *mediate* surrounding conflicts and contending interests and, depending on how they do this, so they serve variously to either enhance or undermine the 'public sphere(s)' of engaged citizenship. In social democracies such as Britain, TV news, because of its institutional position of (quasi-) independence from the state and its statutory obligations towards impartiality and public service ideals, can serve to facilitate that 'realm of social life' which is available to all citizens and in which and through which 'something approaching public opinion can be formed' (Habermas 1974: 1989). To what extent and in what ways news *in fact*, *in part* or only *potentially* contributes to such an ideal of the 'public sphere' requires, of course, careful thought and systematic analysis. It also demands consideration of what exactly is meant by 'citizenship' and the role that television generally, and TV news particularly, can play within this. It is simply insufficient, for example, to assume that news, or 'the public sphere', can be confined to processes of 'information transmission' and/or rationalistic processes of opinion formation.[1] Active and engaged cultural citizenship involves much more than this; it necessarily involves social conflicts, the play of discursive positions and the struggle by different interests for cultural recognition and public legitimacy.

Graham Murdock has usefully identified four sets of basic cultural rights that together help to flesh out ideas of 'cultural citizenship' – that is, citizenship enacted in and through the media (Murdock 1999; see also Husband 2000). First, cultural citizenship includes *rights to information* where citizens have access to 'the widest possible range of relevant information about the conditions that structure their range of choices, and about the actions, motivations and strategies of significant social, political and economic actors'. Secondly, cultural citizenship also involves *rights to experience* where citizens have rights of access to 'the greatest possible diversity of representations of personal and social experience'.

Thirdly, cultural citizenship must necessarily involve *rights to knowledge*. That is, access to 'frameworks of interpretation' which can help to point to the links, patterns and processes that provide explanations by connecting the particular to the general, the micro to the macro, biography to history. These 'frameworks of interpretation' are invariably fractured and contested but they are deemed vital for an understanding of the issues at stake, as well as the differences at play, since 'knowledge is no longer a gift carefully wrapped by experts' but is rather 'the stake in a continual contest of positions'. Fourthly, cultural citizenship also involves *rights to participation*. Today various social groups and interests now demand 'to speak about their own lives and aspirations in their own voice, and to picture the things that matter to them in ways they have chosen' (Murdock 1999: 11–12). Questions of cultural citizenship and representation, then, encourage us to examine issues of access and how the different genres of broadcasting, for example, contribute to, or constrain, the public sphere(s) of engaged citizenship:

> Questions of representation are, first, questions about social delegation, about who is entitled to speak for or about others, and what responsibilities they owe to the constituencies whose views and hopes they claim to articulate. But they are also questions about cultural forms and genres, about ways in which the raw materials of language and imagery are combined in particular expressive forms – documentaries, episodes of soap operas, single plays – and about how well these contribute to the resources of information, experience, interpretation and explanation required for the exercise of full citizenship. (Murdock 1999: 13)

Murdock is surely right to open up questions of cultural citizenship in relation to the full spectrum of TV genres, but this deeper appreciation of cultural citizenship is no less relevant to the genre of news[2] which is, and remains, for most of us the citizenship genre *par excellence*. We need to examine how the genre of TV news delegates access and conditions public participation and the representation of contending views and experiences. Here we must inquire further into the conventionalized and changing forms of news presentation as well as the hierarchies that these variously set up between news producers, accessed news voices and news audiences. We need to know more about the discursive opportunities as well as the forms of discursive containment that these create, and examine how these are managed and manipulated in practice by involved social actors. And we also need to know how these are differentially distributed across the changing TV news landscape – a landscape that is characterized by more difference than is often acknowledged by theorists of 'the news' (Cottle 1993a). In short, we must attend to the various 'cultural forums' provided by TV news and how these variously serve to *enact* the cultural rights of citizens or *detract* from them. This is, of course, an ambitious, if necessary project involving interrelated aspects of news production, news access and news representation (Cottle 1995; 1999; 2000a, b, c). In this chapter, I will focus on the presentational formats that routinely structure and condition news access and participation and which, in so doing, shape the public elaboration and engagement of contending 'interpretive frameworks' and experiences. Given the fundamental role played by these in *mediating* social conflicts it is perhaps curious that formats of news presentation should escape the critical attention of major theoretical approaches to news study.[3] Only by attending to the presentational 'arenas' of news can we begin to critically appraise the current state of British TV news and its contribution to democratic processes of representation and citizenship.

The discussion now turns to a close-up look at a major news story and how different presentational news formats package the voices and contending discursive positions at play. The news story selected for illustrative purposes concerns the demonstrations mounted in London and Seattle in the US in November and December 1999 by a broad coalition of social groups and activists against the World Trade Organisation; a 'story' which attracted considerable news interest at the time. The discussion helps to illustrate the profound impact that presentational formats can have on the public definition of newsworthy events and the discursive contestation that inevitably inform them. Having examined how different news formats variously serve to either detract from, or enact, cultural citizenship in the context of this major news story, the discussion then turns to a systematic review of the range, extent and patterns of presentational formats currently found both within and across the major outlets of British TV news. On the basis of these qualitative and quantitative findings we can begin to see how presentational forms of news currently restrict and contain, as well as expand and open-up, opportunities for access, discursive contestation and public participation and we can thereby begin to critically appraise the contribution of British TV news to a public sphere of engaged citizenship.

Contested spaces and places: news formats and demonstrations

The following examines close-up the range of presentational news formats that 'mediated' the story of the anti-World Trade Organisation demonstrations in Seattle and London towards the end of 1999. These demonstrations involved a broad range of activists and different social groups protesting against the effects of free trade upon the environment, labour rights and the poor around the world. This 'creative cacophony' of latter-day environmentalists and loosely affiliated activists and protestors (Castells 1997: 110–33) also made effective use of the Internet in coordinating their activities across time and space. Our focus of interest here, however, is upon how these events were mediated and represented within the presentational formats of TV news delivery. Specifically, how did these variously constrain or enable the contending voices and viewpoints involved, and how did they contribute to the public 'framing' of these events?[4]

The basic news report: 'framing by default'

To begin, we can first briefly note how incredibly 'restricted' some news formats are when reporting news stories. For example, following the demonstration in London on 30 November 1999, *Channel 4 News* reported on the aftermath of these events the next day in the following way:

> **Channel 4 News 1.12.99**
> News Presenter: Jon Snow
>
> Here in London five people have been arrested after an anti-World Trade Organisation protest outside Euston station. Three appeared in court today.

Sitting in the news studio the news presenter here speaks direct to camera and with no accompanying visuals. Clearly this format offers no opportunities for non-news voices to directly enter into the news delivery, much less contest the news construction at work. As such, it lends itself to an 'objectivist' news stance that proclaims itself to be simply and accurately reporting objective facts 'out there'. Evidently, the report provides the barest of information, and it remains entirely within the editorial and discursive control of the news presenters. No matter the selection of information, nor its possible dependence upon certain sources and not others, the news presentation serves by default and through its prioritization of 'arrests' and 'court appearances' to define the demonstration and its aftermath in terms of a 'law and (dis)order' frame. No other information is provided that could help to invite a different interpretive framework.

ENG, the archetypal news format: 'sealing the frame'

As we shall see below, the 'restricted' news format is a standard feature of most TV news programmes, but so too is the ENG ('electronic news gathering' or video/film) report.[5] On 30 November 1999, ITN led its main evening news programme with the 'major' story of the anti-World Trade demonstrations in London and Seattle. The full transcript of the ITN news report as broadcast, including the words spoken by accessed voices, is reproduced below:

> **ITN 30.11.99**
> News presenter: Dermot Murnaghan
>
> DM:
> Good evening. Demonstrators have been fighting riot police in central London tonight in the second protest against capitalism this year. It started peacefully but then degenerated into violence at Euston mainline railway station which was closed for public safety reasons. A police van was set on fire, several people were hurt and several people were arrested by police snatch squads. ITN's Terry Lloyd reports:
>
> TL:
> For two hours the atmosphere was carnival-like as hundreds of anti-capitalist demonstrators gathered at Euston station for their last rally of the

day. Some though had threatened violence and vowed to close down the railway station. At seven o'clock they charged police lines, terrifying the lightly armed officers.

(Police shouting: 'Right come on, get out the way . . .')

Railings were ripped apart and thrown and explosions were heard. Fully kitted-out riot police were eventually set in to push the rioters back inside the station and surround them. Several arrests were made and the injured taken to nearby ambulances for treatment. But the demonstrators continued to taunt the police; one of them climbed onto an overturned van wearing a policeman's helmet and bib. Then, with the police and fire services helpless, they set the vehicle ablaze ignoring all risks of another explosion. This is exactly what the demonstrators threatened and the police feared; anarchy on the streets of London, albeit for a few hours. Anti-capitalist demonstrators caused two million pounds worth of damage in the city of London in June. Tonight they rioted and blocked the main Euston road bringing road and rail traffic to a standstill.

Assistant Chief Constable:
I can only say that for a group of about 150 people who were obviously hell-bent on creating a situation of violence and mayhem and damage there can certainly be no excuse. It was not lawful protest.

TL:
Police snatch squads were deployed to pick out and arrest troublemakers who had earlier been identified by undercover officers and photographers. Within the last 90 minutes violence flared again close to Euston station; police baton-charged a group of demonstrators who refused to leave the area. Officers will be kept out in force throughout the night in case protesters congregate elsewhere. Terry Lloyd, ITN Central London.

In many respects this is instantly recognizable as the archetypal TV news format. The news presenter first introduces the news item from the setting of the TV news studio where the story is 'framed' in terms that will be elaborated in the following ENG report. Following the studio presenter's introduction, the news item then moves to a filmed report by a news reporter whose voice-over commentary narrates the story over visually 'authenticating' scenes – scenes, that is, which serve to anchor the reporter's narration firmly within the law and disorder frame. Next the news report includes edited clips from an ENG interview which has been packaged into the final film report. Clearly, this conventionalized TV news format only permits limited forms of access and opportunities for discursive contestation. At no point are the voices of the protestors or those in sympathy with the protest against the World Trade Organisation granted direct access to the news report. The film report is thus effectively 'framed' and discursively 'sealed' by the news producers.

Essentially, as we have heard, the frame mobilized in and through this format is instantly recognizable as the 'law and disorder' frame, a frame that researchers have repeatedly documented in the news portrayal of diverse protests, demonstrations and civil disorders (Halloran *et al.* 1970; Gitlin 1980; Murdock 1981; Waddington 1992; Cottle 1993b). The frame invariably has the consequence of politically 'emptying out' the informing reasons and political motivations that can help to explain protests and the actions of the protestors. The interpretive vacuum is then also invariably filled with dramatic pyrotechnic visuals and sensational scenes – burning, 'rioting', shouting, destruction, violence – scenes that all resonate with deep-seated news values – negativity, conflict, deviance – and which reflect the 'event orientation' of news. When combined with the structural dependence of news organizations upon authority sources, such factors help to explain why it is that protestors are so often linguistically and symbolically labelled as 'other' and their political claims and aims consigned to news oblivion.

When outside voices are granted access in this format they have little opportunity to challenge, much less dislodge, the informing frame of the news producers – assuming, of course, that they would want to. It is apparent that the accessed voice of the Assistant Chief Constable in the ENG report above, for example, only serves to endorse the overall frame and narrative of the news producers. The information presented in this report also illustrates how the news producers have, in fact, relied heavily upon the police as their principal source of information and apparently accepted without question their definition of events as their own. The point here, however, is not that such a format inevitably privileges the voices of established authorities, but rather that it is highly dependent on the journalist's own judgement about how a newsworthy event should be handled and who the legitimate voices are and how they should be packaged, juxtaposed and put to work *inside* the news producers' frame. Consider the following ITN report on the Seattle demonstration, for example, and how this deploys the exact same news format but now provides a slightly more encompassing frame; one that at least begins to acknowledge the role of the police as active participants within, rather than simply as a reactive force to, the 'trouble' and the legitimate concerns of some of the protestors:

ITN: 30.11.99
News presenter: Dermot Murnaghan

DM:
And the London demonstration coincided intentionally with the scheduled start of the World Trade Organisation meeting in Seattle on the pacific coast of America. Thousands of protestors there also clashed with the police. Officers used pepper gas against demonstrators as the demonstration threatened to get out of hand. John Draper reports from America.

JD:
After days of peaceful protest in Seattle today it turned violent.

Sounds of police
'this is your final warning. We will be moving forward. . . .

JD:
Police moved against demonstrators stopping delegates reaching the World Trade Conference and protestors blocked city streets, police used pepper spray and pellet guns and canisters of pepper gas.

Voice of protestor:
The police are attacking the crowd using chemical weapons, gas and pepper spray, and we're trying to protect the crowd.

JD:
Protestors with anarchist flags turned their anger on symbols of wealth. A local TV station witnessed another group smashing a MacDonald's restaurant window. Activists on a huge range of environmental and other issues, many of them clearly having prepared for trouble, are using the meeting at the WTO to vent their frustrations. Police tempers too became short as the day wore on. The conference has now cancelled its first session; the centre of Seattle is at a stand still. Before the rioting started, President Clinton said he sympathized with the protestors concerns. How they react to him, we will know tomorrow, when he flies into Seattle to attend the conference. John Draper, ITN. Washington.

As we can see, this presentational format need not always privilege the voices of authority but can grant access to the voices of the demonstrators. That said, one can't help surmising that in this instance, both the geographical distance involved as well as the involvement of a high status 'legitimate' actor – no less than the President of the United States – are both factors that have helped to broaden the news producers' interpretive frame. The key finding remains, however; namely, that this archetypal format permits few openings for social actors to contest the views of others in engaged dialogue, much less challenge the overall frame of the news producers. At best their views may be juxtaposed in 'pseudo-engagements' subsequently orchestrated from edited interview clips, but they remain dependent upon the news producer's overall understanding of 'the story' and the issues at stake. They remain, in other words, the discursive prisoners of the journalist's conception of what the 'story' is all about and who are deemed to be the legitimate actors and voices. Such is the naturalized status of this 'ineffable' format (Winston 1993), that what appears to be a neutral device facilitating *political representation*, in fact is a highly packaged *re-presentation* of views and voices orchestrated by the new producers – a package, that is, which remains highly dependent on the 'omniscient' insights of the news producers and their interpretations of the struggles and conflicts that they 'report' on.

Formats of discursive contest: 'fracturing the frame'

The 'restricted' news report and the archetypal ENG format of news presentation, as we shall see, are prevalent across the TV news landscape; they do not exhaust the discursive opening and possibilities of news presentation however. More 'expansive' TV news formats also occasionally feature within and across news programmes, and these provide enhanced opportunities for discursive contestation as well as live challenges to the informing 'frames' of the news producers. Channel 4 News programme (1 December 1999), for example, devoted a large proportion ($22\frac{1}{2}$ minutes) of its one-hour news programme to the events in Seattle. This included a complex package of news presentation that sutured together different presentational formats. These included, first, the news presenter Jon Snow introducing the presentation from the London studio; secondly, a reporter's ENG film report from Seattle that included interviews with protestors and scenes and commentary from press conferences with both the Mayor and Police Chief of Seattle as well as three clips from interviews with protestors; thirdly, a live interview conducted by Jon Snow again in the London studio via satellite link to Seattle with one of the march organizers; fourthly, following the commercial break, a film report produced by an activist who, granted editorial control, narrated his own piece and selected his own ENG interview clips; fifthly, a live studio interview back in London by Jon Snow with the veteran campaigner and retired MP Tony Benn and a cyber-activist involved in the demonstration; and finally, sixthly, a live location report by the assigned reporter in Seattle who responded to questions from Jon Snow. Clearly, this represents a complex and, in news terms, relatively generous news package – one that included discursive openings and opportunities for engaged participation. For our purposes, it is useful to consider first the opening 'frames' set in place both by Jon Snow in the studio, and by the reporter in Seattle.

C4 News: 1.12.99
News presenter: Jon Snow
Programme Tease:

JS:
A ring of steel and more arrests as police at the Seattle trade summit get tough (C4 opening music).

JS:
Well, now in about an hour the 135 ministers of the World Trade Organisation summit will sit down to lunch with President Clinton, but so far the actual proceedings have been pretty indigestible. Demonstrators have begun to go back on the streets in force again, only to be confronted by an even bigger and more determined police operation. Seattle's Chief of Police said he was proud of his force's performance yesterday and promised even tougher action today . . .

C4 Reporter in Seattle Liam Halligan:
LH.
The protestors are back on the streets, fewer in number, kept further away from the talks but still out in force. With President Clinton now in town, the combined forces of city policemen and National Guard are determined to keep a lid on any violence. A ring of steel has been enforced for several blocks in each direction around the convention centre. City of Seattle authorities have known about these protests for months, but after yesterday and last night it looks as if they are responding to events the magnitude of which took them completely by surprise. Overnight downtown Seattle was a battle zone. The local mayor had called a state of emergency and police set about imposing a curfew order. But with the National Guard still being scrambled, the local police had to cope on their own . . . There were dozens of arrests, with some sustaining injuries. Police stand accused of inciting violence . . . Some came to Seattle to raise legitimate concerns about the World Trade Organisation. And some just came to wreak havoc. It's difficult to know who was who.

What is noticeable here, is that the opening C4 News tease, news presenter's introduction and reporter's film report all tend to initially frame the events in Seattle in terms of the disruption and violence that has informed the demonstrations with only limited acknowledgement of the protestor's political agenda and the possibility that the police in Seattle have been accused of being heavy-handed. This 'frame' is constructed by the limited discursive opportunities that accompany these formats and which remain, therefore, firmly under the control of the news producers and the editing process. The following live interview format with one of the march organizers, however, demonstrably presents new discursive opportunities. Consider the excerpts below:

C4 News: 1.12.99

JS:

Joining me live now from Seattle is Mike Dolan. He's field Director of the Citizen's Trade Campaign; a civil rights group, and part of Global Watch. He's one of the main organizers of this Seattle protest. Mike Dolan, how would you evaluate what's happened so far? Are you happy or sad?

MD:

Well I'm happy. The reality is, apart from the ugliness at the end of the day yesterday and the ugliness that is going on behind me even more, it's absolutely inarguable that we won the day and in fact are winning this battle. It's a major international mobilization against corporate globalization. I'm very happy; I'm sorry that I got tear-gassed.

JS:

Well, you know, the fact of the matter is it got extremely violent last night. It's violent again today. When you talk about 'that battle' and 'win', you are using, surely, the language of the very people that you are trying to defeat?

MD:

Look, battles have been won non-violently, and there's a couple of good examples that a lot of your viewers will remember: Ghandi, Martin Luther King in this country. And that's what we went out to do yesterday; to accomplish by direct action, civil disobedience . . .

JS:

But Mike Dolan, but here we are on day two of Seattle and we are talking not about the key issues that you want focused upon, but upon the police dragging demonstrators away, about battle, about warfare, not about issues. Therefore you have lost surely?

MD:

On the contrary Jon, on the contrary. The WTO will never be the same. The issues that are being discussed behind closed doors now happen to involve labour rights. Our fair-trade message, while stalled momentarily by the official sources news media's sensational attention on to the brief violence, actually will not be lost. I believe we are winning this battle and that our agenda, the fair-trade agenda of the labour, the environment, the family, the farmers, the consumers and the activists that are here in Seattle, will not be lost. We are peeling off some of the political elites and we have the attention of the international news media now. And I'm very thrilled about it.

Here we see how a live interview, in contrast to a pre-recorded and subsequently edited and clipped ENG interview, permits the interviewee to challenge the news presenter's 'law and disorder' framework as well as his belief (ironic given his own persistent line of questioning) that the demonstration has fogged the issues.

A live studio debate/discussion presents even more generous opportunities for alternative voices to challenge and fracture the producer's news frame and to begin to articulate different 'interpretive frameworks'. Again, an excerpt helps make the point:

C4 News: 1.12.99

Tony Benn:
I'll tell you the problem. You never interview any of these people. You just show them shouting, fighting and in funny hats, making out they're a lot of nutters.

JS:
Well we did have a chap at the top of the programme actually.

TB:
Well I didn't see that, but in general 'protest' is the wrong word; it's the beginning of a political campaign. That's how apartheid ended, that's how men got the vote, that's how women got the vote, it was by putting pressure on parliament.

JS:
Right, do you find yourself identifying with Tony Benn, or is he of a different era and not something you find a resonance with?

Paul Mobbs, Cyber-activist:
I think we're all going in the same direction. Campaigning is all about managing change and different views of how we manage that change. People today are using the Internet, much like in the Civil War people used pamphlets. We've just moved on and it's got a lot more technical.

JS:
There's no real identifiable ideology behind what's going on here in Seattle, I mean.

TB:
It's anti-capitalist, it's anti-capitalist.

JS:
Well, wow! Hang on a minute. Look you were a purist, you wouldn't have bought some piece of equipment from some company that you were protesting against, but there are people there who have got shoes on that were made by people inside the World Trade Organisation.

TB: Look, this isn't really globalization is it? The free movement of capital. You can close a factory in London and open it in Malaysia where the wages are lower but if people from Malaysia want to come to London where the wages are higher, the Immigration laws keep them out. What you are witnessing now, Jon, is the globalization of ideas through the Internet. The Internet is only the street corner meeting on a big scale. And even in the street corner someone was wearing a pair of shoes and stood on a soapbox and so this is really part of a continuing process. My experience of change is that to begin with it's ignored, then you're mad, then you're dangerous, then there's a pause, and then you can't find anyone who didn't claim to have thought of it in the first place and that's what you are witnessing in Seattle.

JS:
You're talking about 'one' problem, but there are people there with problems as disparate as the environment, exploitation, child labour.

TB:
They're all the same issue Jon; they're all about profit. Genetically-modified food is all about profit, the IMF trade is about profit, privatization is about profit.

In the relatively expansive format of a live studio interview, then, accessed voices are able to challenge and occasionally agenda-shift informing news agendas and frames.[6] Here they can also begin to elaborate alternative interpretive frameworks that help to make sense of newsworthy events and even, as we began to see above, set these within necessary historical, structural and political contexts.

Towards formats of participatory control: 'alternative frames'

A final format, rarely used, but one that contains important possibilities for opening up news participation and contributing in a meaningful way to cultural citizenship, is that of ceded editorial control. Here, involved social actors are granted resources and news space to present in their own ways, and in their own words, their own frameworks of understanding. They are enabled to share their experiences with others and can also delegate who they deem to be the 'legitimate' voices in terms of news access. In the same C4 news programme, editorial control was ceded to an involved activist who made and presented his own film report from Seattle. Again, a few excerpts from this help to demonstrate something of the distinctive opportunities and democratic contribution that such a format facilitates:

C4 News: 1.12.99

Rob Newman:
RN: Never before have so many disparate groups from all over the world come to protest as one organization. What's really astounding about this, was until these protests no one had really heard of the WTO or so we thought . . .

Protestor:
Let's put our energies where it needs to go, so that we have a planet for our children to live on, and our children's children to live on. That's what this is about.

Protestor:
We've come down here for the world to see us. We want to put the spotlight on the people in that building up there . . . They're the killers; the people who are tearing this planet apart . . .

RN:
We were angry to see our rights turned over to faceless bureaucrats in Geneva. No globalization without representation.

Protestor:
If people can vote in a voting booth they don't have to come out on the streets. There's no way that we can control these people by voting so this is the only place that people can meet.

Protestor:
The five year record of the World Trade Organisation is that every single environmental, labour or safety law that has come in front of them has been struck down or weakened; and that's true of every law in every country that is a member.

RN:
Thank you very much indeed. Well another inarticulate protestor, another mindless anarchist thug there . . .

RN:
This is Channel Four News in England. Can we talk to you about why you are here today and about the raging grannies.

Elderly protestor:
Basically this is a guerrilla organization that sings satirical songs and takes old tunes and we go where we are not wanted.

RN:
It's great; there's people walking towards us going 'we won, we won'. Not 'we', obviously – as a neutral observer I feel that this has serious ramifications for trade liberalization – they can give it up, they can do it.

Protestor:
I think this is the seeds of a very broad global coalition that will have to continue. It's good to join the fight against the WTO.

From the few excepts above, it is apparent that ceded editorial control has allowed the news presentation to get closer to the people on the streets and their views. Stereotypical news constructions of 'anarchists' and 'thugs' are given ironic short-shrift and the wide-spread coalition of popular involvement – across age-groups for example – is deliberately signalled by accessing ordinary voices including the self-proclaimed 'guerrilla grannies'. Moreover, the pretence of news objectivity is also poked fun at by the presenter's self-reflexivity in respect of his obvious delight at the outcome of the protest in halting the WTO summit on this day. This format, then, is clearly enabling in that it serves to access a different interpretive framework into the public news domain, and it also permits a more experiential dimension to come into view through the shared experiences and feelings of many of the protestors – all vital components as we have heard for cultural citizenship.

British TV news formats: patterns of containment and participation

So far we have seen how different presentation formats variously enhance or restrict opportunities for the public display of contending discursive positions that (inevitably) surround and inform major social conflicts. But to what extent do these respectively feature within and across different British news programmes? Table 4.1, based on a survey of eight different TV news outlets and 80 news programmes broadcast over a two-week period, provides the answer.[7]

As we can see, British TV news makes use of a differentiated range of presentational formats, each providing differing opportunities for access and discursive contestation. For the purpose of this analysis these have been arranged in a hierarchy of 'restricted' to 'expansive' formats (listed 1–10) with each successive format making use of further presentational elements. These, as has already illustrated in part, incrementally enhance the discursive opportunities for accessed voices to put their point of view, contest the ideas of others and potentially challenge the news presentation agenda and its possible informing frameworks of interpretation. Whilst each format could be discussed in some detail, the key finding here is that Formats 1–5 all provide severely restricted opportunities in respect of the above and these remain firmly within the editorial and discursive control of the news presenters. With 507 news items delivered in these formats, these together represent 48.01 percent of all news formats deployed across British television news. Nearly half of all TV news items, in other words, provide few if any opportunities for direct access and discursive engagement by non-news voices, and such voices that are referenced remain the discursive prisoners of the news presenters and their informing news frame.

The ENG format, Format 6, as previously described, provides limited opportunities of access and at 445 news items within the sample represents the single most commonly used of all formats across British TV news at 42.14 percent. Interestingly, rarely is ENG deployed to interview groups (Format 7, 0.09 percent) where accessed voices could then at least potentially contest and engage directly opposing viewpoints and, in so doing, partially escape the news presentation's 'pseudo-engagement' manufactured from clipped voices juxtaposed later in the editing process.

Discursively, as we have seen, Formats 8 (live individual interview), and 9 (live group interview), considerably improve upon the restricted and limited opportunities presented by Formats 1–7. Live interviews afford interviewees an 'extended' opportunity to respond to the interviewer's questions, in their own terms, in chronological time, and in the ways that they feel are appropriate. They may even, on occasion, seek to challenge the interviewer's agenda and informing assumptions, and agenda-shift to different issues and interpretive frameworks and in so doing fracture the imposition of a particular news frame. Live group interviews also afford interviewees an opportunity to not only question informing news frames but also to directly engage the ideas and interpretive frameworks of contending interests represented by other accessed voices. Whilst news interviewers will invariably seek to 'hold the ring' on such occasions, the fact that interviewees are inside the ring potentially enables them to engage the ideas and arguments, the claims and counter-claims of their interlocutors and, in so doing, begin to escape the mediation of the news programme and its informing agenda. These, then, are invaluable and potentially meaningful formats when deployed

Table 4.1 British TV news and presentational formats

Format	Totals	BBCam	GMTV	HTV	News West	C4	BBC	ITN	BBC2 Newsnight
Total Items	**1056**	**193**	**126**	**153**	**125**	**140**	**127**	**119**	**73**
Total %	**100%**	**18.28**	**11.93**	**14.49**	**11.84**	**13.26**	**12.03**	**11.27**	**6.91**
1 Newscaster (NC) only	11	1	2	3	0	2	0	2	1
	1.04%	0.52	1.59	1.96	0.0	1.43	0.0	1.68	1.37
2 Newscaster still	104	30	9	11	5	16	12	12	9
	9.85%	15.54	7.14	7.19	4.0	11.43	9.45	10.08	12.33
3 NC/reporter (rpt) fim/voice-over	354	54	41	64	36	51	47	37	24
	33.52%	27.98	32.54	41.83	28.80	36.43	37.01	31.09	32.88
4 Rpt direct to camera	5	0	4	0	0	0	0	1	0
	0.47%	0.0	3.17	0.0	0.0	0.0	0.0	0.84	0.0
5 NC – rpt dialogue	33	6	9	2	0	4	6	4	2
	3.13%	3.11	7.14	1.31	0.0	2.86	4.72	3.36	2.74
6 ENG interview	445	71	42	63	76	55	62	61	15
	42.14%	36.79	33.33	41.18	60.80	39.29	48.82	51.26	20.55
7 ENG group interview	1	0	0	0	1	0	0	0	0
	0.09%	0.0	0.0	0.0	0.80	0.0	0.0	0.0	0.0
8 Rpt-live interview	61	24	13	6	4	9	0	1	4
	5.78%	12.44	10.32	3.92	3.20	6.43	0.0	0.84	5.48
9 Live group interview	26	1	2	0	1	3	0	1	18
	2.46%	0.52	1.59	0.0	0.80	2.14	0.0	0.84	24.66
10 Editorial control	16	6	4	4	2	0	0	0	0
	1.52 %	3.11	3.17	2.61	1.60	0.0	0.0	0.0	0.0

Note: Column percentage figures under each outlet refer to the percentage of each format deployed by this outlet, permitting comparison across rows and outlets. Absolute differences of broadcast items by each outlet are indicated in top row. Percentages in column one refer to the percentage of formats deployed within the sample as a whole.

in relation to social conflicts where contending interpretive and prescriptive frameworks are at play – and in how many news stories are these not present? Together these formats, however, are only deployed within 8.24 percent of news stories on British television news.

Finally, we come to ceded editorial control, where news programmes afford, as we have seen, an opportunity for social actors to represent themselves, their experiences and viewpoints in the ways that they deem to be valid, fair or useful, and which may well involve them in accessing voices and views not normally granted a prominent role on the news stage. According to our systematic review, this promising format is rarely deployed however, and was found in our sample to only figure in 1.52 percent of all news stories and presentational formats across British television news. Evidently, the example taken from Channel 4 News discussed above is rare indeed.

Conclusion: cultural citizenship and news formats

From the discussion above, it has hopefully become clear that television news is indeed structured and delivered by a range of formats, each of which exerts profound effects upon the public mediation and elaboration of social conflicts and contending views – the latter of which are positioned at the heart of most news stories. As we have seen, these formats variously enable or disable the opportunities of access, discursive contestation and public participation. In such ways, TV news provides a range of 'cultural forums' that routinely structure news delivery and which inform, often in the most decisive of ways, the public representation and elaboration of wider social issues and conflicts. Through its presentational formats, TV news literally mediates the surrounding play of social and cultural power and, potentially, plays a vital role in serving to enact, and thereby enhance and deepen, cultural citizenship. However, many of the formats routinely deployed across the TV news landscape also severely constrain and detract from representational and discursive opportunities for engaged citizenship, whilst purporting to simply 'report' and convey the 'information' needed for public understanding. Increasingly driven by the logics of entertainment and commerce as well as by traditional journalist ideals and the pragmatics of news production, news producers must seek to balance considerations of narrative and a 'good story' with those of public exposition and rational deliberation (Corner 1995). These competing aims and logics no doubt inform their professional judgements and the deployment of conventionalized news formats also (Cottle 1995) and may well help to account for the range of formats distributed differently across the TV news landscape as documented in Table 4.1 above. These different TV news programmes are structured differently in terms of national and regional, serious and popular news agendas and appeals and evidently presentational formats also feature within these differences (Cottle 1993a). In these complex and differentiated ways, then, news formats help to structure our TV news and variously constrain and contribute to a public sphere of cultural citizenship.

Finally, lest we should succumb to the myth of news as simply providing 'information' and therefore conclude that all this attention to formats is misplaced, we need only acknowledge that 'knowledge is no longer a gift carefully wrapped by experts' but is 'the stake in a continual contest of positions'. News can and must respond by providing presentational arenas in which discursive positions are enabled to publicly elaborate and defend their claims in close engagement with contending views and interests. TV news producers and programmes already implicitly acknowledge this in so far as they routinely deploy formats that are deliberately structured around the play of social conflicts and differences of opinion. And occasionally, very occasionally, news producers can even reflexively demonstrate that they are aware of the necessity to move beyond their artificial claims to news objectivity and news omniscience by deliberately conceding editorial control to 'others' – that is, those social actors who may previously only have secured news access as the spectacular 'object' of someone else's discourse. Whether these occasional news openings for cultural citizenship can be built on and extended in the future is, for the time being, unclear. Today's processes of digitalization, technological convergence and increased news competition are all reconfiguring the contemporary news map. How these and other processes of change are now impacting on the 'cultural forums' of news and opportunities for cultural citizenship must become a vital concern for future research.

Notes

1 Arguably Habermas' conceptualization of the 'public sphere' does indeed invite an overly rationalistic conception of the public sphere as 'information transmission' to use one of James Carey's mass communication models – a model that has often privileged analysis of news and factuality forms and political communications (Carey 1975). Carey's second model of mass communication as 'ritual', however, invites a wider appreciation of televisual genres including entertainment forms and encourages an approach to television as a 'cultural forum' (Newcomb and Hirsch 1984) – ideas that are in sympathy with a deeper sense of 'cultural citizenship'. The argument here, then, is that ideas of 'cultural forum' and 'cultural citizenship' help us to get an analytical handle on news forms and in this way we are better able to critically appraise today's news media and its contribution to a 'public sphere' of engaged citizenship. For more critical commentary on Habermas' theory of the 'public sphere' in relation to media see Elliott (1986); Garnham (1986); Curran (1991); Frazer (1992); Hallin (1994); Dahlgren (1995); Thompson (1995).
2 Indeed, Murdock with others has empirically examined different TV genres including different news programmes and how these have variously represented discourses of 'terrorism' (Schlesinger et al. 1986). See also, Altheide (1987; 1995).
3 Currently, two influential paradigms to news study have contributed important insights into the nature of news but neither, it seems, pays

sufficient attention to the important dimension of news formats as characteristic and mediating properties of news and news discourse. Putting matters boldly, the sociological paradigm has prompted empirical explorations of the strategic operations of power in relation to processes of news production, access and representation. Recent studies here, for example, have observed how news sources compete for strategic and definitional advantage and how, despite the unequal weighting of institutional resources and symbolic power across different source fields, news access and representation is not always a forgone conclusion in support of powerful interests. The cultural studies paradigm, for its part, also contributes a powerful optic through which to view news. Informed by a philosophical stance that centres the discursive nature of reality and a political commitment to radical change, cultural studies has produced interpretive analyses of news 'texts' and 'representations' and how these are thought to give expression to (and in so doing contribute to) the wider play of social power and the pursuit of cultural hegemony. While both paradigms contribute invaluable insights into the nature of news as a site of, respectively, strategic and discursive struggle, both seemingly fail to acknowledge the important mediating properties of news and how different formats of news presentation in particular, condition and impact on the public play of strategic and discursive power. My argument here, then, tends to invest news, and news forms, with an important mediating position and cultural 'power' that has so far been overlooked by both sociological and cultural studies approaches. (For a review and discussion of both these paradigms and issues of news access see, Cottle 2000a.)

4 The concept of 'frame' is here used to refer to the informing assumptions and interpretation that help to discursively define, allocate, explain and, often implicitly, prescribe in relation to 'events' and 'processes'. These 'frames', then, help to structure news and wider public discourse and literally 'frame' the meanings and understanding that are publicly made available via news representations. For more on 'frames' and 'framing' see Goffman (1974); Gitlin (1980); Entman (1993). For the purposes of this discussion, attention focuses for the most part upon the verbal accounts and narratives that are facilitated through different presentational formats and does not pursue the contributing role of news visuals. For discussion and examples of the different approaches to, and the role(s) played by, TV news visuals in news representation see Cottle (1998; 2000b).

5 For an interesting historical recovery of the origins of the TV news form see Winston (1993).

6 For a more detailed analysis of studio news interviews and how the conventions of this form influence turn-taking, agenda-setting and agenda-shifting see Greatbatch (1986) and Heritage & Greatbatch (1993).

7 These results are taken from the author's *UK News Access* project that systematically examined patterns and forms of TV and press news access and forms. The two selected sample weeks, Monday to Friday,

began on 23 January 1995 and 5 June 1995. For the purpose of this analysis, news 'presentational format' was coded according to the 'highest' format of presentation involved as set out in Table 4.1 and the list of Formats 1–10, as already discussed. I would like to acknowledge Bath Spa University College for funding this research.

References

Altheide, D.L. (1987) 'Format and symbols in TV coverage of terrorism', *International Studies Quarterly*, 31: 161–76.

Altheide, D.L. (1995) *An Ecology of Communication: Cultural Formats of Control*, Aldine De Gruyter, New York.

Carey, J. (1975) 'A cultural approach to communication', *Communication*, 2: 1–22.

Castells, M. (1997) *The Power of Identity*, Polity Press, London.

Corner, J. (1995) *Television Form and Public Address*, Edward Arnold, London.

Cottle, S. (1993a) 'Mediating the environment: modalities of tv news', in Hansen, A. (ed.), *The Mass Media and Environmental Issues*, Leicester University Press, Leicester: 107–33.

Cottle, S. (1993b) *TV News, Urban Conflict and the Inner City*, Leicester University Press, Leicester.

Cottle, S. (1995) 'The production of news formats: determinants of mediated public contestation', *Media, Culture and Society*, 17(2): 275–91.

Cottle, S. (1998) Analysing visuals: still and moving images', in Hansen, A., Cottle, S., Negrine, R. & Newbold, C. *Mass Communication Research Methods*, Macmillan, Basingstoke: 189–224.

Cottle, S. with the assistance of Mark Ashton (1999) 'From BBC newsroom to BBC newscentre: changing news technologies and changing journalist practices', *Convergence*, 5(3): 22–43.

Cottle, S. (2000a) 'Rethinking news access', *Journalism Studies*, 1(3): 29–44.

Cottle, S. (2000b) 'TV news, lay voices and the visualisation of environmental risks', in Allan, S., Adam, B. & Carter, C. (eds), *Environmental Risks and the Media*, Routledge, London: 29–44.

Cottle, S. (2000c) 'New(s) times: towards a "second wave" of news ethnography', *Communications*, 25,1: 19–41.

Curran, J. (1991) 'Rethinking the media as public sphere', in Dahlgren, P. & Sparks, C. (eds), *Communication and Citizenship*, Routledge, London: 27–57.

Dahlgren, P. (1995) *Television and the Public Sphere – Citizenship, Democracy and the Media*, Sage, London.

Elliott, P. (1986) 'Intellectuals, "the information society" and the disappearance of the public sphere', in Collins, R., Curran, J., Garnham, N., Scannell, P., Schlesinger, P. & Sparks, C. (eds), *Media, Culture and Society – A Critical Reader*, Sage, London: 247–63.

Entman, R.M. (1993) 'Framing: toward clarification of a fractured paradigm', *Journal of Communication*, 43(4): 51–8.

Frazer, N. (1992) 'Rethinking the public sphere: a contribution to the critique of actually existing democracy', in Calhoun, C. (ed.), *Habermas and the Public Sphere*, The MIT Press, Cambridge, Mass. and London: 109–42.

Garnham, N. (1986) 'The media as public sphere', in Golding, P., Murdock, G. & Schlesinger, P. (eds), *Communicating Politics*, Leicester University Press, Leicester: 37–53.

Gitlin, T. (1980) *The Whole World Is Watching: Mass Media in the Making and Unmaking of the New Left*, University of California Press, Berkeley.

Goffman, E. (1974) *Frame Analysis*, Harper and Row, New York.

Greatbatch, D. (1986) 'Aspects of topical organisation in news interviews: the use of agenda-shifting procedures by interviewees', *Media, Culture and Society*, 8(4): 441–55.

Habermas, J. (1974) 'The public sphere', *New German Critique*, 1(3): 49–55.

Habermas, J. (1989) *The Structural Transformation of the Public Sphere*, Polity Press, London.

Hallin, D. (1994) *We Keep America on Top of the World: Television Journalism and the Public Sphere*, Routledge, London.

Halloran, J.D., Elliott, P. & Murdock, G. (1970) *Demonstrations and Communication: A Case Study*, Penguin, Harmondsworth.

Heritage, J. & Greatbatch, D. (1993) 'On the institutional character of institutional talk: the case of news interviews', in Boden, D. & Zimmerman, D. (eds), *Talk and Social Structure: Studies in Ethnomethodology and Conversation Analysis*, Polity Press, Cambridge: 93–137.

Husband, C. (2000) 'Media and the public sphere in multi-ethnic societies', in Cottle, S. (ed.), *Ethnic Minorities and the Media: Changing Cultural Boundaries*, Open University Press, Buckingham: 199–214.

Murdock, G. (1981) 'Political deviance: the press presentation of a militant mass demonstration', in Cohen, S. & Young, J. (eds), *The Manufacture of News: Deviance, Social Problems and the Mass Media*, Constable, London: 206–25.

Murdock, G. (1999) 'Rights and representations: public discourse and cultural citizenship', in Gripsrud, J. (ed.), *Television and Common Knowledge*, Routledge, London: 7–17.

Newcomb, H.M. & Hirsch, P.M. (1984) 'Television as a cultural forum: implications for research', in Rowland, W.D. & Watkins, B. (eds), *Interpreting Television: Current Research Perspectives*, Sage, Beverly Hills, CA: 58–73.

Schlesinger, P., Murdock, G. & Elliott, P. (1986) *Televising Terrorism: Political Violence in Popular Culture*, Comedia, London.

Thompson, J.B. (1995) *The Media and Modernity – A Social Theory of the Media*, Polity Press, Cambridge.

Waddington, D. (1992) 'Media representation of public disorder', in Waddington, D., *Contemporary Issues in Public Disorder*, Routledge, London: 160–78.

Winston, B. (1993) 'The CBS evening news, 7 April 1949: creating an ineffable television form', in Eldridge, J. (ed.), *Getting the Message: News, Truth and Power*, Routledge, London: 73–103.

CHAPTER 5

Authority and authenticity: Redefining television current affairs

Patricia Holland

Image

The image was on the cover of the *Radio Times* of 6–12 November 1999. Headed 'I spy' and captioned 'Why this man has the most dangerous job in television', it showed a burly young man, naked from the waist up, his blue eyes gazing directly at the viewer. Items of recording equipment were taped around his body in James Bond style, whilst the pores of his skin and the hairs on his chest glistened under lighting that would do credit to a feature film. This was glamorous undercover journalist, Donal MacIntyre whose covert camera investigations ran on BBC1 during November 1999.

The cover was promoting journalism with a popular face for a peak time mass audience (9.30pm BBC1). Presented with panache, the image seemed full of self-confidence. But it came at a time when television producers were voicing their concern about current affairs journalism. A report from the Campaign for Quality Television, published only a couple of weeks earlier, had claimed, 'the genre is in crisis, possibly in terminal decline' (Barnett and Seymour 1999: 20). At issue were falling budgets, a lack of commitment from management, and the difficulty of protecting journalistic values in a ferociously competitive environment. One anonymous respondent complained about a shift towards 'manufactured journalism' made up of 'hype, entertainment, infotainment values, in which investigation takes the . . . stunt approach' (p.29). The focus is shifting away from the content of a programme, towards its presentation and its style.

So are programmes like the MacIntyre series merely hype or stunts, or are we seeing legitimate new journalistic forms? The authority of television journalism comes under question when the journalist must be a crowd pleaser as well as a reporter and a programme must earn its place in the schedules by winning audiences which will compare with those of entertainment programmes. In this context, a promotional image like the *Radio Times's* MacIntyre is an important supplement to the programmes themselves, as it sets them up and positions them for the viewer. And this was a particularly knowing image. It promised the type of entertainment generated by vicarious danger, while enjoying a contemporary stylishness which both anticipates and defuses criticism. It is impossible not to smile at the acknowledgement of fictional forms and the nods towards computer games in which muscle bound heroes take on ferocious opponents. At the same time, the promotion was able to present the programmes as authentic and authoritative journalism. In an extra twist to these layers of reflexive understanding, the production of the MacIntyre programmes was monitored by no fewer than two university departments (*Media Guardian* 6 December 1999: 3).

Bearing in mind this complex of understandings, I will be arguing that debates which focus on hype and infotainment do not, by themselves, do justice to the multiplicity of changes that have been happening to current affairs television (Brants 1998). From its earliest days, a tension between a desire to attract an audience and a commitment to journalistic values has characterized the genre. The authority of the journalist has constantly been questioned whilst the nature of the programmes – what I shall refer to as the authenticity of the texts – has also come under scrutiny. In the current climate, I want to focus less on content, and more on the changes and debates around these two areas of authority and authenticity. Such debates have taken different forms at different points in history, and it will be important to note that their limits have always been drawn by the institutional and economic contexts within which the programmes have been produced – just as the current institutional and economic upheavals in UK television have led to contemporary concerns. In its struggle to hold together forces which pull in several different directions, the image of Donal MacIntyre on the cover of the *Radio Times* stands as a sign of the times.

Schizophrenia

Like the MacIntyre image, the contemporary received wisdom just about manages to keep in play two positions that are becoming ever more difficult to reconcile. A commitment to 'journalism of impartiality and authority' (BBC 1992: 28) continues to appear as common sense and desirable, something which few politicians or television policy makers would deny in public. At the same time, a new consensus at the policy-making level accepts that television's position as a business is of prime importance. The talk is of the necessity for British television to 'compete on the world stage' rather than to satisfy domestic needs. As a consequence, many current affairs producers feel that the need to attract audiences now overrules journalistic values (Barnett and Seymour 1999). The conviction that, in John Pilger's words, journalists must also 'tell people things that they do not want to know', or as John Simpson put it, 'there's a duty, regardless of audience figures, to tell the bigger picture and to put it on record', now has to be argued for and cannot be taken for granted.[1]

Until the 1990s the sometimes contradictory imperatives to attract audiences and to put over challenging information were held in balance by the powerful concept of television as a public service. The two approaches could be seen as complementary functions of a democratic television provision (Pratten 1998). The Campaign for Quality Television was set up by senior ITV programme makers in the run up to the 1990 Broadcasting Act, specifically to argue that ITV, although a commercial broadcaster, was effectively part of an overall, diverse, public service *system* (Davidson 1992: 18). But the consensus has moved significantly. By 1999, Richard Eyre, speaking as Chief Executive of the ITV Network Centre, was arguing at the Edinburgh Television Festival that 'public service' is an outmoded concept. A sense of embarrassment and puzzlement now often surrounds the use of the term.

In the new schizophrenic climate, the 'public service' glue that held the diversity of television together has been weakened. Television's business activities and its informational role now imply contradictory ways in which the viewers are conceptualized – the two approaches have different 'imagined' audiences.[2] Current affairs programmes have traditionally been part of an informational approach. They have seen themselves as part of a 'public sphere' in which the audience is considered to be made up of thoughtful, participating citizens, who use the media to help them 'learn about the world, debate their responses to it and reach informed decisions about what courses of action to adopt' (Dahlgren and Sparks 1991: 1). By contrast, for the business dominated view, winning a place in 'the market' and becoming a 'global player' is its own justification. In this view the imagined audience is made up of consumers, wherever they may be found across the globe. Trapped within this contradiction, current affairs journalism has become particularly vulnerable. News is stark and instantaneous. The success of CNN following the Gulf War demonstrated its global marketability. Current affairs is slower and more thoughtful. Its investigations may be long term and costly, and much of the work that goes into it is invisible. Its programmes are more specific, more locally grounded – even when they deal with international topics – and more directly challenging to the audience.

Current affairs

Although commentators now tend to run 'news and current affairs' together – as indeed does the BBC's News and Current Affairs Directorate – in the past practitioners have been careful to mark the longer current affairs programmes (now known as 'long form' journalism) off from news, wanting to preserve their privilege to make criticisms, pose questions, investigate and to challenge. 'If the job of a news service was to tell what was happening at any given moment, then the job of current affairs was to help us understand what was happening', wrote Jeremy Isaacs of his time as producer of *This Week* between 1963 and

1964. 'They had to try to do that', he went on, 'by reporting on situations which persisted over weeks, months and years, and which lay behind and gave rise to events that daily made the headlines. Current affairs has a duty to explain the background for what is going on' (Potter 1989).

This Week reporter Peter Taylor put the point very clearly in a letter to the public relations officer of the British Army, when seeking permission to make a programme in the mid-1970s. 'The television audience', he wrote, 'are now punch drunk with the nightly horrors they see on the news. There is no chance for analysis on these news bulletins, and no possibility to connect all these events in one piece to make sense of them. This is where we hope we can help and inform.'[3]

After Grace Wyndham Goldie took the light-weight *Panorama* and transformed it into a serious political vehicle in 1955, current affairs gained a privileged place in the television scene. Hers was an innovative struggle to create a space on television which would be taken seriously by politicians and the thinking public alike (Goldie 1977: 191). She was clear about the role of the journalist in ensuring that the views of the public are presented to the politicians, and in insisting that the politicians present themselves to their electorate. The journalist's authority came from their role as a mediator, not as a final authoritative voice (Kumar 1977).

The post-war BBC was secure in its public service duty to educate, entertain and inform its audiences without commercial commitments, but in the run up to the establishment of ITV, it was strongly aware of the claims that television should be seen as a business and the challenge that this posed. When ITV arrived, current affairs, of a sort, was part of the new commercial mix. Associated Rediffusion was the first company to launch a series with *This Week* in January 1956. Like *Panorama*, *This Week* began as a multi-item light-weight magazine programme. Its producer, Caryl Doncaster, put its aims in the following terms:

> *This Week* will be a programme of stories behind the news worldwide. It won't be all political. There will be a bit of everything in it, including humour and glamour. It won't be highbrow because we want a wide audience. With everything geared to the commercial element we cannot afford programmes that do not pull their weight in viewer strength. (Courtney Browne 1975: 2)

In those early years, the new television companies could be as brash and open about their commercial intentions as Rupert Murdoch was to be in 1989 (Sendall 1982; Murdoch 1989). However, the journalistic instincts of current affairs producers, including Jeremy Isaacs at *This Week* and Tim Hewat at Granada's *World in Action* (launched in 1963), were backed up by the intervention of the regulatory body, the Independent Television Authority (ITA). In 1968, the ITA ensured diversity in the independent network by creating 'mandated slots' for certain programmes. These included *This Week* and *World in Action* which were required to be transmitted at peak time in the evening schedules. The

ITV companies were not entirely happy with this arrangement. John Freeman, chairman of London Weekend Television (LWT), speaking on their behalf in January 1973, described it as putting on 'unpopular' programmes at a 'popular' time (Potter 1989: 106). But 'commercial' television in the UK had been secured as 'independent' television, a recognized and regulated part of a diverse public service system.

Over the following 30 years the authoritative place of current affairs was accepted on the independent network. Although relations were far from smooth, the sense of confidence was guaranteed by the institutional support of the regulatory body. But it was the very sense of confidence behind *This Week* and *World in Action* during the 1960s and 1970s that led to some stringent criticisms. These included an accusation of *over*-confidence and of too much reliance on the authority of a few, privileged journalists (Potter 1989). At the same time, the fault line between 'exploring behind the news' and 'pulling their weight in viewer strength' that Caryl Doncaster had put into words, remained.

Authority

In current affairs, unlike documentary, a named reporter has the right to address the camera/audience directly, making judgements and summing-up a situation. Questions about who has the right to speak with this sort authority, and what elements in the programme guarantee their speech, have intensified over the years. Doubts have been expressed not least by journalists themselves. Jonathan Dimbleby, whose career began with a prize winning programme which revealed the scandal of the 1972 famine in the north of Ethiopia (*This Week* 'The Unknown Famine'), looked back in 1995 and commented on 'the prism of my own prejudice, which I liked to believe was objectivity' (Sheffield International Documentary Festival 1995).

The authority of the television journalist has been challenged from several different perspectives. *First,* in critiques which became increasingly forceful over the 1970s, it was criticized from the point of view of those outside the mainstream of broadcasting. The argument was that the ideological framework of broadcasting was from a narrow, educated, class privileged base, and that the political consequences of this were that oppositional and working class politics were marginalized. Working class or regional voices were not heard, nor was a working class perspective put (Glasgow University Media Group 1976; Murdock and Golding 1977; Hall *et al.* 1978). Although the rationale behind much of the critique from the academic community was an argument for a major shift of power towards a more socialist form of democracy, a variation on the challenge came from right-wing thinkers and the Conservative Party, arguing that the hidden agenda of many journalists was a left-wing one (Potter 1989: 114). However, the increasingly audible voices of marginalized groups which cut across the major class divide shifted the emphasis away from class politics and drew awareness to a more diverse range of excluded voices. It was pointed out that the heavily masculine culture of the broadcasting organizations led to the exclusion of women and of a feminine viewpoint and that television journalism was ethno-centric and euro-centric (Baehr and Dyer 1987; Gilroy 1987; Dowmunt 1993). This body of work can be described as the critique from the point of view of *'access'*, arguing that the democratic obligation of broadcasters requires a meaningful address to different segments of the population, and also, importantly, that members of those groups should participate in the production of televised material.

In this 'access' challenge, the authority of a journalist becomes particularly suspect when they address those who are different from themselves, and when their 'imagined audience' is presumed to be in need of instruction. This adoption of an authoritative right to speak and to define the situation on behalf of others may be seen as patronizing or as talking down. It may involve a disguised ideological exercise of power, excluding certain important meanings (Hall 1977). Although apparently knowledgeable, it may be based on a form of ignorance – ignorance of experience and of the lived reality of the situations reported on.

The *second* challenge to the authority of the television journalist has come from the *'market'* position, in which viewers are 'customers' to be attracted to programmes and gratified by them in certain ways. In this view audiences may be treated as aggregate numbers, as the 'ratings battles' which regularly feature in the media pages of the quality press demonstrate, or they may be attracted as specific 'niche' audiences, suitable for advertising certain types of product. For example, the History Channel promotes itself to advertisers in the following way:

> The History Channel's viewer is predominantly upmarket and male. Half its audience are men under 45 which makes it an excellent vehicle for reaching this difficult to target but highly lucrative market. (publicity brochure 1999)

In both of these approaches the 'imagined audience' is an audience of consumers and the consumer is king. Any programme which does not 'pull its weight in viewer strength' becomes suspect. In this 'market' critique, viewer choice is what gives authority to television journalism, and much importance is given to market research. If the viewers do not watch, then arrogant broadcasters pursuing their own interests (and awkward and opinionated journalists fall all too easily into this category) have no right to take up space on the airwaves (Murdoch 1989).

Of course, producers have long argued that the desire to attract viewers is not necessarily in contradiction to the desire to produce important and relevant current affairs. Nevertheless, the theme that journalists must be restrained has surfaced several times in the history of current affairs programming. *This Week* was taken off the air in 1978 because, in the words of Mike Townson, the editor of its replacement *TVEye*, it was too journalist centred and had become boring.[4] Townson was one of the first to be credited with 'grafting tabloid style and values on to broadsheet journalism' (Bolton 1990: 31). But his argument was a powerful one. Current affairs, he wrote, 'should be driven by the desire to communicate to as many people as possible about the subjects that matter most to them' (Townson 1990).

A *third* challenge to the authority of the television journalist has been from changing technology, which potentially puts the tools of communication and investigation into the hands of many more people, and is beginning to change the context within which television programmes are received and understood. It is beginning to make nonsense of any hard and fast division between the givers and receivers of information (Holland 2000).

Changes

Over the years current affairs has developed in relation to these critiques. A major shift in ways of legitimating television journalism came with the launch of Channel 4 in 1982, which explicitly recognized the need for new forms of journalistic authority in response to the 'access' critique. As a public service broadcaster the channel was free to set its priorities according to cultural and democratic ends – indeed it was required to do so by its licence conditions (Harvey 1994: 111–17). Current affairs veteran, Jeremy Isaacs, as its first chief executive, led several innovatory moves. First, the main current affairs series was to be made by two companies led by women, one of them from a specifically feminist standpoint (Baehr and Dyer 1987: 117). Another was the creation of a multi-cultural department, with a direct address to people from ethnic minorities by people from those minorities. A third was a recognition of a diversity of opinion, with programmes made from committed viewpoints. And there was a commitment to broadcast journalistic work which originated outside the mainstream – and hence which carried a range of different preconceptions (Isaacs 1989: 126–44). It was a recognition that a move away from the accepted journalistic style was not simply a sign of 'tabloidization'. In addition, Channel 4's mainstream current affairs series, *Dispatches* (1987–) continues to be based on more traditional forms of journalism.

If 1982 had been a pivotal date from an 'access' perspective, 1990 was a pivotal date from the 'market' perspective. The Broadcasting Act created a new sort of ITV whose intentions were expressed by Paul Jackson of Carlton, the company which won the London weekday franchise.[5] In a reference to *World in Action*'s long-term campaigning stance, he stated that television does not exist to get people out of jail. He was clear that, if current affairs programmes did not win their place in the peak time schedule by attracting audience numbers, then they would either be moved, or killed (Edinburgh Television Festival 1990). Although it took several years for the full effects of the change to be felt, the shift to a more commercial ITV, together with a more general move to a business approach, has led to the disappearance of long running current affairs series, including *This Week* (ended 1992), *World in Action* (ended

1999) and *First Tuesday* (1983–93), and the inability to support newer series supplied by smaller companies (*Storyline* (1992–3), *The Big Story* (1993–8)) for more than a short period. *Tonight* with Trevor MacDonald (1999–), at the time of writing the main current affairs series on ITV, has returned to the magazine format with stories that follow the agenda of the tabloid newspapers rather than the qualities. (Despite near universal condemnation, in my view the programme has developed its own characteristic style and stories can be lively and informative.)

It is important to note that the 'market' driven changes of the 1990s have not eradicated the 'access' driven ones of the 1980s. Sometimes the two have played complementary roles, even if at other times they have been sharply contradictory. The newer forms of current affairs programming have themselves become a site of contest between 'market' and 'access' forces.

Authenticity

A current affairs text must carry conviction as it digs into 'the stories behind the news'. Without journalistic authenticity it is nothing, as the Independent Television Commission's investigations into current affairs programmes accused of fakery have demonstrated (*Guardian* 19 December 1998: 9). Each television genre has its own distinct conventions, and the authenticity of current affairs must reside in conventions which are reflected in the 'look' of the programme. During the evolution of the genre, certain elements have become accepted as characteristic of a current affairs text. These include the figure of the journalist visibly reporting from a location – whether drought-ridden Ethiopia, the Prime Minister's office, or a war zone. They have included interviews, which ensure that the audience is presented with named individuals who have something authoritative to say about the situation reported on. Those interviewed may be experts on the subject in hand; they may be official spokespeople, or they may be 'ordinary people' telling of their own experiences. (There has been much debate on the selection of interviewees, see Curran 2000.) The journalist may draw painful, personal stories out of an interviewee or may challenge them with hostile questioning. Either way, the visible presence of the witness is of crucial importance, even when the sensitivity of the material means that they must be seen in the shadows, or partly concealed. Finally, traditional current affairs has included location filming which carries specific visual information and may also act as a background against which commentary can be laid (see Corner 1995: 58–63 for a more detailed discussion of such issues in relation to news).

Over the years current affairs programmes have built on this basic framework, employing an ever widening range of filmic styles, from the use of background music and visual effects, to elaborate dramatic reconstructions.[6] Technological innovations have meant that many different 'looks' are now available – from the distinctive 'spy' effect of the covert camera to the glossy lighting and careful set ups associated with drama or cinema or the graphic sophistication of computer effects (Ellis 2000: 91–6). But the introduction of a wider range of techniques has brought concerns that the authenticity of the text may be undermined. Reconstruction may come close to 'fakery'; sophisticated lighting make the programme look too much like fiction; naturalistic, observational filming may give an impression of false innocence, concealing artifice. In their research into audience opinions on violence in factual television, the Broadcasting Standards Council found that 'some viewers objected to the use of slow motion and elaborate sound effects' in a *World in Action* programme, 'and said they made it more like drama' (Millwood Hargrave 1993: 60).

Just as the authority of the journalistic statement to camera has become suspect, the styles of presentation which have been developed once more balance the need to attract audiences with the need to inform and involve. Although dramatic reconstruction has long been part of the current affairs repertoire, following the success of *Who Bombed Birmingham?* (Granada 1990) – a feature-length drama-documentary made by the *World in Action* team to dramatize their own long-term investigation into a major miscarriage of justice – *World in Action* set up a Factual Drama unit which, it was argued, was also a form of current affairs journalism. It could deal with subjects too difficult to reach in any other way (Paget 1998: 174–5).

Redefining current affairs

In response to technological changes and institutional pressures, as well as to journalistic enterprise, a wide variety of programmes now deal with current affairs material, so that the overall picture is far from gloomy. I do not have the space to spell out specific examples in any great detail, but below I list some of the ways in which the journalistic context has expanded on UK television. In responding sometimes to 'market' demands, sometimes to 'access' demands, and sometimes to both, new ways have been evolved of exploring the authority of the journalist and expanding the authenticity of the text.

Collective memory

One factor is the sheer length of time over which current affairs has been operating. Simple, definitive statements are far less possible when so many layers of history can be brought into play. Scenes can be revisited, events re-evaluated in the light of new evidence (Bloody Sunday; the fall of the Berlin Wall; the disappearance of the Hull trawler, the Gaul). Many records and much filmed material are available to place today's immediate news event as part of a long, slow development (the Balkan wars; Northern Ireland). News stories can be visited by different journalists who may bring very different perspectives to bear (Aids). Long term campaigners can be given a chance to voice their claims over a number of years (Derek Bentley: the Guildford Four, the Birmingham Six). The political scene may be reviewed and major figures re-assessed (*The Thatcher Years* – LWT 1989; *Playing the Race Card* – BBC 1999; programmes made by the journalist Michael Cockerell). Journalists may question previous assessments and make new ones (Jonathan Dimbleby re-assessed his earlier judgements about political changes in Ethiopia and Tanzania). These approaches may sometimes draw on the long-term work of a single journalist, sometimes on the accumulation of archive material available to new researchers. A collective memory of visual documentation is held in film and television archives across the world. The opening of the Russian and other Soviet bloc archives in the 1990s has been a striking example of the availability of new evidence. Digital technology has created an unprecedented ability to store huge amounts of documentation, and, most importantly, to access it. Thus the collective memory on which current affairs programme makers may draw is potentially richer than ever before. Such material, made available through many different types of television programme, rather than through a single journalistic prism, potentially allows viewers to make continuous re-assessments of the authority and reliability of each journalistic presentation, and the use of archive material brings its own type of authenticity to the text.

Beyond objectivity

There has been a recognition that professional journalists may themselves speak in a variety of different registers. Reporters have traditionally been expected to maintain a distance from the situations on which they report. They are expected to restrain their emotions and to conceal their political preferences. Recently, several television series have relaxed these rules and made a space for journalists to step beyond their professional persona and express their private views. The argument for committed journalism, made powerfully by Martin Bell at the time of the Bosnian war has, to a certain extent, been taken seriously. Maggie O'Kane's confrontation with the Serbian warlord Vojislav Šešelj for *Frontline* sticks in the mind (C4 August 1993).

Investigative journalism may be personalised. The two programmes in which John Sweeny tracked down those who had carried out a massacre at the Kosovan village of Little Krusha, followed the processes of his investigation step by step (C4 *Dispatches* April 1999 and November 1999). This approach gives a narrative pull in which the journalist becomes a character in the story as well as the presenter, making such programmes more enticing for an audience. It also allows an account of the process of investigation, allowing the viewer the opportunity to assess the evidence and the steps taken to verify it. In this case the processes of production become part of the story, partly guaranteeing the authenticity of the text.

One further step is the actual involvement of journalists in the events reported on. Many programmes of this type have involved the use of covert filming, with the reporter literally acting a role. In the *MacIntyre*

Undercover programmes Donal MacIntyre became, among other things, a football hooligan, a fashion photographer and a care worker. A landmark example in this sub-genre was the series in which *World in Action* reporter Adam Holloway lived as a homeless person in order to reveal the institutional prejudice and the difficulties faced by those forced to sleep on the streets (*No Fixed Abode* Granada 1992).

The role of the journalist has thus expanded. The introduction of the personality of the journalist and their own commitment to a story has added a different type of authority. The fascination generated by the emotional pull of these programmes means that they respond to the 'market' demand for bigger audiences, as well as to the demand for greater transparency in the journalist's role. A danger may be that the sense of conviction and truth which comes from the added emotional power may be at the expense of careful research and the checking of facts.

Reflexive programming

Television journalism can no longer be innocent. In a media saturated environment, its practices are scrutinised by national newspapers, and by the trade press as well as by academics and other authors. With the growth of the public relations industry, sources of information can rarely be taken at face value. Media literate corporations and government agencies have become more skilled at dealing with interviewers and probing questions, while they may, at the same time, display a pseudo openness. There has been a growth of quasi-journalistic activity, as journalism merges into public relations and spin. Journalists who aim at disinterested reporting must be ever more vigilant.

In these conditions it is hardly surprising that there are now many programmes which explore television journalism itself, discussing its representations, its shortcomings and the political implications of its programme making. Pioneered by Channel 4's *Friday Alternative* (1982–3) and *The Media Show* (1987–91), series have included *The Spin* (BBC2 1995) and *Whose News* (C4 1995). Current affairs series such as *Panorama* and *Dispatches* regularly consider the operations of the media and television journalism's relationship with its sources.

De-professionalization

Many programmes have done away with the professional mediator, the source of so much mistrust, and instead have presented programmes with a real current affairs edge fronted by figures who range from the comic – Michael Moore's outrageous forays into corporate America – to the totally unexpected, such as Channel 4's *Look Who's Talking* season (September 1994), which included investigatory programmes presented by children.

Much of the irruption of 'ordinary people' on to the screen has followed the work by the BBC's Community Programmes Unit, which expanded from its slot in which campaigning groups could argue their case in their own words, to the successful genres of video diaries and video nation (Dowmunt 1993; 2000). The many series in which non-professionals have engaged in programme making of a journalistic type have made full use of developing technology. They have included BBC1's *Private Investigations* (1994) and Channel 4's *Free for all: Speak Out* (1994) which came live from a docklands warehouse littered with electronic equipment, monitors and telephones, and invited 'ordinary people' to conduct their own investigations and phone in for topical discussions. Such programmes tend to be loose and unpredictable, with a visual excitement that is completely different from traditional current affairs. People looking into their own problems can display the distress and anger forbidden to the professional reporter. They have no need to be balanced, they can be rude and can ask impulsive questions. With no journalistic reputation at stake the non-professional need only take responsibility for themselves, and therein lies a different sort of authority.

Other examples include initiatives such as *The People's Budget* (BBC2 1993) and *The People's Parliament* (C4 1994) which shared a low tech aesthetic but gave a cross-section of 'ordinary people' the opportunity to question politicians and others in positions of authority. Formats like these recognise that 'ordinary people', too, may move beyond their own experience. They too can aspire to 'public sphere' discussions, and their contributions need not be confined to opinions grounded in their own lives.

The Community Programmes Unit has continued pushing back the boundaries with programmes such as *Good Morning Albania* (BBC2 1999), four ten-minute programmes which ran in one week and gave a rare insight into the lives of the NATO forces based in Albania after the war in Kosovo. It by-passed the need for a reporter in an extension of the video diary style. In a similar format, *Sarajevo: Street Under Siege* (BBC2 1994), the series of two-minute snippets from a single street, broadcast nightly during the siege of Sarajevo, gave perhaps one of the most important insights into the Bosnian war. Point du Jour, the French company which initiated this venture, has also developed a format in which people across the world, from different or conflicting backgrounds, could get to know each other and compare their lives in real time, using computer-based teleconference techniques and satellite video-links. A recent initiative develops this approach by using the Internet as a means of contact and as a broadcast medium. The *Mad Mundo* format addresses globalisation from the bottom up, in a series in which a professional journalist investigates on behalf of someone who is experiencing the effects of global policitical forces.[7]

Beyond television

The use of the Internet has pushed the boundaries of current affairs beyond the television screen. Programmes now have their own websites so that viewers can instantly feed back their responses and engage in discussion with other viewers. As new formats develop out of the convergence between computer and television technologies, television communication need no longer be uni-directional.

The new, more accessible technologies have posed new challenges to journalistic authority. During the 1999 conflict over Kosovo, the news agency, the Institute for War and Peace Reporting, set up a web site to monitor information about the war from wheresoever it came. Managing editor Rohan Jayasekara, has described how the mass of information from literally hundreds of different perspectives shook his view of the traditional journalistic project. 'I was bombarded by so many different levels, views, and ideas that I felt I could no longer have faith in saying "this is my unequivocal interpretation".' Each piece of convincing information could be supplemented, contradicted or modified by other information at many different levels. 'No sooner had I made up my mind about an issue, than another compelling piece of information came in which made me re-evaluate what I had originally thought.' He added, 'as a news editor I am accustomed to a stream of material. I just hadn't realised how monochrome it had been' (from a talk given at ARTEC July 1999).

The interplay between computer-based and television forms of communication was recognized by Channel 4 with its *Web Wars*, a series of two-minute explorations of the Internet by writers and others as part of the channel's *Bloody Balkans* season (1999), which opened up a new kind of play between apparent fact and the many faceted spectrum of opinions. A series such as *Mad Mundo* aims to explore the most difficult of political and economic problems simultaneously through interactive events, open to spontaneous intervention by anyone involved in the problems, and conventional programmes. In these newer, more open forms of journalism, the audience is no longer merely 'imagined' and the programme is never completely finished. Authenticity is no longer to be found simply within the text itself.

Conclusion

My argument has been that the diversification of television journalism both within the mainstream of current affairs itself and scattered unevenly throughout the television schedules, has had the effect of bringing us closer than ever to some sort of messy representation of the complexities of the contemporary world. There is a wider range of programmes which provide space for what could broadly be described as democratic debate within the public sphere (Dahlgren and Sparks 1991). Current affairs is in many ways more powerful than ever before, even though more dispersed and more fragmented. It has also leaked into the longer news programmes which regularly include themed enquiries and serial reports.[8] This means that the traditional current affairs formats are under pressure from uncertainties which spring from the shifting nature of the genre itself, as well as being at the sharp end of contemporary institutional and ideological changes.

I have not intended this to be a relativistic argument. The expansion of current affairs-type programming across the output should not be seen as undermining the journalist's craft, nor as a reason for abandoning current affairs in its more traditional forms. Indeed it puts the difficulties expressed by producers in the Campaign for Quality Television report into a sharper perspective. Other recent reports have been equally worrying – including those from the Third World and Environment Broadcasting Project (3WE), which monitored UK television's declining interest in the 'developing' parts of the world over a period of ten years (Lay and Payne 1998), and the British Film Institute, which reported that a majority of the television workers whose careers they had followed over a period of four years, felt that standards in ethics and accuracy in factual programming are declining (BFI 1999). Looking at the broader context makes the need to protect a wide diversity of programming even clearer. Only a commitment to a broader concept of objectivity, and to a grounding in wider forms of authority and authenticity, can create the diversity of styles that is necessary for the contemporary scene. This expansion does not detract from the importance of journalists committing themselves to report objectively as they see it, nor does it mean that serious lapses from those standards should not be criticised. A changing relationship between current affairs and its audience should not sound the death knell for tight, planned, and balanced current affairs.

We need to understand the delicate balance which continues to sustain the genre in order to argue for its importance in a multi-channel, commercially dominated television world.

This article is part of a larger project on the history of the current affairs series, This Week, *undertaken by Patricia Holland and Victoria Wegg-Prosser, currently in association with Bournemouth University. Thames Television, now Pearson Television International, has kindly given access to its archives for the project. I am grateful to the Harold Hyam Wingate Foundation for a grant which made much of my research possible, and to my colleagues Victoria Wegg-Prosser and John Ellis for their extremely helpful comments and advice on this article.*

Notes

1 John Pilger is quoted from a talk at National Film Theatre, London 15 April 1998; John Simpson from a symposium at the Sheffield International Documentary Festival, October 1999.
2 Much hinges on the imagined relationship between the programme maker and those whom they envisage as their audience. Formalist critics, such as Seymour Chatman have described the concept of an 'implied audience' – 'implied' because what is at issue is the way the audience is conceptualized by the programme makers, rather than the actual behaviour of real viewers (Chatman 1995: 482). I prefer to use 'imagined' because it implies a consciously thought out, rather than an automatic, taken-for-granted, conceptualization of the audience.
3 From a memo in the programme file.

4 From an interview with Patricia Holland, 1991. There were, of course, many more factors involved in the change from *This Week* to *TVEye* in 1978.

5 At the time of writing, Paul Jackson is Controller of Entertainment at the BBC.

6 Most new formats have, over the years, followed the development of new technologies. However, similar initiatives to most of the 'new' formats I discuss here can be found much earlier in the history of television current affairs and independent film making. Even so, it is only in the last decade that a real variety of styles has become commonplace.

7 The series *Vis à Vis* (1992–4) and *Mad Mundo* (1999–) are produced by Article Z, Paris. Some programmes from each of the series have been broadcast on Channel 4.

8 The longer items which give background to news stories have become known as 'broken news' – as opposed to 'breaking news' which strives to report events as they are happening.

References

Baehr, H. & Dyer, G. (eds) (1987) *Boxed In: Women and Television*, Pandora, London.

Barnett, S. & Seymour, E. (1999) *'A Shrinking Iceberg Travelling South'. Changing Trends in British Television: A Case Study of Drama and Current Affairs*, Campaign for Quality Television, London.

BBC (1992) *Extending Choice: The BBC's Role in the New Broadcasting Age*, BBC, London.

BFI (1999) *Television Industry Tracking Study*, Third Report, BFI, London.

Bolton, R. (1990) *Death on the Rock and Other Stories*, W.H. Allen, London.

Brants, K. (1998) 'Who's afraid of infotainment?', *European Journal of Communication*, 13, 3: 315–35.

Chatman, S. (1995) 'Story and discourse (introduction)', in Boyd-Barrett, O. & Newbold, C. (eds), *Approaches to Media: A Reader*, Edward Arnold, London.

Corner, J. (1995) *Television Form and Public Address*, Edward Arnold, London.

Courtney Browne, R. (1975) 'In the beginning', unpublished paper prepared for Thames Television.

Curran, J. (2000) 'Television journalism: theory and practice', in Holland, P. (ed.), *The Television Handbook*, 2nd edn, Routledge, London.

Dahlgren, P. & Sparks, C. (1991) *Communication and Citizenship: Journalism and the Public Sphere*, Routledge, London.

Davidson, A. (1992) *Under the Hammer: Greed and Glory Inside the Television Business*, Mandarin, London.

Dowmunt, T. (ed.) (1993) *Channels of Resistance*, BFI, London.

Dowmunt, T. (2000) 'Access: television at the margins', in Holland, P. (ed.), *The Television Handbook*, 2nd edn, Routledge, London.

Ellis, J. (2000) *Seeing Things: Television in an Age of Uncertainty*, I.B. Tauris, London.

Gilroy, P. (1987) *There Ain't no Black in the Union Jack*, Hutchinson, London.
Glasgow University Media Group (1976) *Bad News*, Routledge and Kegan Paul, London.
Goldie, G.W. (1977) *Facing the Nation: Television and Politics 1937–1976*, Bodley Head, London.
Hall, S. (1977) 'Culture, the media, and the "ideological effect"', in Curran, J., Gurevitch, M. & Woollacott, J. (eds), *Mass Communication and Society*, Arnold, London.
Hall, S., Critcher, C., Jefferson, T. & Roberts, B. (1978) *Policing the Crisis*, Macmillan, London.
Harvey, S. (1994) 'Channel Four Television: from Annan to Grade', in Hood, S. (ed.), *Behind the Screens: the Structure of British Television in the Nineties*, Lawrence and Wishart, London.
Holland, P. (2000) *The Television Handbook*, 2nd edn, Routledge, London.
Isaacs, J. (1989) *Storm Over 4: A Personal Account*, Weidenfeld and Nicholson, London.
Kumar, K. (1977) 'Holding the middle ground: the BBC, the public and the professional broadcaster', in Curran, J., Gurevitch, M. & Woollacott, J. (eds), *Mass Communication and Society*, Arnold, London.
Lay, S. & Payne, C. (1998) *World Out of Focus: British Terrestrial Television and Global Affairs*, 3WE, London.
Media Guardian (1999) 6 December, 3.
Millwood Hargrave, A. (1993) *Annual Review 1993: Violence in Factual Television*, Broadcasting Standards Council, London.
Murdoch, R. (1989) *Freedom in Broadcasting*, News Corporation Ltd, London.
Murdock, G. & Golding, P. (1977) 'Capitalism, communication and class relations', in Curran, J., Gurevitch, M. & Woollacott, J. (eds), *Mass Communication and Society*, Arnold, London.
Paget, D. (1998) *No Other Way To Tell It: Dramadoc/docudrama on Television*, Manchester University Press, Manchester.
Potter, J. (1989) *Independent Television in Britain, Vol. 3 'Politics and Control 1968–1980'*, Macmillan, London.
Pratten, S. (1998) 'Needs and wants: the case of broadcasting policy', *Media, Culture and Society*, 20, 3: 381–407.
Sendall, B. (1982) *Independent Television in Britain, Vol. 1 'Origin and Foundation 1946–62'*, Macmillan, London.
Townson, M. (1990) 'Backchat', *The Listener* (4 January).

CHAPTER 6

10pm and all that: The battle over UK TV news

Howard Tumber

Television news is at the core of public service broadcasting in Britain. Despite the huge growth in news outlets in terrestrial, cable and satellite television together with the entry of new news providers to the market, the state of both BBC News and Independent Television News[1] is viewed as a key indicator of the health of public service journalism within the public service broadcasting system.

Twenty-five years ago controversies about television news were primarily concerned with questions of impartiality and bias. This was part of a wider sociological debate between two broad sociological paradigms (Marxist and Pluralist) that offered different interpretations of the performance of the news media.[2]

Following the publication of the work of the Glasgow University Media Group (GUMG 1976; 1980), this debate extended to arguments between practitioners working within the media and academics conducting production studies of television news programmes and analyzing the text of news bulletins. Apart from the general antipathy to scrutiny into their 'profession', the central focus of animosity towards the researchers by the journalists and editors were the accusations of structural bias. Academics attempted to show that ownership of news organizations and their bureaucratic routines led to the social construction of reality.

These debates were largely usurped by the transformation of the media landscape from the 1980s to the present day. In particular, the decline of public service broadcasting and the growing concentration of ownership in broadcasting and the press led academics to examine how political and economic factors shape media systems and the products of those systems. The rise of the trans-global media enterprise increased the concentration of ownership and power and, together with the development of satellite broadcasting and all-news radio and television, led to widespread competition among and pressures on journalists and editors. Concurrently, on a wider political stage, the collapse of the communist system together with the crisis of socialist theory and practice necessitated a reassessment of the role of the news media in democracies. The emphasis shifted to a reassessment of some of the main arguments of political theory and liberal democracy and an examination of the role of media systems in the new global landscape.

Questions about the relative openness and closure of the communicative processes are now at the forefront of discussion. Citizen access in public debate and the role that the media play in fostering participation in decision making within public life are closely interconnected. The development of the Internet over recent years has made this an even more important focus of concern.

These debates centring around the changing media terrain led to an interest in the concept of the 'public sphere' and the ideas of Jurgen Habermas whilst at the same time sidelining the 'old' Marxist/pluralist arguments.[3] Habermas saw the 'public sphere' as a realm in which individuals gather to participate in open discussions, 'a time consuming process of mutual enlightenment, for the "general interest" on the basis of which alone a rational agreement between competing opinions could freely be reached' (Habermas 1992: 195). Potentially then, everyone has access and 'no-one enters into discourse in the public sphere with an advantage over another' (Holup 1991: 3). Within this 'space' citizens are able to participate in a 'rational, well-informed conversation between equals capable of resolving their differences by non-coercive means' (Schlesinger and Tumber 1994: 9).

The functioning of the public sphere has been researched empirically by a number of scholars. In particular, interest has focused on how various political actors pursue strategies and tactics across a range of media to achieve their communicative goals and interests. Ideological struggle is fought out within liberal capitalist democracies as different groups attempt to influence public attitudes and beliefs.[4]

However, of more relevance to the discussion of television news is the recent view of the 'desirability of public service broadcasting as a space wherein a wide range of views and perspectives might be articulated' (Schlesinger and Tumber 1994: 10). Public service broadcasting is seen by some as a modern embodiment of the public sphere. By adopting Habermas' ideas, the defendants of public service broadcasting possess a conceptual underpinning in debates over its future.

The arguments over the future of public service broadcasting have dominated the media debate in Britain and elsewhere. The proponents of the crisis argument (Rowland and Tracey 1990; Katz 1996) maintain that fragmentation of the mass market, weakening of public service broadcasting, the minimizing and ghettoizing of current affairs and the loosening of the ties between nation and television are 'weakening the foundations of liberal democracy' (Curran 1998: 175). This view is challenged (at least in the UK) by Curran (1998) who argues that the position of public service broadcasting is more varied and unresolved than the crisis position allows and that British public service broadcasting 'has remained resilient for so long' (p.187). However, whilst attempting to disprove the global crisis of public service broadcasting thesis, Curran admits that a price was paid for its survival: – 'The BBC is a more centralised, less creative institution than it was, whilst ITV has become unduly commercialised' (Curran and Seaton 1997 quoted in Curran

1998: 189). It is two aspects of this 'price' that I want to explore further in relation to television news. First BBC News and second Independent Television's *News at Ten*.

BBC News

The early 1980s were a period of particular upheaval in the broadcasting world. The attacks on public service broadcasting by the ideologues of the right, represented by Margaret Thatcher, led to a period of sustained criticism, particularly on the BBC. The push towards change in public service broadcasting and the setting up of various committees to look into the financing of the BBC, led to a particular defensive posture by public service broadcasters feeling a compulsion to defend themselves.[5] To counteract the assault by the opponents of public service broadcasting, the BBC set out on a journey of changes led by its then Director General, John Birt. A programme of sustained and constant management change was implemented, underpinned by a realisation that the BBC had to compete in a world in which it had previously enjoyed a comfortable position, particularly in regard to television news. As Curran (1998: 188) notes 'The BBC defused right-wing criticism by performing an organisational cartwheel. It introduced an internal market for its services, outsourced some program production and made staff redundant. This generated a wave of protest which government critics found reassuring. The right eventually split between gradualists and fundamentalists over the pace of broadcasting reform, with in the end the fundamentalists being isolated with the government as well as in the country.'

The changes introduced by John Birt had a particular impact on BBC News. Birt's background was from news and current affairs so it was inevitable that the kind of changes implemented within the BBC would have a significant impact particularly on news. Birt was appointed to run the newly created Directorate of News and Current Affairs at the BBC in 1987. BBC News was subject to many criticisms from the Conservative Government and other right wing commentators during the 1980s in particular over its coverage of the Falklands war, the conflict in Northern Ireland and the American bombing of Libya.[6] John Birt was also deeply critical of BBC news output but from a different perspective. In a succession of speeches and statements he criticized some BBC journalists for their interviewing techniques. Birt condemned the confrontational approach favoured by some reporters. Instead he called for and attempted to implement a philosophy of journalism which he had been advocating for many years.[7] An increase in the length (and consequent decline in the number) of news items was introduced in order to provide more in-depth analysis. The Birt changes were deeply unpopular within the BBC and as news operations became more centralized, criticisms emerged from within the Corporation. A number of journalists spoke out publicly against the Birtist line.[8]

BBC News then, has gone through a period of considerable change. In 1998 after ten years of upheaval a review of its journalism provision was undertaken.

The 1998 BBC Review

According to the BBC, the object of the 1998 review was to comprehend the changes which had taken place in the broadcasting market and 'to propose a revised and contemporary role for BBC News' (BBC 1998: 2). In particular, senior editors and controllers were seeking to clarify the purpose of the BBC as a publicly funded news broadcaster in a changed environment where there was a far greater choice of news suppliers for the consumer.

Following an extensive programme strategy review, the BBC produced a report in which aspirations about its role in the new digital age were set out (BBC 1998). The BBC conducted audience research to identify areas where it needed to strengthen its journalism and change its programme portfolio. Amongst some of the results it acknowledged that loyalty to the news among the under 35-year-olds was low. From a reading of the report it is clear that the BBC felt the need to publicize its overall news strategy. The BBC views itself as a trusted guide 'to provide calm, reflective journalism that digs beyond the superficial'. It sets out the aim 'to give everybody access to the knowledge and ideas they need to make sense of an increasingly complex world. Our journalism must be truthful, accurate and impartial' (BBC 1998: 2). Attempting to appeal to everyone the report continues: 'It will be popular with the broad audience, or highly appreciated by smaller audiences but never sensationalist. Our journalism will be distinguished through depth of knowledge, range of subjects and original, first-hand reporting from around the world.' And reiterating its public service ideals, the summary states: 'We have a particular obligation to serve democracy through the provision of impartial, reliable and comprehensive news. For this reason we will strengthen our political journalism and our analysis of complex public policy issues. We also restate our determination to cover international news and business and economic news in a way that gives all audiences insight into the significant issues.' This is clearly a retort to the accusations of dumbing down[9] made against many of today's current news providers but is also a restatement by the BBC of its belief in the pre-eminence of its journalism both in the UK and internationally.

The review made a number of proposals to increase the news on science, the arts, sport and 'personally useful' news. Eighteen months after the report was published, there had been a small increase in science, no increase in the arts but more increase in sport. In addition the report's summary refers to the need to 'make clear the relevance of stories we report, broaden the range of stories we cover and the styles we adopt, focus on using clear, direct language' (p.3). This statement has more meaning for the people working inside the BBC than it does

for the consumer reading it or indeed for viewers, since it is very difficult to judge how these changes might be detected. What BBC News has attempted to achieve is to give more of an identity to the BBC1 1pm, 6pm and 9pm bulletins. These outlets have begun to recruit their own journalism staff again in a reversal of the Birtist changes made some years before in which news gathering and production were separated with the same staff working for all the news outlets. Changes in style have also been introduced and include two new presenters, new sets, warmer colours, the throwing out of the blue regal colours and different introductory and closing music.

The report's summary proposed changes for *Newsnight*, including a regular news bulletin at 11pm together with a business report. In line with the set changes for the main bulletins *Newsnight* would also be repackaged. More controversially, the BBC proposed the splitting of *Newsnight* at 11pm with a separate regional programme for Scotland. This proposal, subsequently implemented, was a direct response to the devolution agenda set out by the new Labour government. A further proposed change was for a relaunched *Breakfast News*, which was to provide news briefings 'to prepare you for the day' (BBC 1998: 3). In fact *Breakfast News* was not relaunched; instead it was combined with News 24, the BBC's 24-hour cable channel. The BBC was finally taking the inevitable decision not to try to compete with the other terrestrial broadcasters for morning television viewers. News 24, according to the report, was to sharpen its focus on providing a dip-in news service. At the current time it is in the process of dropping some of its programmes. *News Online*, the BBC's Internet news service and one of the most popular and used websites, was to be strengthened further.

One of the main problems for the BBC is that it faces a constant threat from other broadcasters. It was heavily criticized for the development and subsequent cost of News 24 which is available for 24 hours a day only through subscription.[10] Critics charged the BBC with spending licence payers' money, in effect a subsidy, on the development of News 24. BBC News 24 began transmitting in November 1997 in competition with Sky News, the 24-hour cable and satellite channel operated by Rubert Murdoch's News Corporation, and CNN. Since its inception, Sky News, although not subject to the same quality requirements as the BBC and ITN, has attempted to apply the ideas of impartiality and accuracy inherent in public service journalism and at the same time distanced itself from editorial control of its owners. Sky News has suffered from the development of BBC News 24. BBC News 24 offers its service free to cable companies who in turn have dropped Sky News from their services, thereby depriving Sky News of valuable income.[11]

Despite competition, BBC News is in a healthy position in regard to its share of total UK viewing and listening to network news and current affairs. According to the BBC, its reach is about 70 percent of the UK population and from its own surveys 51 percent of consumers, when asked who they turn to for news, choose the BBC compared with 44 percent for commercial broadcasters. The audiences for News 24 totals about 6 million people each week compared with approximately 4 million for

Sky News. Overnight audiences on BBC1 however, significantly boost News 24. In cable homes where News 24 and Sky compete head to head, News 24 reaches 1.3 million compared with 1.6 million.

BBC journalism comprises a mixture of traditional public service output allied to an increasing commercial operation and its famous brand is proving very successful in its new online guise. For the time being, its position is relatively safe following the upheavals of the last 20 years. The next few years will show whether it can resist further erosion of serious analytical journalism.

News at Ten

The assault on public service broadcasting during the 1980s was not confined solely to the BBC. The ITV network (Channel 3) was turned upside down by the 1990 Broadcasting Act which laid down new procedures for the awarding of licences. Instead of a pure quality auction, franchises were awarded on the basis of the highest bid subject to a quality threshold. One of the main effects of the Act was the move to consolidation by the winning franchise companies. Mergers and take-overs reduced the number of companies within the ITV system as they strove to maintain profitability in an increasingly competitive market. There are now only three main players in the system[12] and further mergers look certain. It will not be too long before one company will control the whole of Channel 3, finally creating a centralized commercial monopoly. Following the 1990 Act, Channel 4, the other commercial public service broadcaster, whilst asked to retain its innovative programming to minority audiences, was allowed to compete with Channel 3 for advertising revenue, thus putting further commercial pressure on the system.

The competitive pressures on public service journalism following the 1990 Act were soon evident. Six months into the franchise period there was a discussion amongst the ITV companies about the possibility of moving *News at Ten*, the main evening news programme. In 1993 the ITV network centre, representing all the Channel 3 franchise holders, announced its intention to move *News at Ten* from its current famous slot held for over 25 years. The 1990 Broadcasting Act required Channel 3 franchises 'to broadcast . . . news programmes of high quality dealing with national and international matters . . . and interviews . . . and in particular . . . at peak viewing times' (*The Broadcasting Act 1990*.c.42, Section 31 (1)). The ITC defined 6pm to 10.30pm as the period of peak viewing time. All the successful applicants for Channel 3 licences undertook to provide news bulletins in the early evening and during peak time (National Heritage Committee 1992–3). Eight of the fifteen relevant licensees specifically indicated that they intended their peak time bulletin to be *News at Ten*.

There was widespread political opposition to the proposed changes including John Major, the Prime Minister, the Secretary of State at the

Department of National Heritage and many Members of Parliament. The Independent Television Commission (ITC), the regulator, opposed the change threatening legal action against the Network Centre, and the National Heritage Committee produced a report criticising the proposal.[13] Following this opposition, ITV did not submit a formal application to the ITC to move *News at Ten*. However this did not stop the ITV network companies from lobbying for the change to the timing of *News at Ten*.

The main concern for the ITV network was the continuous fall in its share of the total television audience. From 44 percent in 1990, it dropped to 33 percent in 1997 and part of its strategy was to increase that back to at least 40 percent. ITV claimed that there was a big switch off of its audience at 10pm; almost three times the loss of viewers across all channels. In particular in the age range 16–34 there was a 37 percent fall. ITV's main argument was that the position of *News at Ten* directly affects its ability to compete for viewers between 9.30pm and 10.00pm now the peak viewing half-hour of British television. The Culture, Media and Sport Committee (1998), in the conclusions to its report on the future of *News at Ten*, acknowledged the fall in the audience in recent years for ITV but dismissed ITV's claim that it would get a larger audience in total for news if its proposals for a 6.30pm news bulletin and an 11pm bulletin were to come into force to replace *News at Ten*. ITV's proposals 'seem to place very considerable strain on the credulity of the public and Parliament and the ITC' (p.ix). The Committee also compared the fall in *News at Ten*'s audience to the decline in the BBC's 9pm news audience which was even greater than that of *News of Ten* (15.4 percent to 13.9 percent). It pointed out that the BBC's response was a proposal to change the contents of its bulletins rather than changing the starting times of either of its two peak time news programmes. The Committee was not convinced that a change to the scheduling of *News at Ten* was 'a necessary component in improvements in programme quality. Indeed it is arguable that news scheduling has become a convenient scapegoat for other factors behind ITV's decline' (p.ix). The Committee concluded by saying they did not believe ITV had established a case for abolishing *News at Ten* and replacing it with an early and late news bulletin and recommended that the ITC rejected ITV's application to make this change (p.ix).

In the light of this political criticism, the ITV network withdrew its proposal temporarily whilst planning further moves. However, pressure from advertisers concerned at the dwindling audiences for Channel 3 meant that the issue was never far from the surface. Intense lobbying by the ITV companies led finally in 1998 to the ITC examining the issue of rescheduling *News at Ten*. This was part of a wider ranging set of changes to the shape of ITV's weekday evening schedules which was put to the Commission in September 1998. The main plank of these plans was to move the network's flagship news programme, *News at Ten*, from 10pm, a slot it had occupied for 31 years. The ITV network put forward the argument that the change would allow uninterrupted films to run from 9pm immediately post-watershed and to open up scheduling opportunities for new drama, more factual programmes, a

60–minute current affairs slot and cutting edge comedy. The proposal included the move of the main evening news bulletin to 6.30pm with a later, 20–minute bulletin at 11pm. In response to the request by the ITV network, the ITC launched a public consultation exercise and commissioned research from MORI, the market research organization, to ascertain public views on the proposals. Despite intensive lobbying by interested groups and politicians, the decision of the Commission, which it claims was informed by the findings of the likely benefits to viewers and an evaluation of the competitive challenges faced by ITV, was to grant qualified approval subject to the following conditions:

- no diminution in the funding, or in the range or quality of national and international news;
- the scheduling of a regional headline service in the nearest break to 10pm on weekday evenings;
- no diminution of ITV's commitment to public service values and for the more diverse range of programmes proposed from 9pm to 11pm to be delivered;
- the scheduling of an agreed quantity of 30-minute slots for high quality regional programmes in or just outside peak time on weekdays throughout the year. (ITC 1998)

The ITC stated that it would review the changes after 12 months and if there was evidence of a marked deterioration in the audiences for news, ITV would be required to take remedial action. As is often the case, it was not exactly clear what 'marked deterioration' would actually mean in practice. In justifying its decision, the ITC stated that 'it was important to ensure that the ITV schedule as a whole delivers a range of diverse high quality services and it should not stand in the way of changes that have the potential to enhance that diversity' (ITC 1998).

The opinion research carried out for the ITC, by MORI, of a sample of 2,000 adults interviewed face to face, indicated that by a margin of 48 percent to 31 percent the public was opposed to moving *News at Ten*. MORI came to the conclusion that the British public would prefer, on balance, that *News at Ten* should remain where it is on a Monday to Friday schedule by a proportion of five to three. The ITC also used a representative sample of viewers employed by BARB (the main source of television audience research in the UK), with the results closely paralleling those produced by MORI (ITC 1998).

The Commission's justification for the changes to *News at Ten* was put in the context of the background of declining audiences for news. Citing the decline in audiences of 50 percent since 1992, the ITC felt that ITV should be given the opportunity to put its proposals to the test. They also noted the number of quality news programmes on free to air services: the 6pm on BBC 1, the 7pm on Channel 4 and Channel 5, 9pm on BBC and *Newsnight* at 10.30pm, and argued that the ITV proposals should be put in context of the overall amount of quality news on terrestrial television. The Chairman of the Independent Television Commission, Roger Bigham (November 1998) put out a press release justifying the changes on these grounds. The pressure put on the ITC from the ITV companies was considerable. A number of audience targets had been set by Richard Eyre, the Chief Executive of ITV, at the beginning of 1998 and shifting *News at Ten* was part of the strategy of reaching these targets. These audience targets were made public to the advertising industry in January 1998 and indicated a commitment to raise ITV's share of peak time viewing to 40 percent by the year 2000.

The controversy surrounding the move of *News At Ten* continued in the year following the ITC's decision. The total number of viewers for ITV's news programmes fell by 13.9 percent after the changes were introduced.[14] *The Daily Mirror* (1999) newspaper launched a campaign for the restoration of *News at Ten*. A small news item in the paper quoted a poll showing that nine out of ten people wanted *News at Ten* brought back (Lalani 1999: 11). The poll was carried out by Teletext, which in an ironical twist pointed out by *The Mirror*, supplies the on-screen news for the ITV network. *The Mirror* organized a vote line asking its readers whether ITN's *News at Ten* should be brought back. On 17 November 1999 *The Mirror* devoted the whole of its front page to a story showing the decline in viewers for the 11pm ITN news since the changes. In a headline '. . . AND FINALLY' accompanied by a picture of Dermot Murnaghan, the presenter of the late bulletin, together with a graph showing the decline in viewers, *The Mirror*, in an ironic piece stated:

> ITN regrets to announce that this is the last late night bulletin ever. The disastrous ratings decline we've suffered since axing News At Ten means that today – May 17, 2002 – is the day our last despairing, exhausted viewer switched off.

Inside, the paper produced a double page spread, saying that 11.00pm was a disaster, with pictures of news presenters and quotes from various news people arguing for the return of *News at Ten* (Methven 1999: 4).

Pressure to restore *News at Ten* came from Tony Blair, the Prime Minister, Chris Smith, the Culture Secretary, and Gerald Kaufman, the Chairman of the Commons media select committee. The ITC accused the network of 'failing to stem an unacceptable decline in ratings for the replacement news bulletins' (Wells 2000: 1) and gave it three weeks to devise a plan to reverse the decline before it decided on whether *News at Ten* should be restored. The network would not surrender without a fight. It gained £70 million in extra advertising income and one million extra viewers at 10pm since the changes. However, the pressure on the regulator to reverse its previous decision to allow the network to move *News at Ten* proved too great and it ordered the network to move the news back to 10pm. The commercial companies, having fought so hard for many years to move their main nightly bulletin to a later slot, were not prepared to go down without a fight and sought recourse in the courts. However, just before the case was due to be heard a deal was reached between the ITV network and the regulator. Under the terms of the new arrangements, *News at Ten* is to be broadcast on three nights a week instead of the previous five (allowing the ITC to claim it had forced the return of the 10pm bulletin). But in return for moving it back, the network is allowed an extra two and a half minutes of peak-time advertising slots, the addition of programme promotions of up to 20 seconds in centre breaks, and an increased number of commercial breaks throughout the schedule. A good deal for advertisers and the commercial companies.

Conclusion

As I suggested at the beginning, the state of BBC News and Independent Television News can be viewed as a key indicator of the health of public service journalism within the public service broadcasting system. The health of public service broadcasting itself remains under diagnosis. 'Optimists' like Curran (1998), believing that in the late 1990s PSB is looking 'much more politically secure' than it did in the 1980s, have set out their own prescriptions for the future (p.189). Amongst these, the agenda for the future for journalism is one of the weaker elements of the 'renewal'. Acknowledging that the current style of public service journalism is influenced by a patrician and disdainful legacy, together with a dominance by political parties and other elites of news and current affairs programmes, Curran calls for a 'pluralism' requirement to be added to the 'due objectivity' obligation (p.196). He envisages an extension of social access (phone-in programmes, audience participant formats and access slots) as the panacea for revising public service journalism.

He also states that 'the exclusion of news and current affairs from peak time, mass channel viewing – and consequent disenfranchisement of the public – is still an American rather than European phenomenon' (p.179). However, if it is trends that one is trying to assess, although it took the ITV companies six years to achieve, the moving of *News at Ten* to a later slot of 11pm was an important and symbolic moment in public service broadcasting journalism. It is doubtful that the ITC will order a move back following its review. Even if it does, the ITV companies or company as it will surely become, will continue to lobby intensively for a permanent change. Similarly, the BBC, while temporarily secure, will face increasing commercial competition in all forms of news.

Future optimism is based on the belief that Britain now has a more diverse broadcasting system, better able to serve 'many publics with differing demands' leading to 'a more relevant, popular, and genuinely "public" broadcasting than has ever existed in the United Kingdom before' (McNair 1999: 169–70). The view that a plurality of publics will be better served by a new public broadcasting system emerging out of the upheavals of the 1980s and 1990s is similar to the beliefs expressed about the possibilities of the Internet for citizen participation. Sociologically, a redefinition of commonality is emerging which embraces various publics. Whether this means that we now need to view the public sphere as consisting of a variety of separate public 'sphericules', as Gitlin calls them, remains unanswered. The old paternalist mode of control is withering quickly but its replacement is untried and untested fully. One reason why Habermas' ideas on the public sphere were co-opted and embraced by communication scholars was because it was a convenient theoretical device to frame (and defend) public service broadcasting (whilst it was undergoing considerable change and upheaval) as an example of a modern version of the public sphere. One trend of interpretation of the new media landscape appears to confirm a more idealized version of the public sphere with the possibility, should reform be undertaken, of extending this even further. Not all share this optimism or view of the current reformation. Gitlin (1998) sums it up rather well: 'what is not clear is that the proliferation and lubrication of publics contributes to the creation of *a* public – an active democratic encounter of citizens who reach across their social and ideological differences to establish a common agenda of concern and to debate rival approaches' (p.173). Gitlin's argument is with those who view a single public sphere as unnecessary as long as parts of it make up their own 'deliberative assemblies'. But this reconfiguration assumes equal resources amongst the different publics for the 'purpose of assuring overall justice'. (Gitlin 1998: 173).

As we move into the twenty-first century, television news is more varied in quantity and quality. Its future is uncertain and challenges to its existence will continue to arise. The appointment of Greg Dyke as Director General of the BBC may signal a move to a more populist approach to news, and ITN may wither away in the face of the advertisers' muscle. In the face of these uncertainties, the need for continuous vigilance of public service journalism is paramount.

Notes

1 Service provider for Channels 3, 4 and 5.
2 For an overview of these theoretical approaches see Curran *et al.* (1982).
3 Theoretical and empirical research on the sociology of news production and journalism is still relatively buoyant. A useful overview of the three main perspectives: Political economy, organizational and cultural approaches can be found in Schudson (1991). See also McNair (1991); and Tumber (1999). Recent studies have tended to focus on variations of these approaches.
4 See for example Schlesinger and Tumber (1994).
5 There are numerous accounts of the deregulation and liberalization of broadcasting during these years. See for example Palmer and Tunstall (1990); Seymour-Ure (1991); Curran and Seaton (1997). For a more interesting argument see Pratten (1998). For a perspective on broadcasting regulation and the concept of impartiality in the US and UK see Harvey (1998).
6 For an account of the criticism of the BBC's coverage of the Falklands war see Morrison and Tumber (1988) and of Northern Ireland see Rolston & Miller (1996).
7 In 1975, Birt together with Peter Jay wrote a series of letters and articles for *The Times* about television news in which they argued

that there was a 'bias against understanding'. News stories, they argued, were too short and often produced without context. See Franklin (1997: 189).

8 As is often the case, news organization foreign correspondents and other senior ones, feel less threatened and therefore able to speak out more freely against management and editorial changes. In the case of the BBC, a number of foreign reporters (John Humphrys, Mark Tully, Robert Fox for example) publicly criticized some of the Birt changes.

9 'Dumbing down' is the popular phrase used to describe the lowering of standards in news products arising out of a combination of the changes in both the structures of the news media over the last 20 years and in the practices of journalism. Franklyn (1997) using the term 'Newszak' provides a book-long argument to try to prove how developments in news practices together with changes in news media organizations have led to a decline in editorial standards. McNair (1999) takes a more optimistic view; seeing the watchdog role of journalism being maintained through its current 'irreverence' and 'unpredictability'. He regards the significant 'dumbing down' as the property of the 'peripheral cable and satellite sector' epitomized in the now defunct Live TV which included the weather read in Norwegian and the use of a person dressed in a bunny costume to react to the news.

10 BBC News 24 is available to BBC1 viewers through the night and in future will combine with BBC1 Breakfast News.

11 For an account of the development of Sky Television during the Thatcher administration see King (1998).

12 Granada, Carlton and MAI.

13 See Culture, Media and Sport Committee (1998).

14 The combined ratings for the two evening bulletins fell from 9.98 million (April 98–Feb 99)(bulletins 5.40pm and 10pm) to 8.59 million (April 99–Feb 00)(bulletins 6.30pm and 11pm).

References

'AND FINALLY' (1999), 17 November, *The Mirror*.

BBC (1998) *BBC News: The Future. Public Service News in the Digital Age*, BBC, London.

The Broadcasting Act 1990 (1990) HMSO: London.

Culture, Media and Sport Committee (1998) *The Future of News at Ten*, Ninth Report, The Stationery Office, London.

Curran, J. (1998) 'Crisis of public communication', in Liebes, T. & Curran, J. (eds), *Media, Ritual and Identity*, Routledge, London.

Curran, J. & Seaton, J. (1997) *Power without Responsibility*, 5th edn, Routledge, London.

Curran, J., Gurevitch, M. & Woollacott, J. (1982) 'The study of the media: theoretical approaches', in Gurevitch, M., Bennett, T., Curran, J. & Woollacott, J. (eds), *Culture, Society and the Media*, Methuen, London.

Franklin, B. (1997) *Newszak and News Media*, Arnold, London.

Gitlin, T. (1998) 'Public sphere or public sphericules', in Liebes, T. & Curran, J. (eds), *Media, Ritual and Identity*, Routledge, London.

Glasgow University Media Group (1976) *Bad News*, Routledge and Kegan Paul, London.

Glasgow University Media Group (1980) *More Bad News*, Routledge and Kegan Paul, London.

Habermas, J. (1992) *Structural Transformation of the Public Sphere: An Inquiry into a Category of Bourgeois Society*, Polity Press, Cambridge.

Harvey, S. (1998) 'Doing it my way – broadcasting regulation in capitalist cultures: the case of "fairness" and "impartiality"', *Media Culture and Society*, 20: 535–56.

Holup, R.C. (1991) *Jurgen Habermas: Critic in the Public Sphere*, Routledge, London.

ITC (1998) *ITC Gives Qualified Approval to New Weekday Schedule On ITV*, Press Release, 19 November, 105/98.

Katz, E. (1996) 'And deliver us from segmentation,' *Annals of the American Academy of Political Science*, 546.

King, A. (1998) 'Thatcherism and the emergence of Sky Television', *Media Culture and Society*, 20: 277–93.

Lalani, S. (1999) 'Thousands more back News At Ten', *The Mirror*, 16 November.

McNair, B. (1991) *News and Journalism in the UK*, Routledge, London.

McNair, B. (1999) 'Public service journalism in post-Tory Britain', in Calabrese, A. and Burgleman, J. (eds), *Communication, Citizenship and Social Policy*, Rowman & Littlefield, Oxford.

Methven, N. (1999) 'Eleven p.m. is a disaster', *The Mirror*, 17 November.

Morrison, D.E. & Tumber, H. (1988) *Journalists at War*, Sage Publications, London.

National Heritage Committee (1992–3) Sixth Report, *News at Ten*, HC 799, Appendix VII.

Palmer, M. & Tunstall, J. (1990) *Liberating Communications*, Basil Blackwell, Oxford.

Pratten, S. (1998) 'Needs and wants: the case of broadcasting policy', *Media Culture and Society*, 20: 381–407.

Rolston, B. & Miller, D. (eds) (1996) *War and Words*, Beyond the Pale Publications, Belfast.

Rowland, Y. & Tracey, M. (1990) 'Worldwide challenges to public service broadcasting,' *Journal of Communication*, 40(2).

Schlesinger, P. & Tumber, H. (1994) *Reporting Crime*, Clarendon Press, Oxford.

Schudson, M. (1991) 'The sociology of news production revisited', in Curran, J. & Gurevitch, M. (eds), *Mass Media and Society*, Edward Arnold, London.

Seymour-Ure, C. (1991) *The British Press and Broadcasting Since 1945*, Basil Blackwell, Oxford.

Tumber, H. (ed.) (1999) *News: A Reader*, Oxford University Press, Oxford.

Wells, M. (2000) 'ITV ordered to halt fall in news viewing', *Guardian*, 26 April.

CHAPTER 7

British and American television documentaries

Carol Nahra

Documentaries in the 'vast wasteland'

The United States likes to celebrate its heroes, and in the world of broadcast journalism, Edward R. Murrow tops the list. Reporting for CBS radio from London during World War II, Murrow carved a formidable reputation for his skill in bringing the immediacy of the Blitz into the homes of Americans thousands of miles away. After the war, Murrow took his talent to the new medium of television, quickly recognizing its potential to help build an informed, engaged citizenry. In 1951 Murrow founded what was to become a legendary documentary series, CBS' *See it Now*, which for seven years brought social issues of the day to the public's consciousness. His programmes about Senator Joseph McCarthy, which let the Senator's own words expose him as a fraud, were instrumental in bringing the powerful politician down.

See it Now became an early victim of the intensifying commercial pressures facing American journalists. In 1954 the show lost its weekly sponsor, Alcoa, which feared the controversial nature of the topics were bad for business. The programme was cancelled in 1958 due to increasing commercial pressures on networks (Sperber 1986). Later that year, in a speech to the National Directors of Radio–Television News (NDRTN), Murrow spoke of the direction American television was headed:

> Our history will be what we make it. And if there are any historians about fifty or a hundred years from now, and there should be preserved the kinescopes for one week of all three networks, they will there find recorded in black and white, or color, evidence of decadence, escapism and insulation from the realities of the world in which we live ... This instrument can teach, it can illuminate; yes and it can even inspire. But it can do so only to the extent that humans are determined to use it to those ends. Otherwise it is merely wires and lights in a box. There is a great and decisive battle to be fought against ignorance, intolerance, and indifference. This weapon of television could be useful. (Sperber 1986: xx)

Although the speech caused a furore in the media (it was reported much more broadly in print media than broadcast), its most significant effect was the freezing over of Murrow's relationship with CBS. To Americans of today, Murrow's words have an over-dramatic dooms-day tinge to them. But Americans of today are exactly those whom Murrow was speaking to, who decades later are largely living in an escapist and insulated world, thanks in no small part to the failure of their television system to teach, illuminate and inspire.

On the face of it, the United States gestures to the concept that broadcasting should serve the public. The Federal Communications Commission, founded in 1934, granted first radio, and then television licences to commercial broadcasters in exchange for serving 'the public interest, convenience and necessity'. But this phrase, which was borrowed from utilities legislation, was never given regulatory teeth which defined, and then protected this concept (Smith 1995: 52).

Before television was even invented, commercial companies were given power over the airwaves without any clearly thought out way to protect the interests of the public. Any attempts to change this status quo had to face the collective political might of the major US networks: ABC, CBS and NBC.[1] American public television emerged as an afterthought to commercial television, with the Public Broadcasting System not formally established and given funds until 1967, after years of campaigning for educational programmes by special interest groups and educators. The young system found a formidable foe in Richard Nixon, who called it a hotbed of liberalism, and ordered it decentralized, permanently weakening it (*Encyclopaedia of Television*, 1997).

In order to justify television's commercial foundations, American network executives have always been keen to argue that the market system will lead to quality programmes. They are also perfectly willing to deny the reality that television can be used effectively as an information and educational tool. Indeed, when pushed, they will argue against it. In their book *Television: Today and Tomorrow*, ABC executives Gene Jankowski and David Fuchs are dismissive of people's faith in public television to educate and inform:

> In our view, public television is not so much the story of an endangered mission as an impossible one, because it is based on extremely fragile propositions. One is an exaggerated notion of television's natural pedagogical possibilities, the idea that the tube was going to be the long sought for magic classroom, where information and entertainment at last joined hands and lived happily ever after. There is, in fact, only a very narrow strip of activity where this is possible, *Sesame Street* being perhaps the best example. (Jankowski and Fuchs 1995: 167)

In this climate, documentaries were never going to have an easy time. Yet despite this shaky foundation, in the early days of television broadcasting, the United States had a current affairs documentary tradition of which it could be proud. Although American network executives never considered documentaries to be big ratings winners, in the 1950s and

1960s they broadcast hundreds of long-form documentaries looking at weighty domestic and foreign issues of the day. Networks saw documentaries as sources of prestige, and a way to establish credibility over competitors, as well as a way to fulfil their promise to broadcast in the public interest. For some years broadcasters were willing to air news programmes without worrying about how much money they made.

But by the late 1950s the financial incentives to produce highly-rated programmes had heightened significantly. The shift from single sponsored shows – such as the *General Electric Hour* – to advertising slots where networks competed with each other for the same sources of revenue quickened the ratings war. A single rating point over the next network in the season's tallies could mean an extra US$20–30 million in profits. With no firm structures in place to protect them, long-form documentaries became vulnerable (Smith 1995).

The increasing commercial pressures which proved the end of *See it Now* in 1958 were temporarily held in abeyance in the wake of the 1959 quiz show scandals, when the networks, caught rigging the results, worked to regain lost credibility by increasing their documentary output. They also used documentaries to defend against President Kennedy's threat to license the networks, in the wake of Federal Communication Chairman Newton Minnow's famous 1961 speech lambasting television as a 'vast wasteland'. The networks allowed time for documentaries unimaginable in today's schedules: in 1960, CBS presented 765 hours of news and public affairs programming. In all, the three networks produced 387 documentaries in 1962, more than ten times the number produced annually by the networks in recent years (Curtin 1995: 49).

As the quiz show scandals became a distant memory, and financial pressures continued apace, documentaries again grew vulnerable by the mid-1960s. Murrow's co-collaborator, Fred Friendly, resigned in 1966 as head of CBS News to protest the network's replacing live coverage of the Senate Foreign Relations Committee hearings on Vietnam war policy with *I Love Lucy* re-runs. In the late 1960s, networks were searching for new ways of delivering news that would prove more broadly popular with the public. CBS executive Don Hewitt conceived of a programme that would counter long-form documentaries with personal journalism, in a multi-story format. Since its debut in 1968, *Sixty Minutes* has continuously ranked in the top ten rated television shows, making it the most successful and lucrative television series of all time. It has made more than US$1billion for CBS. As Hewitt has said repeatedly, *Sixty Minutes* was bad news for network news, for it demonstrated that news could garner big ratings and profits. From then on the networks would settle for nothing else.

Since *Sixty Minutes* proved so successful for CBS, the US networks have endlessly replicated its format in an attempt to mirror its profits. They have yet to stop trying – the late 1990s has seen the appearance of more newsmagazines than ever before on US television. The drive to replicate is one of the by-products of the tremendous money involved in American broadcasting. When each rating point is linked to millions of dollars of advertising revenue, fear of failure has crippled the networks.

In such a climate, creative risk-taking is rare, with broadcasters instead trying to guestimate what audiences will like through focus groups and surveys.

Newsmagazine formats, usually three 13-minute stories broken up by commercials, are suited to the remote control culture that has come to dominate American television. Viewers who are channel surfing are liable to pick up something tantalizing and early in its story development if they are making new stories every 15 minutes.

Although *Sixty Minutes* is still widely regarded as first-rate journalism, many of its descendants cater to more prurient tastes, featuring plenty of sex, scandal and violence. The multi-story format of the newsmagazine lends itself nicely to the shift across American news media from a journalism ethos to one of entertainment over the last 20 years. The change in content has been dramatic. A survey of 4,000 stories on network news programmes, newsmagazine covers and front pages of major papers by the Project for Excellence in Journalism, found that the percentage of human interest stories, i.e. celebrity, and scandal, increased from 15 percent in 1977 to 43 percent in 1997 (Hickey 1998).

The success of *Sixty Minutes* was a major factor in networks abandoning interest in the long-form documentary. One of the last such series was ABC's *Closeup* which ran from 1978 to 1984. The show was a critical and sometimes commercial success, earning the first network documentary Academy Award nomination in 1979 for an investigation into chemical waste; that same year a film about homosexuals drew a 35 percent audience share.

The programme's producer, Richard Richter, has written bitterly of the climate in which *Closeup* had to struggle: erratic scheduling on low viewer dates, and lack of institutional support helped fulfil the network's assumption that the show wouldn't prove an enormous ratings success. He wrote that, at times, ABC seemed to engage in 'outright sabotage' of successful documentaries, with no linking between public affairs and news. When *Closeup* revealed the shocking conditions at nuclear weapons plants, the ABC news department ignored the story until a *New York Times* piece appeared a full year later (Richter 1992: 39–41).

By the 1970s and 1980s, long-form documentaries had vanished almost completely from the screens of the major networks.

The rise and fall of current affairs documentaries on American television is only one symptom of the detrimental effect that the industry's commercial foundation has had on realizing Murrow's vision for television. As financial stakes rose in the battle for advertising revenue on American network television, the only factual programmes which have survived are those which have proven successful in the ratings game, and which are palatable to audience, sponsors and interest groups alike.

Aside from the newsmagazines, today the only other factual genre found in abundance on the four major networks is 'reality-based programming'. This genre exploits surveillance and camcorder technology, to bring the mean streets of the US into living rooms. At its core are cop shows, which follow law enforcement in its encounters with luckless Americans in every possible setting. Other favourite scenarios are natural disasters, people with home cameras embarrassing themselves, and hospital emergency rooms (Edwards 1998). These programmes provide the magic combination for broadcasters: low costs and high ratings, with the added attraction of selling well internationally.

A web site for GRB Entertainment, a producer of reality-based action programming for television, sums up much of the genre: 'If you have video or film footage of extraordinary, bizarre or unusual events, including: natural and man-made disasters; incredible animal moments; extreme weather; raging fires; underwater creatures, WE WANT YOUR VIDEO!!' (http://www.grbtv.com).

The growth of the cable and satellite industry, and the fragmentation of the broadcast market, has fostered a new age for US television documentaries. Cable stations realized early on that the way to succeed was not by broad appeal, which the networks strive for, but by building demographically select and loyal audiences. Known as 'narrowcasters', cable stations develop tightly defined programming targeted at a sliver of profitable consumers. Discovery Communications is the biggest in the new breed of documentary narrowcasters. The company is crystal clear in its focus on ABC1 viewers, and concentrates on attracting the middle-aged male through science, natural history, adventure, technology, 'boys' toys' and travel programming.

Although they have greatly increased the American public's access to documentaries, the range of programmes on offer by narrowcasters is limited. They are first and foremost corporate entities, avoiding controversy as avidly as the major networks. Any given programme can risk offending audience tastes, sponsor sensibilities, or a parent company; moreover, the US's litigious climate always leaves the door open for lawsuits. Consequently stations of all kinds tend to self monitor, developing safe programming that can't be seen to offend.

Thus American cable documentaries tend to seem washed out, with a literalness and deference that is off-putting to Europeans. Instead of hard-hitting investigations, documentaries are often 'celebrations of'. Historical documentaries covering familiar ground are safe territory, as are cultural documentaries and affirming human interest stories.

Noncommercial stations in the United States, striving to offer an alternative to the parade of bland programming on offer by the networks and commercial cable, are home to a wider, if limited, range of documentaries. Public Television's *Frontline* is an acclaimed investigative journalism series which has been running since 1983; its *P.O.V.* series airs authored documentaries documenting minority viewpoints. But continuous budget constraints prevent public television from developing a commissioning structure to support independent film-makers – *P.O.V.* instead accepts only completed or near completed films.

PBS is also well known for its occasional grand-scale documentary series, most notably those produced by brothers Ken and Ric Burns, such as *Civil War* and *Baseball*. Underwritten by a number of foundations and major corporate sponsors such as GM, the programmes draw heavily on archived footage, celebrity voice overs and stirring music. The series are instantly recognizable and are used extensively for educational purposes; they've earned a core following among viewers, making them one of public television's greatest successes.

Although PBS was set up to provide alternative, intelligent fare to the network diet, it often finds itself facing similar constraints as commercial stations. Programmes depend heavily on corporate underwriting, and therefore have to be considered a good risk ratings-wise, as well as inoffensive to sponsors and viewers. The US stations most free from commercial pressures are pay stations such as the Home Box Office. As a pay noncommercial cable station, HBO has something in common with the BBC – it does not have to consider advertising pressures. It can also circumnavigate the taste and decency standards that govern other stations. To make this distinction clear, it features much nudity, foul language and topics taboo on network television. Its drama and comedy series, including the *Larry Sanders Show* and *The Sopranos*, are admired internationally for their wit and edge. In the past several years it has also built a reputation for commissioning documentaries with an edge, such as Nick Broomfield's *Fetishes*, about a high end New York S&M club, and *Paradise Lost: The Child Murders at Robin Hood Hills*, Joe Berlinger and Bruce Sinofsky's tale of three teenagers accused of killing children in a satanic ritual.

But as a for-profit company with an ongoing eye on attracting more subscribers, HBO is a corporate machine, looking to attract viewers. It therefore draws from a narrow brand of programming topics, namely sex, violence, and celebrity. Moreover as part of a mass conglomeration, – HBO's parent company is Time Warner – there are many topics which are off limit as critical studies. Sinofsky and Berlinger have said the station gives them 'golden handcuffs': large sums of money to make documentaries, but a narrow range of topics to draw from (Nahra 1998: 10).

While financial pressures have always been a dominant force in shaping US programmes, in the 1990s they have intensified sharply. The 1996 Telecommunications Act's deregulatory measures have resulted in even further corporate gigantism. Increasingly, the power to control the information available to the American public rests with a small handful of conglomerations, which have no direct accountability for the information they provide (Grossman 1991). As television's financial stakes spread further away from broadcasters, the pressures upon journalists to cut corners – to provide entertainment over news, and graphics over depth – is acute. A 1999 survey by the Pew Research Center for the Press and the Public found that amongst broadcast journalists and news executives, a 53 percent to 38 percent majority say that pressure to make a profit is hurting the quality of coverage rather than just changing the way things are done. This opinion has reversed since 1995, when the national television media split 37 percent to 46 percent on this question ('Striking the Balance: Audience Interests, Business Pressures and Journalists' Values', The Pew Research Center for the Press and the People, March, 1999).

On the surface, Americans today have an abundant range of news and factual programmes to choose from. A plethora of 24-hour news stations, such as CNN and MSNBC, now appear to fill the need of any

American news junkies. But despite the burgeoning number of outlets, the range of information available to Americans remains relatively narrow, with news stations competing heavily for the same handful of big stories dubbed 'be there' journalism (Casey 1999). As Harold Evans commented in a *Guardian* piece: 'They have discovered that the only way they can keep an audience is to hit a single story with everything they have got. OJ Simpson, Monica, Princess Diana, Kosovo, school shootings . . . when stories like these are running, nothing else in the world is happening. The stations don't care that they are not doing justice to the rest of the news.' (Evans 1999).

With the emphasis on either breaking news or pure entertainment, the documentary genre on US television still remains in the early stages of development. One of the largest information gaps is the arena of serious, challenging documentary programming: in depth current affairs, investigative journalism, and international documentaries.

Another gap is the absence of documentary programming providing insights into average American lives. Observational films are almost non-existent; the cumulative effect of their absence means that television remains the domain of either beautiful people or exploitative chat shows. Yet observational programming has obvious appeal to American audiences. Michael Apted's *Up* series has a loyal following in the US, as did the British docusoap *The House* when it aired on public television. But observational programmes don't always sound sexy on paper – or to focus groups – and the American networks have been reluctant to experiment with such programmes, unless they cover the familiar terrain of crime, sex, and violence.

Spend time watching American television, and a third gap appears: the complete lack of artistic documentaries. Independent documentary film-makers in the US are admired worldwide for their irony, style, and dedication to the genre – observational film-makers such as Frederick Wiseman, and D.A. Pennebaker are leaders in the documentary film movement, influencing many British film-makers working today. But documentary makers wanting to exercise creative editorial control operate outside the US television system. A few auteur films will achieve theatrical release, usually after years of personal struggle and personal financial investment; most are limited to festivals.

The many years of neglect of the documentary genre in the US, and the narrow channels along which it has now developed, means that documentary remains in the periphery of most Americans' experience. Moreover the blandness which characterizes much of American documentary programming has not endeared itself as a genre that the American public feels passionate about. For most Americans, the term documentary means worthy, but dull. Consider this attitude of *People Magazine* television critic, Joe Queenan towards public television and cable documentaries:

> Over the centuries, mankind has developed many cruel and unusual punish-
> ments: the rack, the Iron Maiden, the Super Bowl half-time show. But is
> there anything more sadistic than the long-winded documentaries that flood

the airwaves at this time of year? Ever since Ken Burns won all those awards with his masterpieces about baseball and the Civil War, well-meaning TV programmers seem determined to drive the country completely bonkers with epic documentaries about subjects we already know by heart, or don't really want to know.

Queenan goes on to complain about series covering country music, European cinema, and automobiles, saying 'In each there was lots of vintage footage, a regiment of know-it-all talking heads and a plodding voice-over by a star who hasn't had a hit lately.' (Queenan 1996).

This opinion of US documentaries is echoed by observers across the Atlantic. Nicholas Fraser's views are typical of many British programme makers, if more outspoken. In the *Faber Book of Documentaries*, the BBC commissioning editor attacks the bland formula of cable and public television documentaries:

> ... I suppose most of all, I dislike The Great American Wind Film. This comes from PBS, usually, or Discovery. It deals with a historical subject, almost invariably American and excessively well-known; and reverence is written into the script courtesy of an earnest, pseudo-authoritative commentary, and a lustreless score. (Fraser 1996: 368)

Significantly, Fraser's comments were written before the announcement of the forging of a $660 million global alliance between the BBC and Discovery Communications. The deal is one sign of how the two very different worlds of British and American television documentaries are converging.

British television documentaries

Whilst the US from the outset let market forces rule with minimum regulation, Britain always regarded broadcasting as a medium that needed to be reined in. As early as 1926, British broadcasting policy explicitly avoided going the American way, which was perceived to be too commercial (Blumler 1991: 62). With the establishment of the BBC as a monopoly, and the introduction of licence fees to allow for editorial independence, British broadcasting set down a very different path from the Americans.

The first director general of the BBC, John Reith, was instrumental in articulating a public service vision that is still a strong part of the culture today. He was adamant that broadcasting should exist for the 'education and moral improvement of the people'. He was quick to recognize that pandering to perceived public tastes could lead to 'lowest common denominator' programming; he once wrote: 'he who prides himself in giving what he thinks the public wants is often creating a fictitious demand for lower standards which we will then satisfy.' (Blumler 1991: 60).

From the start, Britain took its public service philosophy seriously by giving it regulatory teeth. Every major step in broadcasting – including the launch of new television channels – has been accompanied by mechanisms to protect the public service foundation (Smith 1995: 50).

Documentaries have always been a critical tool in fulfilling the 'inform and educate' portions of the public service remit. Over the years, British broadcasters have experimented with the documentary genre, bringing the godfather of British documentary, John Grierson's definition of documentary as the creative treatment of actuality to the small screen.

In the early days of BBC television, documentary styles tended towards the paternalistic and patronizing. In the 1950s and 1960s, the BBC, influenced by US programmes such as *See it Now*, began to develop a more personalized style of journalism that spoke directly to, rather than down to, the people (Tracey 1995: 126). During these decades, current affairs programmes such as *Panorama* and *World in Action* helped to shape the UK's status as a world leader in the provision of news and information. At the same time, British film makers carved a reputation for observational documentaries. This subgenre allows the British to indulge their infinite capacity for 'navel gazing' – exploring the most minute aspects of everyday life in an effort to understand British culture, its commonalities and differences. The launch of ITV in 1955 spurred the BBC out of a complacency it seemed to have fallen into, and caused it to liven up its broadcasts. The launch of Channel 4 in 1980, with its remit to cater to underserved sectors of the population, opened up a raft of documentary opportunities for independent producers.

Although the fortunes of the documentary genre in Britain have ebbed and flowed over the years, throughout it has enjoyed more favourable conditions than across the Atlantic. The public service philosophy, backed up by regulation, has ensured that documentaries have been integral to schedules throughout the years. The broadcasting culture has also permitted risk-taking, and, by definition, failure. With fewer financial constraints, broadcasters have been able to nurture intellectual creativity, throwing up to audiences a mixture of programming, to challenge, prod, and stimulate. The ability to nurture projects over time, and a broadcasting environment where many of the executives come from documentary rather than business backgrounds, have also eased the way.

The use in Britain of the camcorder exemplifies the ways in which the industry has fostered the documentary genre. As camcorder technology developed, allowing for broadcast quality films to be made by a single person, the BBC began exploring how it could be used to provide access to a broader range of voices. While in the US, the camcorder on network television has spurred a rash of cheap reality programming documenting misfortune and embarrassment, in Britain it has been responsible for a multi-pronged revolution within the landscape of television documentaries.

In the late 1980s, the BBC's Community Programmes Unit launched *Video Diaries*, which commissions members of the public to make 50-minute films. The success of *Video Diaries* in turn spawned *Video Nation*, which provided a cross-section of Britons with camcorders. The project was conceived without any clear notion of how the material would be used. Its main byproduct, *Video Nation* shorts – two-minute films about topics of relevance to the contributor – have succeeded in introducing a wide range of viewers to an equally wide range of perspectives.[2] Today, camcorders are used widely in a variety of formats in British television, and have succeeded in greatly democratizing the documentary field by lessening the chasm between film-maker and subject, and by giving voice to a greater number of film-makers (Nahra 1999: 22).

The 1990s have proven a particularly lively decade for British television documentaries. A combination of increased competition and a looser regulatory structure has weakened the infrastructure in Britain supporting challenging documentaries. The 1990 Broadcasting Act, which introduced more competition and free-market mechanisms, soon had an effect on documentary output, most notably in the steep drop in the number of international documentaries (Cole 1996: 17). A report by the Campaign for Quality Television found that foreign coverage's share of current affairs fell from 29 per cent in 1977–8 to just 19 percent 20 years later. ITV's foreign investigations fell most precipitously from 25.6 percent in the 1970s to 6.8 percent in the 1990s (Donovan 1999: 9).

Within this context of intensifying competition, documentaries came under threat in the early 1990s. Although still plentiful on television screens by US standards, they seemed to be losing ground on the agendas of commissioning editors. Then, in the mid-1990s a new documentary subgenre exploded onto television screens: the docusoap. The docusoap formula, following several colourful people in a given industry or location, has been replicated at an alarming pace, so much so that by 1999, more than 65 series had appeared on British TV.

In its brief history, the docusoap has been intensely controversial. The term itself – now listed in the *New Oxford Dictionary* – has become a lightning rod for debates about the dumbing-down of the television industry. The genre has been accused of making caricatures of its subjects: television voyeurism in the pursuit of popular entertainment. Critics say the docusoap is a discredit to the documentary genre, if it can even be called a documentary, and that its success has come at the expense of quality informational programming. Supporters say the docusoap has pushed out comedy and drama in the schedules, rather than other documentaries; and that the best of docusoaps can be enlightening and illuminating programming.

What is irrefutable is the fact that the docusoap phenomenon played a major role in re-invigorating interest in factual programming in the mid-1990s. Like the success of the newsmagazine in the US, the docusoap has demonstrated the potential of factual programming to achieve high ratings at a low cost. Broadcasters realized that documentaries could now be responsible for all three prongs of the public service remit: information, education and entertainment. By the late 1990s, broadcasters were running more factual programmes than ever before. At first, documentary makers revelled in the renewed focus on their craft, and with enthusiasm began producing factual entertainment programmes. By the end of the decade, however, a number of factors have contributed to an increasingly negative climate and growing complaints about the 'industrialization' of British documentaries.

The complaints reflect the heightened market pressures facing all UK broadcasters, including the BBC. In order to help define a station's 'brand', documentary makers are asked to shape their films into products which will fit into programme strands, making it difficult to find room for one-off films. More often than not, challenging content is losing out to human interest stories: sexy topics taking precedence over serious issues. Whereas in the past, commissioning editors enjoyed editorial autonomy, increasingly power is being centralized in station controllers, leading to less hands-on care and nurturing of documentary makers. Documentaries are also at the mercy of shifting schedules, as the terrestrial stations juggle their programmes to gain the competitive edge.

Chief among complaints is the pace of activity in this new documentary climate. Producers are asked to turn around films very quickly, forcing them to cut corners and rush editing, pressures which work against in-depth journalism and analysis. A British Film Institute survey of TV programme makers found that more than half are under pressure to distort factual programmes to create exciting programmes; almost three-quarters thought programme quality was declining (Arlidge and Collins 1999). A growing number of film-makers are being left out of the editing process altogether, simply providing footage to others to shape, damaging an apprenticeship culture which used to be rich.

Another factor in the industrialization of British documentaries is the increasing desire to compete in the international marketplace. The fragmenting broadcasting landscape, and the need to produce more programmes for the same money have contributed to a growing number of documentaries co-financed with international partners. This has raised conflicts in a British documentary industry that prides itself on editorial control and challenging viewing.

The BBC–Discovery partnership has realized some fears over the loss of editorial control, as programmes co-produced have to fit within the Discovery 'style'. The partnership was always going to be a challenging one. The two companies don't make the most natural bed partners: one a cable narrowcaster, deliberately setting out to deliver programmes to a small elite sliver of the American public; the other a public service broadcaster responsible for touching everyone. The differences are fully acknowledged by Discovery, which is very explicit about its focus on ABC1 viewers. As a Discovery European executive commented at a UK documentary festival: 'Ultimately every decision I take is a commercial decision. It might be fine to reach old age pensioners for public service broadcasters, but not Discovery.' But the venture is allowing the BBC to significantly increase its overseas presence. It has led to the launch of BBC America on digital television, which is introducing Americans to a range of new factual programmes, including the docusoap.

On British television, the docusoap formula is wearing thin among viewers and programme makers alike. Ways in which the industry is moving away from the docusoap are indicative of the ongoing faith in documentary programming as of relevance and interest to British viewers. Broadcasters are frequently blending the docusoap and other documentary formulas to create new subgenres. An example is the Channel 4 series *1900 House,* which recruited a family to live like Victorians in a house renovated entirely as it would have been in 1900. A factual hybrid, the *1900* series combines four different subgenres: docusoap (tracking the family during time); video diaries (family members recording their experience on camcorders); lifestyle programming (the first episode focused on the house's renovation, and the experts behind it); and history programmes.

There are also signs of a backlash against the subjects most accused of contributing to the dumbing-down of British television. Channel 4 has warned independents against proposing films about police, crime, sex and relationships, asking them instead to consider 'blurring of gender and sexuality, things to dread in the new century, changing family structures and the collision between personal freedom and collective responsibility' (Plunkett 1999: 9). Meanwhile, the BBC, in a leaked report on the future of factual programming, advises programme makers to produce 'a new generation of observational documentaries' rather than continue with old formulas. The report urges programme makers to avoid programmes which could be perceived as dumbing-down, noting: 'The controller feels that the audience would not be surprised and charmed by some of the current offers; they lack originality in some cases.' (Keighron 1999).

Such top down advice is encouraging, as the British documentary industry seeks to find the right balance of challenging and popular documentary. It is also testimony to the faith that television executives have in the sophistication of the audience, and their need for television that is original and charming, challenging and educational.

Critically, the market-driven changes introduced by the 1990 Broadcasting Act were made to a public service foundation that has had decades to strengthen and penetrate the culture. By American standards, the British public is amazingly tele-literate. Words like strands, programming, remit, commissioning, educated citizenry, pepper newspaper columns, talk shows and radio debates. Having paid its licence fee, the public expects the right to demand great things from its television. One of these is the right to access challenging documentaries – even if it doesn't always choose to exercise the right to watch them.

As Britain has headed into a new broadcasting environment characterized by competition and fragmentation, documentaries are an essential ingredient of competitive strategies for terrestrial broadcasters. Factual television is integral to the BBC's distinguishing itself as a public service broadcaster, and justifying its licence fee in terms of the educational services it provides to the British public. At the same time, ITV and Channel 4 are focusing on providing enough informational programming so that the BBC can no longer justify the licence fee.

Conclusion

Americans find the British licence fee structure peculiar. The notion that you would have to pay to watch the basic stations, and that if you don't, you might get caught out by television police, helps Americans to be smug about their 'free' system. But the cost that Americans have had to pay for their free system is an enormous one. Although Americans still spend many hours a day watching television, cynicism reigns among viewers and critics alike. Since the mid-1980s, American's faith in the credibility of news media has dropped across media; for network news Americans' evaluations of the news media's credibility have declined since the mid-1980s, with network news believability down an average of 11 percent ('Internet News Takes Off', The Pew Research Center for The People & The Press, June 1998).

Most dismaying of all, perhaps, from an American perspective, is the utter lack of understanding among the general public of just how much their television system has let them down. Soon after making his NTRDN speech in 1958, Murrow wrote to a friend that he had no hope it would help to change a television industry 'which seems determined to destroy itself'. He wrote: 'This could be the most exciting and fruitful method of communication yet devised, but it is in the hands of timid and avaricious men and the public appears to be incredibly apathetic.' (Sperber 1986: xx). This apathy has intensified in the intervening decades. Amongst the mainstream media, there is no public discourse about how broadcasting might be improved. Advocates of educational television in the US remain marginalized, operating very much outside of the mainstream. Even within public television, there is ambivalence about the role of documentaries, with many of the best programmes airing erratically at off-peak viewing times.

As generations of Americans grow up on a television diet of commercials and entertainment, Murrow's warnings of American escapism and insularity appear to have been borne out. Few images of the world out-side of the US can be found today on television; when they do appear they are usually in the form of natural history programmes or disasters occurring in faraway places on the evening news. This failure of American television to make the outside world real, along with an equally insular education system and geographic isolation, has contributed to a culture which continually astonishes the world in its failure to demonstrate either a basic understanding, or glimmer of interest in other countries.

The changeover to digital television has given some advocates for educational television hope that the US can finally re-visit a broadcasting structure that was cemented in the 1930s. But early signs have not been promising. An advisory committee on the public interest obligations of digital television broadcasters, known as the Gore Commission, submitted its final report to Congress in December 1998. Although early drafts were encouraging, the final report bowed to pressures of television executives on the committee, and recommended only minimal regulation of digital broadcasters.

The report did include a recommendation that would free broadcasters from any public interest obligations but would require them to pay into a fund which would be used for educational programmes. The proposal is similar to one put forth by Murrow in his NRTND speech that corporations should pay a 'tiny tithe' to a pool to fund public affairs programmes. At the time his idea was met with a combination of patronizing derision and admiration, and ultimately ignored. Forty years later, the Gore Commission has resurrected the idea and made it one of their key recommendations. It has yet to be acted upon (Hickey 1999).

Notes

1 The fourth major network, Fox, was not established until 1987.
2 Although only a tiny percentage of *Video Nation* contributors' footage ever sees air time, all material is logged and cross-referenced to form a mass archive documenting British life in the late twentieth century. There are now more than 10,000 hours of videotape in the archive, which is earmarked for the British Film Institute's National Film and Television archive.

References

Arlidge, John & Collins, Michael (1999) 'TV Accuracy and ethics at all time low', *The Observer* (23 May).

Blumler, J. (1991) *Television and the Public Interest*, Sage, London: 62.

Casey, Ginger (1999) 'Beyond total immersion', *American Journalism Review* (July/August).

Cole, William Rossa (1996) 'The decline of dissent: the effects of the market on British television documentaries', *Dox* (Autumn): 16–18.

Curtin, Michael (1995) 'The discourse of "scientific anti-communism" in *The Golden Age of Documentary*', in Newcomb, Horace (ed.), *Television, The Critical View*, Oxford University Press, Oxford: 49.

Donovan, Paul (1999) 'Report attacks TV trends of the 1990s', *Broadcast* (29 October): 9.

Edwards, Ian (1998) 'Reality check: peep show', *Real Screen* (May).

Encyclopaedia of Television (1997) Museum of Broadcast Communications.

Evans, Harold (1999) 'From the world to the web,' *Guardian Media* (8 November).

Fraser, Nicholas (1996) in Macdonald, Kevin & Cousins, Mark (eds), *Imagining Reality: The Faber Book of Documentaries*, Faber and Faber, London: 368.

Grossman, Lawrence K. (1991) 'Regulate the medium, liberate the message', *Columbia Journalism Review* (November/December).

Hickey, Neil (1999) 'Beachfront property on the cyber sea,' *Columbia Journalism Review* (September/October).

Hickey, Neil (1998) 'Money Lust,' *Columbia Journalism Review* (July/August).

'Internet news takes off', The Pew Research Center for the People & the Press (June).

Jankowski, Gene & Fuchs, David (1995) *Television: Today and Tomorrow*, Oxford University Press, Oxford: 167.

Keighron, Peter (1999) 'What do you really really want?', *Guardian*, (25 October).

Nahra, Carol (1998) 'Golden handcuffs', *Dox* (August): 10–11.

Nahra, Carol (1999) 'Video nation and Britain's camcorder citizens', *International Documentary* (May): 21–2.

Plunkett, John (1999) 'C4 tells Indies to stay off beaten track', *Broadcast* (29 October): 9.

Queenan, Joe (1996) People Magazine website, pathfinder.com/people/ 960708/picksnpans/tube/index.html.

Richter, Richard (1992) Commentary, in Cook, P., Gomery, D. & Lichty, L., *The Future of News*, The Woodrow Wilson Center Press, Washington, DC: 37–43.

Smith, Anthony (1995) 'Television as a public service medium', in Smith, Anthony (ed.), *International History of Television*, Oxford University Press, Oxford: 48–53.

Sperber, A.M. (1986) *Murrow: His Life and Times*, Freundlich Books, New York.

'Striking the balance: audience interests, business pressures and journalists' values' (1999), The Pew Research Center for the People & the Press (March).

Tracey, Michael (1995) 'Non-fiction television', in Smith, Anthony (ed.), *International History of Television*, Oxford University Press, Oxford: 118–45.

PART III

Problems of accountability

Reporting changing democracy: Commercial radio and news in the UK of regions and nations

Michael Bromley

Until the 1990s radio in the UK was dominated by a national (public) service ethos first articulated 70 years earlier. While the BBC intermittently comprised local and regional, as well as national broadcasting, the non-metropolitan commitment, as a head of programmes for BBC Wales put it in the 1960s, was determined by 'tentativeness, almost an evasiveness' (the regions were known inside the Corporation as 'London's babies') (Davies 1965: 5). Attempts to address the issue in the early 1960s through the establishment of a network of local radio stations were often seen as acts of democratisation: what was called 'community radio' was meant to reflect and enhance 'community life' with news at its core (Barton 1976, Crisell 1998: 25–6). At its advent in 1973, commercial independent local radio (ILR), established on the model of independent television (ITV) broadcasting, was constrained by the same nationally construed public service requirements (Crisell 1997: 186–7). This led, on the one hand, to attempts to redefine (local) 'news' more liberally, and, on the other, to a heavy reliance on common denominators in (national) 'pop' music tastes. For most of the 1970s and 1980s ILR attempted, generally unsuccessfully, to satisfy demands for both community access and relevance, *and* commercial enterprise and vitality (Crisell 1994: 34–6). The liberalization of commercial radio regulation in 1990 tipped the balance in favour of the latter, and has resulted in the rapid expansion of the commercial radio sector based on the crudest forms of formatting (Crisell 1997: 232–4). Requirements to maintain overall broadcasting 'quality', to ensure the local relevance of output, and to increase diversity in programming, it is argued, are sacrificed to competition and commercial viability, creating 'a massive disenfranchised audience', according to the former head of music of an independent station subsequently taken over by a conglomerate (Osborne 1999). Evidence for this is seen primarily in the continued proliferation of 'pirate' stations, which has been a traditional indicator of the need for innovation and change in mainstream radio, as radio has been consigned formally to the role of a provider primarily of standardized music output with 'less effect on diversity of view'[1] than any other measured medium.

Yet the UK is characterized by an increasing diversity in political and social cultures. Many significant groups feel consigned to the margins of commercial radio: in the mid-1990s, it was noted, 'multi-racial and multi-cultural London still has no black music station' (Kendall 1997). Women have found it difficult to correct commercial radio's 1990s trajectory from the merely 'male' to the outrageously 'laddish' (Carter 1994; Snoddy 1999). This has been consistently recognized as a regulatory issue. Two specific attempts have been made to regulate for diversity – 'incremental' licence awards in 1986 and small scale alternative location local licences (SALLYs) in 1996, both of which were intended to create opportunities for non-corporate broadcast groups. ILR having been established as a public service, the UK Government retains a commitment to regulation for 'diversity and choice . . . Commercial radio in the UK is a branch of public service broadcasting', the Culture Secretary Chris Smith told a seminar held to mark the 25th anniversary of the introduction of ILR. 'And the clearest demonstration of its public service is its local community relationship' (Williams and Tacchi 1999: 4; Radio Authority 1998a). Nevertheless, ILR in Britain has failed to deliver differentiated community-based radio and instead has been consumed with 'standardised radio formats' (Crisell 1998: 30; Williams and Tacchi 1999: 2).

Recently diversity within the UK has been most conspicuously formulated around concepts of nations and regions with a measure of autonomy and self-government being granted to Scotland, Northern Ireland and Wales (for Wales, see Osmond 1998). This has the potential to reverse the tendency to couch 'diversity' in commercial radio in terms of the specificity of music output, and the capsuling and packaging of more loosely defined news and information in the margins of broadcasting; and to prioritize speech output again as a key component (see Beech 1970: 5). Questions of what constitutes the 'national' and the 'local,' the relationships between them, and of linguistic variance, are likely to lay bare tensions between the editorial independence of individual stations in their locales, and national public service and (commercial) programming expectations as expressed by the UK regulatory body, the Radio Authority (Crisell 1998: 28–9).[2] It is pertinent, therefore, to question the democractic fitness of metropolitan UK regulation of 'local' radio in the newly reinvigorated nations and regions.

Radio news and news values

Radio news is still somewhat inchoate. Indeed, it is too reductionist to use the unexpanded category 'news' in this context. In many respects, this is a print concept (Crisell 1997: 61); and one which, initially, was forced on radio in the 1920s. Not surprisingly, radio has borrowed heavily from both print and other media, notably the cinema, in constructing its news (Bromley 1997: 337; Crisell 1997: 56). Unlike television, radio has chiefly occupied a space somewhat uncomfortably between the private/ domestic (the radio set as 'part of the furniture' to personal possession) and the public;[3] a situation which has been reinforced since the 1950s by its (trans)portability (Crisell 1994: 28–30; Crisell 1997: 54). From 1928, features, and in the 1930s talks and documentaries, and the 'news magazine', extended the core notion of 'news' to the broader generic category most commonly used today – 'speech' (Crisell 1997: 36–7). In 1926, and again between 1939 and 1945, the BBC carried not 'speech' *per se* but 'national interest speech', a distinctive category in its own right (Crisell 1997: 18– 19, 55–7; see also Nicholas 1999). The BBC was mobilised by the UK state, and its speech-based programming (which in both instances involved actual reporting and more generally news-making) included accepting censorship, permitting the blocking of access and broadcasting blatantly heavy-handed propaganda and public information on behalf of the state: as Sian Nicholas (1999) has pointed it, the BBC both created and then co-opted a middle-class based national consensus as its main contribution to a constructed national effort. The situation of speech in this project is clear: for example, during the war, the *Nine O'Clock News* attracted audiences of 17 million; Churchill's speeches 21 million, even J.B. Priestley's *Postcripts* 10 million; the King's statement on the eve of D-Day had an audience of 28 million and the 1940 *War Report* 10–15 million. These figures can be put into some perspective when compared to the audiences for the BBC's immensely popular comedy show *ITMA* which had listenerships of between 10 and 15 million.[4]

The radio news was listened to by between 43 percent and 50 percent of the national population, and an average of 60 percent tuned in to Churchill's 'broadcast orations' (Crisell 1997: 56; Nicholas 1999: 74). Moreover, news and talks, features and documentaries, enjoyed a symbiotic relationship: for example, talks which immediately followed the *Nine O'Clock News* attracted the largest audiences for the genre. The permeability of the boundaries between 'information and education', on the one hand, and entertainment, on the other, were evident in *The Brains Trust*, described by Nicholas (1999: 84) as 'an uncategorisable hybrid'. All this output was underpinned by painstaking scripting, and over-production. This was foreground radio meant to be listened to after deliberation – not background noise, wallpaper, or radio 'on tap', as the *Radio Times* put it (Nicholas 1999: 65).

In 1945, radio news had to be defined over again. Moreover, from 1946 (until 1955, when separate TV news services were inaugurated at the BBC and through ITN) news included television news (always a problem). The most obvious starting-point was the press model (Bromley 1997: *loc. cit.*; Crisell 1997: 92). As TV news subsequently became more genuinely 'telegenic' (Crisell 1997: 93) and the audience shifted from radio (46 percent of people regarding it as their main source of news in 1957 but only 17 percent in 1962), attempts were made to yet again re-define radio news and news values. News and current affairs magazines; packaging, capsuling, repetition, segmentation; chat, phone-ins and information packages all became more commonplace, leading to format radio (Crisell 1997: 142–5). Content, however, was still an issue. The news was supposed to be the news, and while many Reithian ideas were being discarded, others were more resilient.

Most of the newer formats of information and education emerged in local radio. Nevertheless, the content objectives were still couched in familiar terms. Frank Gillard, then director of sound broadcasting at the BBC, wrote:

> Each [local radio] station would undertake a continuous and detailed task of modern radio-journalism, aiming to present on the air, in many different forms and through a multitude of local voices, the running serial story of local life in all its aspects. Through the direct and intimate medium of broadcasting, the local radio station would try to parallel the service which a *good local newspaper* can and does provide for its public. (Gillard 1963: 9)

Reviewing the first decade of local radio, Michael Barton, who was the general manager of BBC local radio, regarded information as 'the bedrock of . . . radio in the community'. Orthodox news output was based on 'the traditions of the BBC' (Barton 1976: 6). In the 1960s it was envisaged, even by the Director General Hugh Carleton Greene (1963: 6), that this day-time output would give way in the evening to educational programming as a localized alternative to what was to become the Open University as the 'University of the Air'. The basis of the BBC's vision of local radio was that:

> The day-by-day news of the community, local ultility information on traffic, weather, tides, shopping, agricultural and stock market prices, local government in all its aspects, the activities of churches, the youth clubs, the sporting organisations, industry and commerce, the voluntary societies and public bodies, the music clubs, drama societies, entertainment organisations – all these and much more would be covered . . . up to five hours a day of really lively community material, which would be transmitted in the peak hours . . . From mid-evening onwards a full curriculum of education programmes would bring an immense stimulus and enrichment . . . *Can the communities of Britain afford to be without this valuable new instrument* . . . (Gillard 1963: 11 – my italics)

The purpose of this agenda was important, too: regional and local radio were regarded by the BBC primarily as news gathering resources for Broadcasting House; what Barton called '20 exclusive local news agencies' providing a steady flow of copy to London (1976). In the 1970s, there was a shift of focus to properly local, rather than English regional radio (which ended in 1983) – from what the controller of English regions called the 'convenience' of regional radio as an alternative to London to the supposedly genuinely community based nature of local radio (Beech 1970). A key element in this arrangement was the 'two-way radio' – participation, access broadcasting, d-i-y radio, phone-ins, chat and education (for example, see Carleton Greene 1963: 6). At its instigation, ILR adopted this extended definition of news but at the same time argued that this would provide 'a news service that offered listeners the tools to better understand their world and play a more effective part in it' (Local Radio Workshop 1983: 49, 59–60). This mixture of arguably more accessible formats and didactic purpose meant that news on ILR could be presented, in the words of one anonymous executive, as 'Reithian but not po-faced'.

Wales

While the English regions were 'partly natural, partly expedient', in Wales there were 'common bonds of interest, whose characteristics coincide'. This meant that 'information broadcasting' (defined as 'news, topical, current affairs programmes') was viable in the national regions, including Wales, where it was not in the English regions. 'The national regions . . . [believe] it is part of their job to cherish their sense of entity . . .' (Davies 1965: 6–7). By way of contrast, the English regions had no 'territorial consciousness or patriotism' (Beech 1970: 5). This distinction was continued into the 1980s in Wales, most noticeably in the development of BBC Radio Cymru and the television service Sianel Pedwar Cymru (S4C). The nature of the relationship between the media and identity in Wales has been a persistent theme of both scholarly debate and public discussion (for an introduction, see Allan and O'Malley 1999). Most extremely, Wales became, in the celebrated if overdone phrase of John Davies (1994), 'an artefact created by broadcasting'. Although both Radio Cymru and S4C were predominantly Welsh language services there was not just a language dimension to this. In the 1960s it was evident that Welsh news *per se* had specific characteristics: it was more 'political' than in the UK as a whole. More significantly, it was, and is, more Welsh. The demand for Welsh news, and especially Welsh political news, has only been encouraged by devolution. In 1999, 30 percent of BBC Wales's news output was 'Welsh'/national news – what a former Secretary of State for Wales Ron Davies called the 'reporting on those elements of our national life that do not exist in England or the English regions' (*The Record* 1999). It was evident to both the BBC and HTV (the Independent Television Channel 3 provider) that viewing of factual programming had increased. Forty percent of television viewers said they were very or fairly interested in politics. Interestingly, 53 percent (a third more) of *radio* listeners held this view. Moreover, the most noticeable decline in consumption of news and current affairs was in television – particularly in satellite and cable homes. There is also a high dependence on public service broadcasting: 48 percent of viewing and listening in Wales is to the BBC (about a quarter higher than in England). However, whilst the BBC accounts for an even higher percentage of viewing and listening in Welsh (67 percent), it is significant that a combination of independent local radio, S4C and a very small Welsh language press actually accounts for a third. Local radio, Elin Jones, a National Assembly Member (AM), noted in an Assembly debate on broadcasting, 'is increasingly popular in Wales and is an important medium to reflect regional and local differences within Wales' (*The Record* 1999). Despite its importance, ILR in Wales cannot be quantified straightforwardly. Nevertheless, by common consent there are nine stations, of which seven broadcast in Welsh, although the only genuinely bilingual broadcaster is Radio Ceredigion. Nevertheless, another AM, Cynog Dafis, has argued that 'It is extremely important to safeguard the contribution of local radio to Welsh language radio' (*The Record* 1999).

All this evidence[5] points to the central importance of Welsh (in both national and linguistic terms) news and speech output on local independent radio. How has the Radio Authority responded to this?

Case study: the Bridgend ILR licence

Three consortia bid for the Bridgend ILR licence in 1999.[6] A key factor in constructing the bids was the provision of speech content, and especially news – if only to meet the Radio Authority's remit to ensure that new licences add to listener choice and pluralism in output (Crisell 1998: 28–9; Barnard 2000: 54). There is very little speech on independent radio in South Wales: the minimum day-time weekday output is about 20 percent on Swansea Sound, 15 percent on Red Dragon and 10 percent on Galaxy 101. Not unexpectedly then, each bid emphasized the extent to which news (and other speech) both established its local credentials and would act to promote wider local identity. All the bidders claimed that market research indicated a strong demand for local news. Two of the bids, Bridge FM and Celtic 105, proposed broadcasting between 25 percent and 35 percent of weekday daytime speech output. The third bidder, Bridgend Radio, offered a lower figure: 15–20 percent. The *qualitative* differences in the proposals were more striking, however. Despite its proposed lower level of speech output, Bridgend Radio – wholly owned by The Radio Partnership, which controls both Swansea Sound and Valleys Radio – claimed to have identified a need for local news set within 'a regional and national (Welsh) context' in which coverage of the National Assembly would play a central part. Its news operation was to be an extension of the Swansea Sound newsroom, but also drawing on Valleys Radio to provide the regional/national dimension. Key to this would be the deployment of the Swansea Sound Welsh Affairs (reporting) Unit. The bid specifically identified MPs, AMs and the local council as important sources of news. The station would also broadcast news bulletins in Welsh.

Celtic 105, a local bid backed by the radio developer UKRD (which held a 50 percent interest), made the greatest claim about audience demand for local news: 96 percent. Thus, the bid argued that news would occupy a place of 'cardinal importance' in its output. It, too, recognised the Assembly as a key source of news, and Assembly responsibilities such as education and economic development as vital news topics. It would broadcast in Welsh, and its senior journalist would also act as the station's 'Welsh supervisor'.

The third bid, Bridge FM, originated with the same local group (divided acrimoniously in October 1998). It found the smallest local demand for news (64 percent) and 70 percent of those it asked did not want extended news programmes. So, the proposal contained schedules for short, sharp bulletins to act chiefly as a 'hook' for the mainly music content. The bid claimed that the top priority among the prospective audience was for local weather and travel information rather than news. The news in demand was local and international, but not *Welsh*. There was no mention of covering the Assembly or local authorities, and it was asserted that there was no local demand for Welsh language broadcasting, even though up to 29 percent of the 'target' population in and around Bridgend is Welsh-speaking (it is lower, at 16 percent, in the town itself).

This is the bid which was awarded the licence on 4 November 1999. The Radio Authority's public assessment of the winning application reveals little. It extended to three paragraphs over about half a page of A4 paper. A major factor in the decision was the composition of the consortium, which was made up of Chrysalis Radio (a UK media conglomerate), the local newspaper (the *Bridgend and District Recorder*, which is owned by an English publishing company which controls about 80 titles) and local business interests. In the view of the Authority, this gave Bridge FM 'a balanced blend of business and media experience . . . capable of delivering the proposed service' (Radio Authority 1999b). This particular allocation would appear to confirm broad UK experiences with ILR licences that large, corporately-backed bids win out irrespective of local needs (see Kendall 1997). However faithful the Radio Authority is in implementing its statutory obligations, the overall effect has been to create 'by stealth' a national network out of local radio (Barnard 2000: 55).

Perhaps the most instructive element in this small individual case is the role of Chrysalis. Bridge FM represented a relatively new arm of Chrysalis Radio (Chrysalis Radio Investments) begun in 1998 'to support, on a selective basis, community-based applications for small-scale radio licences'. The pattern so far has been for Chrysalis to take a 25 percent share in the bid consortium and to offer a share to a local newspaper. Chrysalis's first successful foray into this arena was with Telford FM in the English Midlands, which began broadcasting in May with 15 percent news and information content (Chrysalis Group 1998; Telford FM 1999; Radio Authority 1998b).

In its bid for the Bridgend licence, Bridge FM promoted Telford FM as the 'model' for the new proposed service. The intriguing question is how a licence in the English Midlands could act as a prototype for a licence in the 'new Wales' where nearly a third of the population speaks Welsh. But, then, the Radio Authority shows little awareness of Welshness. There is no Welsh member on the board (although one has to be appointed under devolution legislation). It also lists Marcher Radio, which is based in Wrexham but covers Chester, too, as an *English* station (although there is no reciprocity, as Galaxy 101, which Chrysalis publicizes as a Bristol/Cardiff station is NOT listed as Welsh). And the Authority finally got round to publishing its first licence advertisement in Welsh only in 1997.

Conclusion

The myth is vigorously promoted that independent radio in the UK is founded on the freedom of the market. Listener choice is supposedly primary. Licensees must satisfy varied tastes (music, entertainment) and interests (speech). From its inception, local radio in the UK has found itself caught in an uncomfortable space between community and commerce. As references by people in radio to local newspapers suggest, this is not a situation unique to sound broadcasting. Critics of the local press have argued that since the 1970s newspapers in the UK have consistently chosen commerce over community (see Franklin and Murphy 1997). Unlike the press, however, ILR is regulated, although in practice, this regulation has increasingly aped the 'free market'.[7] What emerges from this approach is that the measures applied are inherently biased towards national rather than local considerations (Barnard 2000: 54–5). These prioritize taste (music and entertainment) over interest (speech), a tendency noted by the Government as a major reason for continuing with regulation (Radio Authority 1998a). As an example of the proliferation of media outlets, ILR typifies the dilemma of maintaining the vibrancy of 'distinctive cultural voices' in the ensueing cacophony (Allan and O'Malley 1999: 145). If local broadcasting were merely a 'convenience', a result of accidents of geography, then it might not matter so much. In a UK consciously constructed of variegated cultures, the regulatory regime applied to ILR appears to run counter to formal declarations of multi-culturalism and relative autonomy. Such regulation impacts not only on the mediascape in Wales but also on the very idea of what Wales is.

This line of argument has general applications, of course; but in terms of the specificities considered here are, the failure of the Radio Authority regime for licensing ILR lies in its inability or unwillingness to acknowledge that a crucial part of what Wales is, is a speech (and perhaps no less, a news) nation.

Notes

1 The designation is that of the Department for Culture, Media and Sport.
2 Although the focus has been on television rather than radio, this shift is already evident (see Ferguson and Hargreaves 1999 and Waters 1999).
3 In 1941 the magazine *Picture Post* published a photograph 'Listening to Churchill' in which three people were shown in the street listening to the radio through the open window of a house. This picture is reproduced in Nicholas 1999: 74.
4 The figures are taken from Crisell 1997 and Nicholas 1999.
5 The figures in the previous paragraph are drawn from *The Record* 1999; Talfan Davies 1999, and contributions by Elan Closs, chair of S4C, and Menna Richards, then head of HTV Wales, to the Royal Television Society/Wales Media Forum conference held in Cardiff (11 November 1999).

6 The data and information in this section have been drawn from the formal applications submitted by the three bidding consortia made public as part of the process of allocating the licence. Copies of the applications were consulted in Bridgend public library.

7 One example of this was the replacement of 'promises of performance' by 'formats' by which stations would be allowed 'more scope to make changes within their remit boundaries' (Radio Authority 1999a).

References

Allan, S. & O'Malley, T. (1999) 'The media in Wales', in Dunkerley, D. & Thompson, A. (eds), *Wales Today*, University of Wales Press, Cardiff: 127–47.

Barnard, S. (2000) *Studying Radio*, Arnold, London.

Barton, M. (1976) *BBC Radio in the Community*, BBC, London.

Beech, P. (1970) *New Dimensions in Regional Broadcasting*, BBC, London.

Bromley, M. (1997) 'The end of journalism? Changes in workplace practices in the press and broadcasting in the 1990s', in Bromley, M. & O'Malley, T. (eds), *A Journalism Reader*, Routledge, London: 330–50.

Carleton Greene, H. (1963) 'Local broadcasting and universities of the air', *Yorkshire Post* (10 December) repro. in *BBC and Local Broadcasting*, BBC, London: 3–7.

Carter, M. (1994) 'A new wave of the airwaves', *Independent*, 13 December: 28.

Chrysalis Group (1998) Annual Report: Divisional review radio http://www.chrysalis.co.uk/index_corporate.html: accessed 23 November 1999.

Crisell, A. (1994) *Understanding Radio*, 2nd edn, Routledge, London.

Crisell, A. (1997) *An Introductory History of British Broadcasting*, Routledge, London.

Crisell, A. (1998) 'Local radio: attuned to the news or filling in with tunes?', in Franklin, Bob & Murphy, David (eds), *Making the Local News: Local Journalism in Context*, London, Routledge: 24–35.

Davies, H. (1965) *The Role of the Regions in British Broadcasting*, BBC, London.

Davies, J. (1994) *Broadcasting and the BBC in Wales*, University of Wales Press, Cardiff.

Ferguson, G. & Hargreaves, I. (1999) *Wales in the News*, Wales Media Forum Working Paper, WMF, Cardiff.

Franklin, B. & Murphy, D. (1997) 'The local rag in tatters: the decline of Britain's local newspapers', in Bromley, M. & O'Malley, T. (eds), *A Journalism Reader*, Routledge, London: 214–28.

Gillard, F. (1963) 'Radio station in every city', *Yorkshire Post* (11 December) repro. in *BBC and Local Broadcasting*, BBC, London: 8–11.

Kendall, A. (1997) 'The campaign for more choice for London', *AirFlash* 59 http://www.commedia.org.uk/airflash/af-59/choice.htm: accessed 13 July 1999.

Local Radio Workshop (1983) *Nothing Local About it: London's Local Radio* rev. edn, Comedia, London.

Nicholas, S. (1999) 'The people's radio: the BBC and its audience, 1939–1945', in Hayes, N. & Hill, J. (eds), *Millions Like Us? British Culture in the Second World War*, Liverpool University Press, Liverpool: 62–92.

Osborne, B. (1999) 'Pirate radio rules', *The Times* 2 (9 April): 40.

Osmond, J. (ed.) (1998) *The National Assembly Agenda: A Handbook for the First Four Years*, Institute of Welsh Affairs, Cardiff.

Peak, S. & Fisher, P. (1999) *The Media Guide 2000*, Fourth Estate, London.

Radio Authority (1998a) 'Lively discussion and debate at Radio Authority's and RSA's seminar to celebrate 25 years of independent radio', Press Release 109/98, 22 October, http://www.radioauthority.org.uk/Information/Press_Releases/98/pr109.htm: accessed 8 July 1999.

Radio Authority (1998b) Assessment of winning applicant [Telford] (n.d.) http://www.radioauthority.org.uk/Information/Appraisal/telford_fm.htm: accessed 22 November 1999.

Radio Authority (1999a) 'Formats to replace Promises of Performance for Radio Authority licensees', RA news release 14/99, 21 January http://www.radioauthority.org.uk.Information/Press_Releases/99/pr014.htm: accessed 7 July 1999.

Radio Authority (1999b) Assessment of successful application by Bridge FM, 23 November: http://www.radioauthority.org.uk/Information/Appraisal/bridgend.htm: accessed 11 August 2000.

Snoddy, R. (1999) 'A well-deserved slap for radio's unacceptable face', *The Times*, 3 (17 December): 41.

Talfan Davies, G. (1999) *Not By Bread Alone: Information, Media and the National Assembly*, Wales Media Forum, Cardiff.

Telford, F.M. (1999) http://www.realtelford.com

The Record (1999) the official proceedings of the National Assembly for Wales, 'Broadcasting in Wales', 16 November.

Waters, D. (1999) 'News "London-centric" says Humphrys', *Western Mail*, 9 October, http://www.totalwales.com/news/: accessed 15 December 1999.

Williams, B. & Tacchi, J. (1999) 'Spaces of innovation in UK radio', *Journal of Radio Studies*, forthcoming.

CHAPTER 9

Who listens to radio? The role of industrial audience research[1]

Jo Tacchi

Abstract

This chapter looks at the role of audience research in the UK radio industry. The chapter is based on fieldwork carried out from 1993 to 1997 – a crucial time for the industry as commercial radio was expanding at unprecedented rates, providing established commercial stations and the BBC with increasing competition. This chapter investigates the role of audience research in the battle for listeners. A commercial radio example serves to illustrate how and why commercial stations are 'narrowcasting' and constructing 'streamlined' audiences. A BBC example illustrates how and why the BBC is fighting to maintain its broad appeal (through 'broadcasting') and through the creation of concepts such as the 'sophisticated' audience. The crucial role played by audience research and measurement is examined. Finally, two local commercial station listener panels are described to examine what happens when 'researched audiences' meet 'real audiences'.

Introduction

The radio industry in the UK is an expanding media sector. Whilst the BBC began its life as a commercial company in 1922, and became a public corporation in January 1927,[2] commercial radio in this country has a shorter history. The first independent local radio (ILR) station broadcast to London in 1973. While at first the number of commercial stations grew very slowly, restricted by tight regulation, in the late 1980s and early 1990s, deregulation allowed commercial radio to expand more rapidly. There were by 2000 over 240 commercial stations in the UK, including three national commercial services, Classic FM, Talk Radio UK and Virgin 1215.

When I first began to look at the radio industry in 1993, there were several independent stations in existence. Over the next three years, helped by changes in the ownership rules, and by further deregulation promoted as facilitating greater choice and diversity, fewer and fewer independent stations survived take-overs, and four or five radio groups emerged as the market leaders. Radio in the UK has become an increasingly important and lucrative business enterprise. As Curran points out, 'deregulation' when applied to the media industries, is a misleading term; 'What deregulation means, in practice, is not the removal of all state controls but their relaxation in ways that will assist the leading communications conglomerates to expand at the expense of broadcasting diversity' (Curran 1986: 126). Whilst the Radio Authority states that plurality of ownership and diversity of output remain the foci of its attention (Stoller 2000), Wall (2000) describes the ways in which legislation and regulation serve to limit such goals. Tacchi and Williams (forthcoming) provide a case study, which demonstrates the regulatory obstacles for new and small radio operators in the UK.

It is the contention of this chapter that the situation created by deregulation and increased competition has resulted in an increased importance for industrial audience research. Industrial research on radio audiences can be seen to form one of the foundation stones of the expanding radio industry today. However, audience research in this context is not simply about finding out about audiences. In order for radio companies and stations to achieve success, consumers of radio sound are used as pawns in a business/promotion enterprise. Other bodies, the Board of Governors and the government for the BBC, the Radio Authority and advertisers for commercial radio, are the people who need to be satisfied that audiences exist in quantity and that their needs are being addressed. This is demonstrated through the audiences who are presented to them, once they are constructed and defined through elaborate and expensive audience research.

This is not to say that industrial research does not have something to say about radio as it is used by the population at large, but it rarely gets close to gaining an understanding of how and why, in complex domestic environments, this is so. Moreover, actual audiences and service providers rarely come face to face. Listeners are presented to programmers, managers and advertisers through the mediation of the research process. Through examination of one of those rare situations where listeners and programmers do meet – listener panels – my research reveals what can happen when 'real' listeners do not accord with the ideas of 'researched' listeners, and how, consequently, 'researched' listeners may become more 'real', from the institutional perspective, than 'real' listeners.

The radio industry's research is designed to measure, define, construct and ultimately to build, audiences. There are particular structural reasons why this is so. The commercial sector must sell audiences to advertisers and sponsors. Public service radio research has tended to define its research goals as understanding listener choices and needs, with measurement being used to assess the extent of its success in meeting them. The philosophy of public service broadcasting means that the needs of all potential radio listeners should be addressed in output. However, with governmental threats to the universal licence fee, and the increasing emphasis within the BBC on accountability and efficiency, the measurement and definition of audiences has also become a prime goal for the BBC. Any previous distinction between attempts by commercial, and by public service radio institutions to 'know' their audiences is blurring fast. Commercial stations need to sell their audiences to advertisers. To do this they need to construct them. Public service radio, subjected to governmental scrutiny, and faced with a rapid growth in competition, must justify its use of licence fee money, and persuade the government that this is the best way of funding the BBC. These imperatives motivate audience research and affect the ways that both commercial and BBC radio 'view' audiences. These views of audiences together make up an 'institutional point of view' (Ang 1991) that will be examined here.

I will first examine the ways in which audiences are constructed by ratings, before looking at a commercial example, then at a BBC example, of how in-house research is added to ratings to reinforce their market positions. The ways in which they define their audiences are directly linked to justification of their business, market and broadcasting (or narrowcasting) aims. Finally, an examination of a rare situation where consumers and producers meet face to face is explored, and the role of the 'researched listener' in this relationship is examined.

Constructing the audience

Writing about research on television audiences, Ang (1992) and Morley (1986) suggest that the actual activity of audiencehood, as it is 'embedded' in the social and cultural activities of everyday life, does not constitute a neatly definable entity. Ang proposes that there is 'no such thing as "watching television" as a separate activity' and 'if . . . the boundaries of "television audience" are so blurred, how could it possibly be measured?' (1992: 139–40). In his study of family television, Morley shows that ' "watching television" cannot be assumed to be a one-dimensional activity which has equivalent meaning or significance at all times for all who perform it' (1986: 15). Ang demonstrates how the US TV industry needs 'the audience' to be unproblematic as it provides them with their 'currency' – the same is true of the UK radio industry. Talking about 'the audience' as if it can be clearly defined, is like talking about 'population', 'nation' or 'the masses' (Ang 1991: 2), and as Raymond Williams points out, there are no masses, 'only ways of seeing people as masses' (Williams quoted in Ang 1991: 2). Thus, what Ang calls 'the social world of actual audiences' is articulated in 'a discursive construct' of the 'television audience' produced by industrial research, and the reading of that research (Ang 1991).

Attaching meaning to the concept, 'television audience', can never be definitive, because there are 'infinite, contradictory, dispersed and dynamic practices and experiences of . . . audiencehood enacted by people in their everyday lives' (Ang 1991: 13). There will always be a 'surplus of meaning' that will not fit the construct of the audience (ibid). Ang's analysis of industrial research shows how there is 'a profound disparity between everyday practice and official or professional discourse' (1991: 2). The US television institution is not interested in 'getting to know what real people think and feel and do in their everyday dealings with television. Institutional knowledge about the television audience inevitably abstracts from the messy and confusing social world of actual audiences, because this world is irritating for the institutions . . .' (ibid: 7). Audiences are not homogenous entities, and they resist being constructed as such. The institutions, however, continually aim at such a construction – in Ang's terms, a 'streamlined audience'.

All of the unmanageable aspects of audiencehood are excluded from the concept of the streamlined audience. Variations are contained in 'types' and 'patterns'; developments over time are straightened out in terms of 'trends' (Ang 1991: 65). Through this streamlining procedure, a filtering-out of impurities takes place, and people's viewing activities are represented 'in a smooth, totalized but adaptable map':

> The map is very handy indeed for the industry: it supplies both broadcasters and advertisers with neatly arranged and easily manageable information, a form of knowledge which almost cannot fail to provide a sense of provisional certainty, as maps generally do. (Ang 1991: 65)

The research that produces ratings is the primary means used to construct the 'streamlined audience'.

Radio ratings

In 1992, the commercial and public service sectors of the radio industry came together to form RAJAR – Radio Joint Audience Research. RAJAR carries out nation-wide research for both sectors of the industry. For commercial radio, the motivation for setting up RAJAR was simple. Radio, as an advertising medium, prior to 1992, was seen as second rate; its share of the total media advertising cake was just 2 percent. One of the reasons for this was the lack of a credible audience measurement system.[3] Forming a research alliance with the BBC would allow it to gain credibility in the eyes of advertising agencies, which would bring about the necessary increase in advertising revenue essential to finance the continuing growth in numbers of commercial radio services. RAJAR has proven to be a key factor in the success of the commercial radio industry since 1992 – its annual share of total media advertising having increased from 2.8 percent in 1992 to 4.9 percent in 1997 and in the 12 months to September 1999 to 5.5 percent.[4] In 1996, the managing director of the Radio Advertising Bureau (RAB) predicted that it would 'probably' reach 6 percent by the year 2000.[5] For the BBC, RAJAR also made economic sense, offering a means of measuring audiences that would be less expensive than its own survey (Daily Survey). In addition, it fits in with its move towards greater accountability, allowing it to measure its performance – in terms of how many people BBC radio reaches – in a more publicly accountable way.

RAJAR research is contracted out to an independent market research company, Ipsos-RSL. At the time of the research reported on here, samples of the total population aged over 4 years were surveyed using a self-completion diary. The diaries included some general questions about radio, television, cinema and print media – which stations have been listened to in the last year, which television channels are watched most frequently, how often the cinema is visited and which newspapers have been read. The diary listed all of the radio services available in the area in which the respondent lived. A separate page was supplied for each day, divided into time slots of 15-minute intervals (30 minutes overnight). If the respondent had listened to a radio station for at least five minutes they were required to place a mark in a box showing the time of day and the station listened to. In January 1999, RAJAR launched a new methodology – the result of a £500,000 investment in research and development work over two and a half years.

The key changes to the methodology were necessary because of the rapid increase in numbers of stations available. The diary method was retained, but now each respondent creates his or her own personalized station list, making the diary more manageable in areas with high numbers of radio stations such as London. Prior to January 1999, whole households were given diaries, although the researcher briefed only one household member. Now only one household member is asked to take part. These and other changes to the methodology, according to RAJAR, increase the sample reliability and produce more robust data.[6] The first results using the new methodology were reported in June 1999.

RAJAR reports its findings as 'weekly reach', 'average hours', 'total hours' and 'share of listening'. The *weekly reach* gives the adult population which listened to a particular station for at least five minutes in an average week (averaged across the quarter). This figure shows the numbers of listeners in terms of the total potential audience for each service. The *average hours* report one figure for listening across the total population of the UK or area, and another across those who listen to any radio service in the UK or area for at least five minutes in an average week. These figures, then, give average listening hours across the potential audience (whether or not they listen to any radio), and for the 'actual' audience (those who listen to any radio at some time in an average week). *Total hours* are the overall number of hours of adult listening to a station in an average week, as calculated from the samples tested. The *share of listening* is the percentage of total listening time that is accounted for by a station in the UK or area – the station's total hours as a percentage of all of radio listening in the area that it serves. In addition to these published results, stations subscribing to RAJAR receive more detailed breakdowns of results set against demographic variables (RAJAR 1997). Stations can only publish these results if they conform to a strict publication code.

The weekly reach and share of listening are the figures that are most often talked about in the industry, and are generally referred to as the 'ratings'. The importance of ratings figures within the industry should not be underestimated. A senior radio programmer from a London-based radio group equated waiting for the publication of ratings to waiting for examination results.[7] Ratings are one of the industry's most important measures of success.

The battle for listeners

As commercial radio in the UK expands, and deregulation continues, competition for listeners becomes more and more fierce. In the battle for those listeners, the use of research is an important weapon. Public service radio is not a neutral bystander as the battle rages. Rather, the BBC is a key player in the fight for listeners. In recent years, the BBC has been under increasing pressure to justify the universal licence fee, and its programming output. Like the commercial sector, BBC radio has constructed and used 'the audience' for business reasons. The hitherto apparently timeless institution of public service radio is now under threat, and the BBC is using 'the audience' to justify its existence.

Nicholas Garnham describes the changes in the structures of public communication that are currently underway in the West, as character-ised by:

> a reinforcement of the market and the progressive destruction of public service as the preferred mode for the allocation of cultural resources; by the focus upon the TV set as the locus for an increasingly privatised, domestic mode of consumption; by the creation of a two-tier market divided between the information rich ... and the information poor ... [and] by a shift from largely national to largely international markets in the informational and cultural spheres. (Garnham 1991: 104–5)

Deregulation and privatization are seen by Garnham as just two of the aspects of the current shift in communication structures which are having profound effects on society. The 'unholy alliance' between western govern-ments and multi-national corporations have produced the 'information society', which has driven the balance of power away from public ser-vice institutions, and into the path of the market. This has meant a shift in 'the dominant definition of public information from that of public good to that of a privately appropriate commodity' (ibid: 105). Garnham sees serious implications in this shift of emphasis, as he sees public communication channels as integral to the democratic process (ibid).

In 1986, Curran reviewed the different perspectives on media reform that he observed at that time. He grouped together some of these per-spectives under the label 'neo-liberal market approaches'. The 'New Left' and the 'New Right' had come together with the paternalist centre, and under Thatcherism, apparently formed an 'unstoppable' coalition (Curran 1986: 90). Generally, they argued for a free market approach to broadcasting. Some were influenced by a desire to change the hierarchical structures in broadcasting which have a few individuals at the top, protecting their own interests and positions. These few were seen to make decisions about programming based on assumptions about what the public wanted or needed. The free market model was favoured by these 'neo-liberals' as a means to allow the paying viewer, rather than the 'small elite', more control over programming. More channels and stations, greater competition, and fewer state controls should result, according to this way of thinking, in greater variety and greater consumer control (Curran 1986: 90–8).

On the other hand, those who favoured a 'public service approach' felt that the lack of a commercial imperative allowed public service institutions to deliver high quality programming and variety. They could afford to appeal to minority interests and groups, whilst maintaining these high standards. Advocates of maintaining public service alongside the free market, felt that in a mixed system the consumer has the best of both worlds. In this system, the BBC must compete for audiences, and will therefore maintain its high quality programming, whilst commercial services, through competition with public services, will need to match those high standards. Thus, a high quality broadcasting system is ensured (Curran 1986: 98–109).

Curran warned that, unless proper political attention was given to media reform, the free market model would continue to dictate the direction in which the media industries were moving. Into the new millennium, the long-term future of the BBC is still uncertain. This chapter demonstrates one of the ways in which BBC radio is, on the one hand, investing in expensive audience research to ensure that audiences are being reached, and, on the other hand, using audience research strategically to reinforce its position as a public service broadcaster in an increasingly competitive and deregulated environment. At the same time, one of the largest commercial radio groups in the UK, GWR Group plc, which has benefited from deregulation, invests heavily in audience research which has a direct relationship to programming decisions and design, and is used to justify its market dominance. Whilst both the commercial and the public sectors, explicitly and implicitly, talk about changes in radio broadcasting as democratic (giving the listener what he/she wants), the imperative of the market can be seen as both omnipresent and omnipotent.

An ILR example: the 'streamlined audience'

Much of my research on the radio industry was focused on one commercial radio group, and in particular, on two of its local stations. During the time of my fieldwork, GWR Group plc became the largest UK radio group by number of stations owned (over 30). GWR is the largest partner (57 percent) in the consortium, which was awarded the first and only national commercial digital multiplex. This multiplex will support several national digital radio services, and the consortium, Digital One Ltd, is proposing to deliver ten. In market capitalization terms GWR was worth £225.8 million in early 1997.[8] At the time GWR Group spent around £200,000 a year on research, which represented 0.4 percent of its turnover.[9] GWR used (and continues to use) research strategically, to promote service rhetoric, justify its programming decisions, and sell airtime to advertisers. This is one of the cornerstones of GWR's success. Research has been used to create programming formats that deliver high ratings. Within the industry GWR was often criticised for producing 'bland' radio, resulting, some would say, from its implementation of research findings. In simplistic terms, there were until recently two camps in the UK radio industry: those who believed programming decisions should be led by 'gut feel', and those who thought programming should respond to 'researched audience needs'. GWR fell firmly into the second camp, and its strongest defence against allegations of bland programming was that it gave people what they wanted, with its success reflected in the ratings. In many ways GWR could be seen as the group responsible for bringing the now dominant styles of research (and the resulting formats) to the UK.

In Bristol, GWR has two stations; one on the FM waveband (GWRfm), the other on AM (Brunel Classic Gold). These two stations are very similar in output to their other stations across the country. The FM station is targeted at 25–35 year olds, the AM at a 35–55 age group. GWRfm knows its audience well; it actively targets a predominantly female audience, aged between 25 and 35 years, and this is the audience it packages and sells to advertisers. Whilst one can be critical of the attempt to streamline audiences, the format created by GWR, which it claims to be directly related to 'researched audience need', is popular among the audience it targets. RAJAR figures reinforce this – GWRfm's weekly reach figures for the period 20 September–19 December 1999 were 33 percent of the adult population in the area it serves. This compared to BBC Radio Bristol's 21 percent, and, nationally, BBC Radio 1's 24 percent.[10] GWR has identified the largest single audience that its research can define in the area (which may in fact consist of the 'types' of people most visible to market research), and has produced a tailored service for that researched demand (and, crucially, sold the audience to advertisers). Although GWR's audience can be described as 'large', it nevertheless is segmented, and ignores many other audiences, and audience needs. GWR does not attempt to broadcast and serve the whole adult population. It segments that population and streamlines it. GWR's research machine, operating in accordance with a market model, identifies only narrow audience demand, and produces what can be defined as 'narrowcasting' in radio output. Like the audience, this output is also streamlined, mechanized (through the use of computerised playlists), and carefully controlled.

The period of this research marked a key point in the transition of the UK radio industry in relation to research and formats and the increasing concentration of ownership. At the 1995 Radio Festival, which is an annual conference for the UK radio industry, one of GWR's area programme directors defended 'format radio' with the tongue-in-cheek tale of his personal evolution from 'Nerd DJ' to 'Format Man'. The mission of 'Nerd DJ from Hell' was to destroy all music forms by saying and doing 'nerdy' things on the radio, while Format Man fights for the listeners. (The hero of commercial radio is always likely to be described by those within the industry as male, reflecting the overwhelming gender power relations that prevail (see Baehr and Ryan 1984; Gill 1993).) This particular story went: the evolution of Format Man began when GWR changed its objectives from the sort of radio service that suited the station staff to the sort of service that suited 'researched audience needs'. In the old days, he said, programmers were little more than 'witch doctors', not understanding how or why programming ideas succeeded. With the development of in-house audience research came the realization that, among other things, listeners want less chat from their presenters, but like them to have personalities. Research findings like these led to the development of a 'soft ac' (adult contemporary) format long before other stations began to use it. The ego of the presenters can be a big block to this kind of format radio, so they need to be carefully controlled. Presenters on GWR, he told us, had become more like actors who rehearse, than after dinner speakers who ramble on and on. Through implication, the 'witch doctor' of old was no more than a 'good guesser', while Format Man, whose programmes, according to researched audience needs, understand how and why programming works. In fact, what the research appears to tell them, is not how and why things work or do not work, but quite simply when they work. Explanations are then sought for success or failure. This is all undertaken under the banner of 'scientific research' which might, in fact, be better understood as 'formatted research'. Based on this 'scientific' research, they believe that successful programming can be maintained and built upon.

Between the two camps of 'gut feel' and 'researched audience need' there used to lie a more moderate position that recognized the importance of research but apparently also recognized its limitations. According to Richard Park, Group Programme Director of Capital Radio plc, 'research should never dictate content. Good programming comes from a gut feeling', but research has an important place in programming, so that 'what used to be done on gut feel must now be supported by qualitative and quantitative research if you are to avoid certain errors such as playing music people don't want to hear or running too much news' (Park, quoted in Carter 1995: 7). This moderate position seems to have shifted since then, with more radio groups subscribing to the kind of research software that GWR uses.[11]

My access to information on research at GWR was very easy, despite the fact that, generally, stations are not happy to discuss their research with people outside their companies. This was due to GWR's belief in its use of research, which is evangelical in character. Consequently, I describe a particular type of commercial station which, at the time of my fieldwork, could have been described as atypical, but which has now become typical. GWR demonstrates a highly sophisticated use of research, and provides a model that many other stations followed in the search for high ratings and financial success.

Streamlining output

The music that GWR plays is strictly controlled by a playlist for each service (AM and FM). The playlists are held on computer. The computer operates software called Selector, which holds 1,000 songs for each service. This type of computerized playlist is now widely used by music radio stations, and very few radio presenters choose their own playlist. The use of a computer ensures that songs are not played too regularly, and that a song with, say, a relaxing feel, is not played back-to-back with a heavy rock song. Following the news and weather (which, GWR feels, holds the potential to cause audiences to feel depressed), Selector would programme an up-tempo song. In this way one could say that the mood of the output is computerized.

The playlists are constructed through 'music research'. There are two panels of 700 people, one for each type of service. This research is carried out over the telephone. GWR has found that music tastes do not vary in any significant way across the country, so these two panels, consisting of people who live in the South West, serve to provide music research for the whole group of stations. One of GWR's slogans is 'Local Radio Nationwide'. The idea is that if one travelled across the country, GWR stations would be recognizable by their sound. The station creates a list of songs (changed monthly), including current regular players, some newer songs, and songs that have not been used for a while. The respondents are asked to give each song a score, from 1 to 7. The results are used to construct a mean score for each song, with the best scores getting entered onto the stations' computerized playlists. Those songs that show a high 'burn out' factor – ones that people have heard too much of – are removed from the playlist. Fifty songs are assessed in this way each week for each service (AM and FM). One of the criticisms of this kind of music research, and the restrictive use of playlists, is that new bands and songs rarely get aired. For songs to be successfully tested in this way they need to be already recognizable to the respondents through short snippets played over the telephone.

GWR's tracking research consists of 100 telephone interviews a week in each area. For its four biggest stations this takes place all year round, whilst the smaller stations are covered by this research twice a year for six weeks. Questions asked in the tracking research include which radio station is most listened to by respondents, what other stations are heard, when the respondents would usually be listening and for how long. Over a six-week period, the demographic profile of respondents in each area would be corrected, although age and gender are the only factors taken into account. Through the tracking research, and the playlist compiled using the music research, GWR has developed its own particular 'format' for its stations.

This serves to demonstrate how, along with the streamlined audience, comes streamlined programming. It is a logical step, because although research can give an idea of what has been successful in terms of attracting audiences, it does not say exactly why it has been, and cannot predict future successes (see Ang 1991: 65–6). So a repetitive, familiar, some would say unimaginative, format is designed, that irons out any inconsistencies or variables, just as the streamlined audience does. This is seen and promoted by GWR as responding to researched audience needs, and it maintains that, because of its tightly controlled format and playlists, anyone can tune into their stations at any time and know what to expect. This it sees as an advantage in a growing radio market. In fact, when it is re-launching a station – which happens every so often as it revamps a station that it has bought from another company, or give an existing station a 'face lift' – it restricts its playlist. That is, it plays fewer records than usual, more often, in order to give any new listeners who might tune in a better idea of the station sound – a more condensed version. Its research is designed to create the commodity of the streamlined audience, attracted through streamlined output.

A BBC example: appreciating audiences

The BBC has its own Broadcasting Research Services, which has researched audiences since 1939, and includes research on audience appreciation, as carried out through methods such as the Daily Survey, focus groups, panels and advisory councils. In 1994, the BBC launched the Radio Opinion Monitor (ROM), which is a service that is contracted out to the same company that operates RAJAR (Ipsos-RSL). One difference between RAJAR results and the results of in-house research is that, with the latter, it is not necessary to publish results. The BBC has, over the years, collected masses of information that has never seen the light of day outside of the Corporation.

As a public service institution, the aims of BBC Radio are different to those of commercial radio. In its audience research it also demonstrates clear differences. The BBC began to claim, during the early 1990s, to place more emphasis on 'reach' figures (how many of the population listened to BBC Radio for at least 5 minutes in the course of an average week) than on 'share' (the percentage of the total listening time in an area accounted for by a particular station). This was in the face of a dramatic increase in competition, which had resulted in a reduction of the BBC's listening figures. In fact, it could be said that the BBC defended itself with reach figures while it still measured itself with share figures. If we look at the changes in its figures over the last few years we can see why this might be so. In quarter 2, 1993, the total BBC share of listening was 57 percent, compared to the total commercial share, which was 38.9 percent.[12] A year later, the BBC had fallen to 50.3 percent, whilst commercial radio had risen to 47.4 percent. In quarter 2, 1995, the BBC had suffered a further fall to 47.9 percent, whilst commercial radio had, for the first time, broken the '50 percent barrier' with 50.1 percent. One year later (1996), the BBC had regained some ground, with a 48.6 percent share, as commercial radio dipped under 50 percent at 49.3 percent. During 1997, for the first time, commercial radio gained higher figures than the BBC through each quarter (RAJAR/RSL). In 1995 the managing director of radio at the BBC had predicted a decline in share, which would level off in the new millennium to around 30 percent (*The Radio Magazine*, 11 November 1995: 15). At the same time, the BBC began to talk in terms of concentrating on reach – that, as a public service broadcaster, it should try to provide programming for everyone at some time, rather than settle with some of the people, most of the time (see BBC 1995). This should also be seen in the context of political discussions going on at the time about the future of the universal licence fee. In fact, during 1998 and 1999 the BBC gradually recovered its share of listeners, overtaking the commercial share in early 1999 (50.3 percent compared to commercial radio's 47.5 percent), and generally maintaining its lead since then with a share of 51.3 percent in the last quarter of 1999.[13]

The BBC shows a keener interest than the commercial sector in reactions to programmes or stations, known as 'appreciation indices'. The recently established Radio Opinion Monitor (ROM), and its predecessor, the Daily Survey, are a testament to this. ROM gathers audience reactions to BBC network radio (Radios 1, 2, 3, 4 and 5 Live). Each radio programme is given a Reaction Index (RI) which will range from 0–100, with a high RI indicating a high level of appreciation (RSL April 1995). Ang notes that public service broadcasters 'often display a confident disrespect toward [commercial broadcasters] . . . "Giving the audience what it wants", a principle celebrated within commercial rhetoric as a triumph of cultural democracy, is deeply distrusted in public broadcasting circles, connoted as it is with submission to the easy, unprincipled path of populism' (Ang 1991: 102). BBC Radio, as demonstrated by the scale of its research, which aims to do more than simply measure audiences, has different goals from commercial radio. Rather than increasing its audience size, in order to sell it to advertisers, the BBC, as a public service broadcaster, aims to demonstrate 'appreciation' amongst the general public. As Ang points out, however, this is not as clear a distinction as it might at first appear:

> The appreciation index is a kind of fetish for public service audience measurement: it is seen as the key difference between public service and commercial research. But the privileging of 'appreciation' as the pre-eminent variable to capture viewers' subjective responses to television also presents problems, signifying an unprompted, contradictory capitulation to the logic of the market after all . . . what is exactly measured here is not particularly clear: many varieties of 'appreciation' are lumped together into a one-dimensional scale of something like 'general satisfaction'. (Ang 1991: 144–5)

According to Ang, appreciation measurements do 'nothing other than register the volume of applause' (ibid: 145), which is a narcissistic act on the part of the institution. As such, it mobilizes and quantifies subjective feelings of audiences 'in the service of institutional self-confidence' (ibid). Thus the audience remains abstracted, a more sophisticated version of ratings serves merely to measure audiences' reactions to its own performance whilst avoiding the 'specific and probably complex and contradictory responses of actual audiences. The audience remains an abstracted, objectified other' (ibid). Rather than using research to get to know how actual audiences use and respond to radio in their everyday lives, 'Audience measurement information tends to be used as a form of public relations, as a sustainer of legitimacy, as a means of probing market conditions, in short, it provides the broadcasters with a discourse of symbolic reassurance' (ibid: 146). This is very necessary for the BBC in the current broadcasting and political environment.

The sophisticated audience

In-house research by the BBC has been utilized for promotional purposes and for 'symbolic reassurance'. An interesting example of this is the BBC's publication, *People and Programmes* (BBC 1995). Seen in the light of increased competition from commercial stations, and growing pressure to demonstrate value and relevance, both to its licence fee payers and to the government, this publication could be seen as an attempt to satisfy all interested parties that the BBC is responding to researched audience needs and trends – a defence to criticism that GWR commonly uses.

According to Liz Forgan, former managing director of BBC Radio, 'successful radio understands how its audience thinks and reacts'.[14] To achieve this would be quite an accomplishment, considering the myriad ways in which radio is used and consumed, the heterogeneity of audiences and the aim of the BBC to serve the total population of Britain. *People and Programmes*, a glossy publication that covers BBC television and radio programming, admits that the BBC is not yet reaching all of its potential audiences, but claims to provide evidence that it is at least listening to audiences. *People and Programmes* claims to be the result of the 'largest research project in the BBC's history' (BBC 1995: 19). It places the results of listening to audiences in the wider context of social trends, and predicts 'likely changes in audience need' (ibid). It reports that it has uncovered a picture of audiences that is 'very unlike the unspoken but acutely patronising view of them that has influenced at least some of the debate about the development of broadcasting in the UK' (ibid), which, by implication, is the way in which the BBC used to view its audiences. The audience is found to be capable of thinking and talking fluently about broadcasting, of analyzing and deconstructing programmes 'on the spot'. The BBC names this new discovery 'the sophisticated audience'.

No piece of research can ever be 'neutral'; there will always be a purpose behind both the commissioning and the presentation of the research. The purpose behind this BBC report will be connected with a desire to be seen as more publicly accountable and responsive to 'researched audience needs'. In contrast with the commercial streamlined audience, the BBC has created the sophisticated audience, an audience that would resist streamlining. This allows the BBC to demonstrate that ratings are less significant than appreciation. The BBC anticipated that it would lose out in the ratings game, as new stations come on air. It wanted to be in a position to demonstrate that it was nevertheless responding to the researched needs of the 'sophisticated listener'.

The collision of 'real' and 'researched' audiences

Tracking and music research are seen by GWR as its 'scientific research'. Along with RAJAR, this provides the foundation for its view of 'the audience'. For a period of two and a half years during my fieldwork, GWR set up two listener panels in Bristol, one for each service (AM and FM). This it referred to as its 'qualitative' research. I attended most of the meetings, which took place once every three months for each panel.[15] They provided interesting examples of the ways in which 'real' listeners do not necessarily fit the station's construction of 'researched' listeners. In most cases, when differences were made apparent, the 'researched' listener's opinion, as expressed through scientific research, was put forward by the station as more substantive information. After all, the panels only had 12 members each, whilst several hundred people are contacted each year to take part in their scientific research.

The panels were organized and chaired by an external broadcasting consultant. A member of programming staff was present at most meetings. The meetings followed a fairly flexible pattern where, at some time during the two hours, every member fed back their thoughts and feelings about the station's output since the last meeting. Although in the consultant's reports on the meetings written afterwards (and available only to station staff) he usually managed to indicate areas of the services on which the panel members' views constituted a consensus, what were very apparent from the meetings were the differing points of view and opinions that individual members expressed. Even if they all 'liked' something, the degree of 'liking' varied, as did the reasoning behind it. At some meetings, members of staff, such as presenters or the news editor, were invited to attend. Meetings usually finished with the programme controller updating the panel on the latest station news.

For the first 12 months, one senior member of staff, the station manager, took responsibility for the panels and attended regularly. As staffing structures changed, the panels were taken over by the programme controllers from each service (AM and FM). During the first 12 months, a good relationship appeared to develop between the panel members and the station. Initially, the station manager was liable to counter criticisms put forward by panel members by quoting research statistics. Over the year, he became much less inclined to do so, and there was a much less defensive air about his responses. Other staff members were occasionally invited to meetings, and they often seemed uncomfortable to be in a situation where they were meeting listeners 'face to face'.

One of the reasons that this situation might be intimidating for the staff is the way in which, over time, the panel members appeared to have developed, or increased, their sense of 'ownership' of the station, giving them a greater confidence in expressing their views. They were often told that the station valued their views and that the station considered all of their comments and suggestions. When specific complaints were made – for example, a record might have been played twice within a few hours – they were assured that it would be investigated. These sorts of statements suggested to the panel members that they were being listened to, and their ideas were being taken on board. Panel members often commented, to me or to the meeting, that their suggestions had been responded to by the station, often reporting this with an air of surprise. Changes that were made to the output were often seen by panel members to be related to their own expressed opinions. Members were sometimes encouraged to feel involved in the station, with comments like 'I'm letting you into a secret now'. On one occasion, one of the programme controllers implied to the panel that he had gone against management in order to test one of their suggestions.

Livingstone and Lunt (1994) point out an opposition between commercial and public service broadcasting. Commercial broadcasting is often promoted as a sort of democracy, while public service broadcasting is seen as a form of elitism (Livingstone and Lunt 1994). Commercial broadcasters have been inclined to justify their programming decisions, as having taken account of audience tastes. In this way, they claim to respond to audience needs in a democratic fashion; 'The problem is that commercial interest uses an emancipatory rhetoric offering the illusion of involvement relative to public broadcasting' (1994: 22). The contributors to Keat et al. (1994) discuss 'The Authority of the Consumer' in the new relationships that have emerged between producers and consumers. They show that there are many ways of interpreting these new relationships, some of which acknowledge consumer authority, whilst others see it as existing in producers' rhetoric. The type of emancipatory rhetoric that Livingstone and Lunt refer to was evident in the interactions between station staff and the listener panels. The use of emancipatory rhetoric in these settings had some interesting outcomes over time.

The AM panel, who were especially encouraged and 'massaged' by the programme controller responsible for that service, became very confident in expressing their ideas and opinions. At one meeting, the news editor talked to the panel about the news service. A very lively, at times, quite aggressive debate took place. The news editor appeared totally unprepared for the response; it was as though he had expected the panel members to respect his knowledge of radio news and how to deliver it. They in turn saw themselves as the experts on what 'the audience' required from the news editor. The news editor talked about what audiences wanted from news, regarding the audience as a separate definable entity. Panel members responded aggressively to this, as they did not recognize themselves. The AM panel had generally felt that they were being listened to, which perhaps gave them the confidence to react to the news editor in this way. The FM panel, on the other hand, appeared to become less and less involved with the station, and more at odds with it, as time went on. Unlike the programme controller for the AM panel, the programme controller of the FM service did not appear to be keen to encourage the panel members to give their views. Emancipatory rhetoric was not convincingly used with them, and when it was, there was an air of disbelief and suspicion. Some of the panel members felt that they were not taken seriously (see Tacchi 1998).

One of the things that happened when panel members and station staff were in disagreement, or simply not communicating well, was that the staff reverted to the use of research statistics to reinforce their position. The news editor at the AM panel meeting became very defensive, and used research to back up his statements. The panel members were unimpressed. In fact, they often questioned the scientific research, especially the music research. The FM panel rarely did so with any confidence.

The listener panels set up by GWR make an interesting case study if one is attempting to understand the ways in which broadcasters define audiences, as they provide a rare instance where 'real' audiences and broadcasters come together. Ang calls TV audience ratings a 'focal site of the inherently contentious relationship between industry and audience, a site in which a battle between television and its audiences is constantly being fought out, but never absolutely won or lost' (1991: 50). According to Ang, ratings are primarily used to control 'the audience'. This is not control in real terms, but symbolically. Ratings produce a discourse 'which enables the industry to know its relationship to the audience in terms of frequencies, percentages and averages' (ibid). A discursively constructed audience inhabits the symbolic world created by ratings, and it is this audience that the broadcaster 'knows' and uses to establish programming schedules which such an audience 'wants'. Because it is discursively constructed, the industry is continually battling to maintain 'the audience'. The listener panels are interesting in terms of their negotiated relationships with the members and the station, and in how they changed over time. The panel members resisted incorporation into the 'streamlined audience', not through some deliberate act, but because they are complex individuals, who are prone to unpredictable thoughts and opinions, and are essentially 'un-streamlined'.

Station rhetoric

Despite GWR's interest in finding out about audiences through the panels, the station's use of 'scientific research' claims a higher position in a hierarchy of information and knowledge. GWR's research bases its claim to validity in the interaction that takes place with 'actual audiences' in the gathering of information. Its use of such information, however, is selective, as it constructs the discursive concept of the streamlined audience so that any incorporation of the social worlds of actual audiences into this concept 'cannot go beyond the horizon of the institutional point of view' (Ang 1991: 10). UK radio research, like US television industry research, with 'its aura of scientific rationality, has acquired an entrenched position in the institution as a whole' (ibid: 22). In the face of criticism, scientific rationality can be used to defend controversial moves. This Ang names 'the rhetoric of quantitative justification' (1991: 22).

The 'rhetoric of quantitative justification' is well used by GWR. It also uses its research to create a more general station rhetoric, one that works towards promoting familiarity with GWR among listeners. The station sound, the music, the way music is presented, and importantly, the research: all of these things come together to create a streamlined, tight package. The rhetoric tells the listeners that it is a success. On air we are told that GWR listens to us, the audience, and is giving us what its research tells it we want, it is in touch with the audience. At one listener panel meeting, a panel member commented that sometimes this appears to be a little overstated, so that it sounded a bit like the station was saying 'this is what you are going to listen to, whether you want to or not'. In response, the group programme controller said that it is the intention of GWR to 'sound invincible', he recognized that it had a very 'brassy' image on air, and said that this was deliberate. Through these kinds of rhetorical devices, through repetition, and through a carefully controlled playlist (underpinned by 'scientific' research) the sound of the station is reinforced.

Listeners are continually reminded that the station is giving them what they want, that it is based on extensive research, and that it values the musical choices of its listeners and therefore does not talk over the records. The music is reinforced by the rhetoric. Nothing is left to the individual whims of presenters; they read from cards, like 'trained actors'. In the slick, repetitive, recognizable presentation there are no gaps or pauses; they pump out continuous sound that is in line with the station's mission or ethos, which is constructed for business reasons. The competition for listeners has never been fiercer. Because of this competition, the audiences that ILR stations target will become ever more streamlined, as stations attempt to corner the market in their particular targeted audiences.

This is quite different to the way listeners see themselves and describe their relationships with the radio. Many of the listener panel members came to the panel with this relationship in mind, only to find that there was someone between them and 'their' station – the 'streamlined' audience member who may only exist in the discursive realm, but who is a very real commodity in the world of commercial radio.

Conclusion

Alongside the construction of the sophisticated or streamlined audience, the sophisticated and streamlined researcher has developed. Within the radio industry there is no straightforward or somehow independent correlation between research and the application or publication of research results. Research is used to achieve objectives and to affect specific audiences (including politicians and advertisers). Some commercial stations like GWR have, for some time, been telling their audiences how the station listens to them, in order to provide the service that the listener wants. Research provides a base for promoting the particular brand of service on offer. The BBC is telling its listeners that it understands their complex and different needs, and that it will do its best to meet them. In both cases, research underpins the station's rhetoric and its promotion.

Research, as I have shown, plays an important part in the creation and maintenance of a strong station rhetoric. The research is used to construct a listenership which is 'sold' back to individual listeners. In the case of commercial radio, this use of research can be seen as functionally appropriate in a competitive market. Success could be related to a successful definition of 'the audience'. The BBC's *People and Programmes* is significant as it demonstrates the use of research in a promotional exercise comparable with the commercial sector's enterprise of rhetoric creation. The BBC states that one of its 'central justifications for existing' is to be a '*universal* public service broadcaster, funded by all to make programmes for all', which means that it has to reach out 'to previously neglected audiences' (BBC 1995: 31 – emphasis in original). This apparently presents them with a dilemma, as 'it would be destructive – and pointless – to adopt a programme strategy which in striking out in search of new audiences, neglected or undervalued the loyal audiences the BBC already has' (ibid). However, it also gives it a defence – for a shrinking share of audience.

The BBC is presenting itself as attempting to deal with issues like quality versus popularity, and neglected versus loyal audiences. When combined with the growth of competition and threat to the licence fee, these things could be seen to account for the birth of the concept of the 'sophisticated audience'; an audience constructed through the creative use of research – which deserves to be, and is, listened to. Just as commercial radio's research constructs the audience to sell it to the advertisers, then BBC research could be seen to be constructing the 'sophisticated audience' to sell to its licence fee payers. 'Sophisticated' listeners would understand that the BBC will not necessarily attract high ratings compared to commercial radio. Just as with commercial stations, this creative use of research can be seen as functionally appropriate to the situation the BBC finds itself in.

Thanks are due to Peter M. Lewis and Martin Spinelli for comments on earlier drafts of this chapter.

Notes

1 This chapter reports on fieldwork carried out between 1993 and 1997, funded by the ESRC. The main focus of the work, undertaken

for a PhD in the Department of Anthropology at University College London, was the domestic consumption of radio sound in a city in the South West of England (Tacchi 1997; 1998). As a part of my research I also spent some time looking at how the radio industry measures, researches and constructs audiences. This chapter is a result of that aspect of my research.

2 See Briggs (1961; 1965; 1970) for radio's early history, and Scannell and Cardiff (1991) for a social history of early BBC radio.

3 There are other reasons, including the lack of a national commercial service. Commercial television began in 1955, while the older medium of radio had to wait until 1973 for its first commercial service, which broadcast to London. The first commercial national radio service did not come into being until 1992.

4 Commercial Radio Marketplace Reports, Radio Advertising Bureau (RAB) www.rab.co.uk.

5 Doug McArthur, managing director RAB, *Media Week*, 23 August 1996: 12.

6 www.rajar.co.uk/rajar99_1/booklet.cfm

7 Richard Park, Capital Radio, at the RAB conference 1995.

8 Personal correspondence from GWR's director of human resources and public affairs, 7th February 1997.

9 Ibid.

10 RAJAR/RSL Quarterly Summary of Radio Listening, survey period ending 19 December 1999.

11 This includes Capital Radio itself, Chrysalis, Classic FM (which used it before GWR, and is now owned by GWR), and Virgin, which bought its results from Classic FM (personal communication with GWR groups Research Manager, February 1997).

12 The figures do not add up to 100 percent because of 'other listening' which would include listening to stations which are not legal, and, listening to stations which are outside of the survey area in which the listener lives.

13 RAJAR/RSL Quarterly Summary of Radio Listening, survey period ending 19 December 1999.

14 Voice of the Listener and Viewer Autumn Conference, November 1994.

15 I also attended a BBC Local Radio Advisory Council (LRAC) meeting, which I do not report here due to limitations of space.

References

Ang, I. (1991) *Desperately Seeking the Audience*, Routledge, London.

Ang, I. (1992) 'Living-room wars: new technologies, audience measurement and the tactics of television consumption', in Silverstone, R. & Hirsch, E. (eds), *Consuming Technologies*, Routledge, London.

Ang, I. (1996) *Living Room Wars: Rethinking Media Audiences for a Postmodern World*, Routledge, London.

Baehr, H. & Ryan, M. (1984) *Shut up and Listen! Women and Local Radio: A View from the Inside*, Comedia, London.

Briggs, A. (1961) *The Birth of Broadcasting: The History of Broadcasting in the United Kingdom, volume I*, Oxford University Press, London.

Briggs, A. (1965) *The Golden Age of Wireless: The History of Broadcasting in the United Kingdom, volume II*, Oxford University Press, London.

Briggs, A. (1970) *The War of Words: The History of Broadcasting in the United Kingdom, volume III*, Oxford University Press, London.

BBC (1995) *People and Programmes: BBC Radio and Television for an Age of Choice*, British Broadcasting Corporation, London.

Carter, M. (1995) *RAB Conference Special Issue, Marketing Week*.

Curran, J. (1986) 'The different approaches to media reform', in Curran, J., Ecclestone, J., Oakley, G. & Richardson, A. (eds), *Bending Reality: The State of the Media*, Pluto Press, London.

Garnham, N. (1991) *Capitalism and Communication: Global Culture and the Economics of Information*, Sage, London.

Gill, R. (1993) 'Justifying injustice: broadcasters' accounts of inequality in radio', in Burman, E. & Parker, I. (eds), *Discourse Analytic Research: Repertoires and Readings of Texts in Action*, Routledge, London.

Keat, R., Whiteley, N. & Abercrombie, N. (1994) *The Authority of the Consumer*, Routledge, London.

Livingstone, S. & Lunt, P. (1994) *Talk on Television: Audience Participation and Public Debate*, Routledge, London.

Morley, D. (1986) *Family Television: Cultural Power and Domestic Leisure*, Comedia, London.

RAJAR (1997) *Rajar Service Overview*, 4th edn (May).

RSL (1995) *Radio Opinion Monitor Reference Manual and Users' Guide*, issue no.1 (April).

Scannell, P. & Cardiff, D. (1991) *A Social History of British Broadcasting: Volume One 1922–1939 Serving the Nation*, Blackwell, Oxford.

Stoller, T. (2000) 'The future of radio regulation in the UK', *International Journal of Cultural Studies*, Vol. 3, No. 2.

Tacchi, J. (1997) 'Radio sound as material culture in the home', PhD Thesis, University College London.

Tacchi, J. (1998) 'Radio texture: between self and others', in Miller, D. (ed.), *Material Cultures: Why Some Things Matter*, UCL Press/University of Chicago Press, London.

Tacchi, J. & Williams, B. (forthcoming) 'Spaces of innovation in UK radio', *Journal of Radio Studies*.

Wall, T. (2000) 'Policy, pop and the public: the discourse of regulation in British commercial radio', *Journal of Radio Studies*, 7, 1:180–95.

CHAPTER 10

How broadcast journalism training in the UK is adapting to industry changes

Heather Purdey

Introduction

For many journalists working in British broadcasting today the industry seems to be changing beyond all recognition. Technological advances are revolutionizing delivery and production methods and de-regulation is fragmenting audiences and changing organizational structures. A highly competitive marketplace is leading to new programme formats and presentation techniques and there are fears that serious news is being ousted by consumer-driven coverage, which focuses on lifestyle issues at the expense of political and industrial stories (Barnett and Seymour 1999).

Meanwhile, political and social changes in the last quarter century have produced contradictory and confusing repercussions. The anti-union legislation of the 1980s removed occupational and internal-promotion barriers, allowing new entrants without formal training to surge through the system, often at the expense of older, more experienced hands, while at the same time, the drive towards mass education has appeared to 'professionalize' the industry with around 70 percent of journalists attending university or college (48 percent graduating) in the mid-1990s (Delano and Henningham 1995) compared to just 30 percent of specialist reporters who had a degree 30 years ago (Tunstall 1971). A survey by the National Training Organisation, Skillset, showed that nearly 70 percent of broadcast journalists had a first degree (Skillset 1995/1996b).

At the same time as these changes within the broadcast industry, a plethora of 'media' or 'journalism' courses have sprung up around the United Kingdom. The UCAS web site alone, which lists courses available at higher education institutions, mentions 83 courses which include journalism in the programme, 34 which include broadcasting, and 1,136 with media in the title (UCAS). Nor do they include the hundreds of well-established courses in 'media' which are run at further education colleges around the country.

In the past, most new recruits into radio journalism – few young people leapfrogged directly into television – had followed one of two time-honoured routes; either they completed three years of indentures on a local newspaper, passed the nationally recognized National Council for the Training of Journalists proficiency certificate and then applied for a reporter's job on the local radio station, or they spent a year on one of the few postgraduate courses in radio journalism, validated by the Joint Advisory Committee for the Training of Radio Journalists (JCTRJ). In both cases, training was structured and validated by industry-recognized bodies.

Now, journalism training generally is a 'mess', according to the National Union of Journalists, (Corbett 1997) and students are faced with a complex array of qualifications, courses and entry routes which try to match the industry's diverse and rapidly changing requirements.

Many observers have decried the huge growth in media courses with headlines such as 'Lured by media hype' (*The Times* 1996) and 'Students "misled" over jobs in the industry' (*The Sunday Telegraph* 1996). Skillset estimates that 32,000 students were on 'media' courses in 1995 and employment outcomes varied widely between courses (Skillset 1995/96a). But journalism training has always been a source of contradictions and debate. Carr-Saunders and Wilson believed nearly 70 years ago that the range of activities within journalism was so great that a connecting link was impossible to find, making training difficult (Carr-Saunders and Wilson 1933), and discussions about what constitutes 'merit' when employers differ in their expectations and requirements (Boyd-Barrett 1970), what should be included in a journalism curriculum and whether students are better off with vocational skills or a general education have been raging since formal training programmes were established for journalists in the 1950s. These questions about how journalists should be trained mask the underlying debate about what journalists are being trained for, and what the journalist's role is and should be in today's society.

The industry context

The debate today appears more concentrated because of the rapidity of change within the broadcast industry in the UK. Some changes have been fundamental. Two successive Broadcasting Acts in 1990 and in 1996, which de-regulated the industry, changed the face of British broadcasting. New rules on ownership within the independent television network allowed 15 licences to be consolidated into the hands of seven companies. The number of independent radio companies rose from about two dozen in 1980 to over two hundred in 1999, including three national stations, with a handful of major groups holding many of the licences (CRCA 1998). Cable and satellite services have become affordable and easily available. Technological advances mean that analog broadcasting is being augmented in both radio and television by digital services, enabling hundreds of new stations to come on stream over the next few years and the drive to digital is now gaining momentum with the Culture Secretary's announcement that analog services will be switched off within ten years (Smith 1999). The interactivity made possible by digital technology will also fuel competition, with viewers able to dictate programming more obviously and rapidly than ever before. This already highly competitive marketplace can best be illustrated by the formidable growth of the Internet. So-called 'light-touch' regulation has also allowed broadcasters a freer rein in the scheduling and the broadcasting of news. The Radio Authority has loosened its requirements with the introduction of format statements rather than promises of performance, signalling a less rigorous regulatory system. Chris Smith has hinted at plans to streamline what is seen as the confusing and unnecessary number of regulatory bodies (ibid) and is under increasing pressure from commercial broadcasters to relax regulations governing independent television in the run up to digital (Eyre 1999).

Meanwhile structural changes within, particularly, television but also radio have meant that working practices have been altered fundamentally. The weakening of unions coupled with the concentration of ownership and the mushrooming of outlets have meant that broadcast journalists are now expected to be both multi-skilled and multifunctional. What began in broadcasting, amid heated debate in the mid-1990s, with the introduction of the video journalist who shot pictures as well as carrying out interviews, has culminated in the BBC's multi-media approach to journalism, incorporating radio, television, Ceefax and on-line, and a computer system installed in both the BBC and ITN (ENPS) which enables broadcast journalists to produce complete packages for broadcast almost single-handedly. This 'multi-skilling' approach had already been well-established in most areas of radio broadcasting for many years. Most journalists had been reporting, editing and presenting their own bulletins since the 1970s (Chantler and Harris 1997), doing away with the need for dedicated editors or newsreaders, but the advent of journalism on the Web has seen radio journalists too under pressure to extend their working practices[1] and while re-purposing material, which has already been broadcast elsewhere, for the Web is still more usual, some journalists working on-line believe that the face of journalism could be transformed by reader involvement and feedback (West and Eedle 1999) and the possibilities of convergence are thought not to have been fully recognized or explored by the broadcast industry yet (Bromley and Purdey 1998).

This disintegration of independent skill areas has led to ineffectual yet heartfelt allegations of de-skilling from some areas, countered by protestations of 'up-skilling' from others but, in fact, the decade of multiskilling when broadcast journalists, particularly those employed by the BBC, were expected to excel at a variety of different media, is being replaced by a more pragmatic approach. The BBC now admits that the 'super journalist' is hard to come by and it now requires what is being called a 'diversity of excellence', recognising that convergence does not mean that one person needs to have all the skills.[2]

However, the concept of 'multi-skilling' is not confined to skills. Few journalists in either the BBC or the commercial sector are any longer unaware of the implications for their own news agendas of the regular audience research undertaken both by their own employers and by research companies. Being able to interpret audience research is thought of as desirable by around a fifth of editors from both the BBC and the commercial sector.[3]

The discrepancies within the broadcast industry between the way services are funded and the amount of money available for news and factual programming have also led to a vast difference between accepted working practices. Whereas mainstream broadcasters such as terrestrial television stations may still have well-defined career routes or 'occupational areas', cable or community stations operate in a much more flexible way, allowing new recruits to take on more responsible jobs and move through the system more quickly.[4] Likewise, trends in broadcasting, driven either by financial imperatives or fashion, mean new skills are needed. Journalists are required to be interviewed in live 'two-ways' as well as to conduct live interviews and to be able to process news to feed a variety of programmes.

The context, therefore, in which broadcast journalists currently operate, is complex and varied and is constantly subject to the uncertainties of the marketplace and technological developments. While this is nothing new for journalism – debates surrounding multi-skilling and new technology have dogged the industry from the beginnings of photojournalism in the nineteenth century (Bromley 1997) and reached their nadir in Rupert Murdoch's battles with the print unions at Wapping (Shawcross 1992) – the sheer volume of journalistic outlets and the number of occupations which have a journalistic component makes the debate about how journalists should be trained, and what they should be trained for, immeasurably more complex. And while the debate is most usually focused around pre-entry training, it should not be forgotten that many new journalists begin their career by freelancing and, in common with other freelancers in the broadcast industry, are less likely to have access to – or the money for – additional training to ensure their skills remain consistent with the demands of the rapidly changing industry in which they are working (Skillset 1995/96b).

The training context

Despite the plethora of 'media' programmes on offer in the British education system, one of the most traditional, and indeed recommended routes for students who want to enter the field of broadcast journalism has been by way of the courses validated by the cross-industry validation body, the Broadcast Journalism Training Council, which is made up of industry, union and college representatives (NUJ 1998). Originally the Joint Advisory Committee for the Training of Radio Journalists, it was formed 20 years ago because of the growth in radio journalism and the recognition that a training in print journalism was not suitable for a radio journalist.[5] The BJTC and the courses it accredits have continued to fulfil a role which both the commercial and public broadcasting sectors have in the main ignored. The BBC has largely concentrated its resources on internal training (even though its new entrants schemes would attract thousands of applications for about two dozen places), while the few new-entry training initiatives by commercial radio have failed in the past, largely through lack of industry-wide support. Commercial television companies have in the past recruited experienced journalists from radio or print. According to a survey by Skillset, the broadcast industry training organization, 35 percent of those entering the industry in the 1990s had a postgraduate qualification in journalism, of which 35 percent said the qualification was approved by the BJTC (Skillset 1995/96b). In an industry which is geographically widespread and with increasingly diverse needs, those figures are significant.

The BJTC, from its very start, has adopted a 'core skills' approach to training. In this it is very similar to the National Council for the Training of Journalists, the equivalent body for the print journalism sector. This policy, shared by both training bodies, has been informed by the industry which has insisted on new recruits being equipped to do the job in the shortest possible time. It also accepts the premise that journalists practising in any area of broadcasting essentially need the same skills and knowledge; that is reporting, interviewing, writing, researching, relevant technical skills and a knowledge of media law and public administration. This approach has been reinforced by the developments in internal industry training. Skillset, which developed the National Vocational Qualification in Broadcast Journalism, a work-based qualification, rejected from the outset any separate qualifications for radio and television journalism and is encouraging cross-industry co-operation in the future. A cross-industry committee, the Journalism Forum, has been formed to discuss common issues and approaches. The emphasis throughout has remained on practical journalism training. The BJTC's guidelines for courses, which must be met for accreditation purposes, have been extended, rather than substantially altered, to satisfy industry developments. Thus television guidelines were bolted on to the original radio guidelines when the BBC signalled its bi-media initiative, and standards for on-line journalism were adopted when new media outlets were developed by the BBC and ITN. Both sets of guidelines adhere to the 'core skills' approach supplemented by additional media-specific competencies (BJTC 1999).

Although courses are free to choose which media to teach, nevertheless, industry convergence is having major implications for training. Students are expected (and expect) to grasp different working practices for different media in a limited amount of time – most of the courses are nine months long. Courses are aware that any dilution of core skills could mean the loss of accreditation. However, the more diverse a course attempts to be and the more skills it attempts to teach, the less relevant it becomes for specific sectors. Conversely, the more focused a course decides to be, the less appeal it may have for students who want to be able to have as wide a choice of employment as possible when they graduate.

The emphasis on practical training, meanwhile, also has implications for courses, which are run within educational establishments and are therefore subject to the organizational requirements of higher education. At the same time as having to grapple with the rapid developments within the broadcast industry, broadcast journalism training finds itself caught up in key educational debates about what constitutes 'graduate-ness', the concept of life-long learning and the implications of funding a mass education system. In particular, the tensions inherent in running a vocational programme within an educational environment impact on broadcast journalism courses. The more emphasis is placed on voca-tional skills, the less time remains for any broader reflection of other issues. This can cause particular tensions on undergraduate courses where the twin goals of intellectual development and employability are finally balanced. Indeed, some course leaders at both postgraduate and undergraduate level are driven to emphasize that they are involved in both journalism training and journalism education, and not just straight-forward skills-development.[6]

It is ironic that while the 'profession' versus 'craft' debate is rarely an issue for journalism – few of the criteria for a profession are met (Parsons 1968) – broadcast journalism training itself is becoming ever more 'professionalized'. It is closely scrutinized by its own peer-group validation body, the BJTC, which has the ultimate sanction of being able to withdraw accreditation. Tutors are required to have considerable journalism experience and are increasingly under pressure to have a degree[7] and to undertake research which can be accredited within a higher education context.[8] Thus, broadcast journalism training can seem at odds with what appears to be a fiercely 'craft-based' industry.

Furthermore, when looking at employment patterns generally, it appears that, while validating only a small number of highly professional courses, the industry at large is much more flexible about where it recruits its labour from and despite the excellent employment record of BJTC-accredited courses, recruitment by the broadcast journalism industry, is by no means uniform.[9]

The industry's needs and the 'ideal' journalist

The research conducted in 1997 shows that organizations in different industry sectors, which employ broadcast journalists, recruit from a variety of different sources. The BBC would seem to be more closely bound to the 'traditional' training ground of validated courses. More than 80 percent of BBC news editors who responded said they recruited more often than not from BJTC-accredited courses and this is supple-mented by their own in-house trainees. The commercial sector, how-ever, recruited from more diverse sources; just over 64 percent usually recruiting from the validated courses and this dropped to only 52 per-cent of editors in commercial television (Table 10.1).

Although these statistics do suggest that the commercial sector is more likely to cast its net wider for recruits, some BBC managers believe that recruiting from outside the formal training courses is healthy. Reasons ranged from the equal opportunity aspects – course fees on postgraduate courses can have the effect of excluding the less well-off, affecting the BBC's policy of diversity – to a feeling that some students, who were not suited to a career in broadcast journalism, were nevertheless

Table 10.1

Question: When you recruit, how often do you take people on from a validated course?

	BBC Radio	Commercial Radio	BBC TV	Commercial TV
More than 50% of the time	78.1%	67.7%	83.3%	52%
Less than 50% of the time	18.7%	30.2%	8.3%	44%
No answer	3.1%	2.1%	8.3%	4%

Table 10.2

Question: From where else do you recruit?

	BBC Radio	Commercial Radio	BBC TV	Commercial TV
Own training scheme	68.8%	25%	91.7%	20%
Journalism PG course	87.5%	63.5%	100%	52%
General PG course	6.3%	14.6%	25%	8%
Journalism degree	56.3%	53.1%	58.3%	40%
Media-related degree	15.6%	32.3%	33.3%	20%
General degree	25%	21.9%	75%	40%
Media-related FE	12.5%	21.9%	41.7%	8%
General FE	0%	9.4%	8.3%	0%
School	3.1%	5.2%	0%	4%
Formal work-placement	37.5%	47.9%	41.7%	24%
Informal work-placement	18.8%	30.2%	33.3%	12%
Other media	9.4%	7.3%	8.3%	4%

applying successfully to these courses because there were no other formal routes into the media.[10] A significant number of both BBC and commercial sector editors said they recruited from other, less specialized, educational courses, particularly degree courses, and particularly people who had been on work experience with their organizations (Table 10.2).

Despite the fact that journalism generally is becoming a largely graduate occupation, employers will accept a wide range of qualifications (Table 10.3) and a small number (2.1 percent) of independent local radio news editors said they were content to accept recruits with no minimum academic qualifications, this despite the fact that, of the 17

Table 10.3

Question: Which of the following qualifications would you expect as a minimum?

	BBC Radio	Commercial Radio	BBC TV	Commercial TV
Journalism qualification (postgraduate)	68.8%	41.7%	41.7%	44%
Journalism qualification (not PG)	65.6%	39.6%	41.7%	48%
NVQ/SVQ	3.1%	6.3%	8.3%	4%
Degree (any subject)	37.5%	31.3%	25%	56%
Journalism degree	3.1%	31.3%	8.3%	8%
Media degree	0%	8.3%	0%	8%
HND	3.1%	6.3%	8.3%	4%
Media HND	0%	6.3%	0%	0%
HNC	0%	0%	0%	0%
Media HNC	0%	1%	0%	0%
A-levels/ Scottish Highers	50%	27.1%	66.7%	28%
Media A levels/ Scottish Highers	0%	1%	0%	0%
B.Tec	3.1%	0%	0%	0%
Media B.Tec	0%	5.2%	0%	0%
City & Guilds	0%	1%	0%	0%
Media City & Guilds	0%	4.2%	0%	0%
GNVQ/GSVQ	0%	1%	0%	0%
Media-related GNVQ/GSVQ	0%	1%	0%	0%
GCSE	0%	17.7%	16.7%	12%
Media-related GCSE	0%	5.2%	0%	8%
None	0%	2.1%	0%	0%

accredited broadcast journalism courses, all are at post or undergraduate level. It is even more surprising when one considers that nearly half a century ago minimal educational requirements were deemed essential by The Royal Commission on the Press (*The Royal Commission on the Press* 1949) and the National Council for the Training of Journalists indicates that it is rare for a newspaper trainee to have less than two 'A'-levels or equivalent (NCTJ).

Employers are not only willing to accept a range of educational qualifications but they also value the personal qualities of new recruits more

Table 10.4

Question: What would you say is the most important in a new recruit? Skills, knowledge or personal qualities?

	All	BBC Radio	Commercial Radio	BBC TV	Commercial TV
Personal	55.4%	56.3%	50%	66.7%	76%
Skills	35%	31.3%	41.7%	16.7%	16%
Knowledge	7%	12.5%	5.2%	8.3%	8%
Don't know	3.8%	6.3%	3.1%	8.3%	0%

Table 10.5

Question: Which personal qualities do you think are essential for a new recruit?

All	BBC Radio	Commercial Radio	BBC TV	Commercial TV
Enthusiasm (96.8%)	93.8%	96.9%	91.7%	100%
Good voice (90.4%)	90.6%	96.9%	75%	68%
Learn quickly (88.5%)	81.3%	91.7%	83.3%	84%
Withstand pressure (86.6%)	78.1%	91.7%	75%	80%
Positive attitude (85.4%)	84.4%	85.4%	75%	84%
Team work (82.2%)	90.6%	81.3%	91.4%	72%

than the skills and knowledge they bring with them. 55.4 percent of respondents said that personal qualities were more important than either skills (35 percent) or knowledge (7 percent) (see Table 10.4).

Employers were particularly interested in new recruits who displayed such qualities as enthusiasm, the ability to learn quickly and to work as part of a team. There was a consistency in response which indicates that such personal characteristics are deemed necessary and, indeed, desirable by all sectors of the broadcast journalism industry (Table 10.5).

Conversely, certain qualities, such as an enthusiasm for social reform, having strong opinions, a sense of public duty, ethics or fair play, did not strike the majority of editors as essential qualities (Table 10.6).

This heavy emphasis on personal qualities, at the expense of skills and knowledge, is replicated by the recruitment practices of those broadcast journalism courses which are validated by the industry body.

Not only do they value personal qualities over both skills and knowledge – 72.7 percent of those surveyed said personal qualities were most

Table 10.6

Question: Which personal qualities do you think are essential for a new recruit?

	All	BBC Radio	Commercial Radio	BBC TV	Commercial TV
No opinions	1.3%	0%	1%	0%	4%
Enthusiasm for social reform	2.5%	0%	4.2%	0%	0%
Strong opinions	7%	3.1%	9.4%	0%	4%
Sense of public duty	12.7%	25%	5.2%	50%	16%
Lots of outside interests	15.3%	9.4%	16.7%	0%	20%
Strong sense of ethics	21.7%	25%	17.7%	25%	28%
Sense of fair play	25.5%	31.3%	25%	25%	20%

Table 10.7

Question: Which personal qualities do you think are essential for a new recruit?

	Trainers
Enthusiasm	90.9%
Curiosity	90.9%
Listening ability	90.9%
Learn quickly	81.8%
Withstand pressure	81.8%
Positive attitude	81.8%
Ability to analyse	81.8%
Ability to communicate	81.8%
Good voice	81.8%

Table 10.8

Question: Which personal qualities do you think are essential for a new recruit?

	Trainers
No opinions	0%
Enthusiasm for social reform	0%
Strong opinions	0%
Lots of outside interests	0%
Sense of public duty	18.2%
Ambition	18.2%
Strong sense of ethics	27.3%
Sense of fair play	27.3%

Table 10.9

Question: What overriding factor would make you accept a new recruit?
(Answers given by more than 10% of those who responded included)

BBC Radio	Commercial Radio	BBC TV	Commercial TV	Trainers
Talent (21.9%)	Good voice (16.7%)	Talent (50%)	Enthusiasm (24%)	Enthusiasm/ communication skills/commitment/ curiosity (18.2%)
	Enthusiasm (15.6%)	Hunger for news (16.7%)	Talent (20%)	

Table 10.10

Question: What overriding factor would make you reject a new recruit?
(Answers given by more than 10% of those who responded included)

BBC Radio	Commercial Radio	BBC TV	Commercial TV	Trainers
No enthusiasm/ Poor voice (15.6%)	Poor voice (19.8%)	No enthusiasm (25%)	No enthusiasm/ apathy/ arrogance/poor communication skills (12%)	Poor voice/ poor communication skills/no curiosity (18.2%)
Arrogance (12.5%)	Arrogance (15.6%)			

important, compared to 18.2 percent and 9.1 percent who cited skills and knowledge respectively – but they also valued the same essential qualities (see Tables 10.7 and 10.8).

Such commonality between trainers and employers is testimony to the closeness between the industry-accredited courses and the broadcast industry itself. This is underlined by other close similarities in recruitment practices and in what is thought to be essential professional practice.

Employers and trainers were largely agreed on both the overriding factors which would make them accept (Table 10.9) or reject (Table 10.10) a new recruit. Similarly, trainers and employers agreed on the importance of what should be taught to trainee journalists (Table 10.11).

Thus, according to the research, the 'ideal' journalist would be highly motivated with a positive attitude, someone who is enthusiastic, curious, quick to learn and works well in a team. A strong sense of ethics or an enthusiasm for social reform are not essential qualities.

Table 10.11

Question to employers: Are the following topics which are taught on accredited courses important?

News writing	98.1%	Keyboard skills	91.1%
Feature writing	68.2%	Shorthand**	54.1%
Subbing	63.1%	Use of audio	92.4%
Production	83.4%	Camera work*	28.7%
Research	89.2%	Picture selection*	27.4%
Sources of news	94.3%	Bulletin compilation	96.8%
Media organizations	40.1%	Newsreading	97.5%
Reporting	94.9%	Feature production	66.9%
News values	96.2%	Ethics	79.6%
Newsroom practice	93.6%	Interviewing	97.5%
Technical skills	93.6%	Public administration	78.3%
Editing (technical)	92.4%	Media law	96.2%
Editing (editorial)	93%		

* Camera work and picture selection both scored highly with TV editors but low with radio editors.
** Neither trainers nor editors can agree on the value of shorthand. The BJTC advises courses to teach shorthand but it is not a compulsory subject.

Contradictions

The evidence would seem to suggest that those validated courses, which are carefully constructed to receive industry approval and take great care to acquire the latest (and often expensive) industry-standard hard- and software, ideally match the needs of the industry they serve. However, the research masks a number of different influences, both current and historical, which serve to explain the reality; namely that broadcast news editors, and in particular those in the commercial sector, take their new recruits from a variety of different routes, of which the industry-validated courses are simply one.

Because of the way journalism training generally has evolved, the specific likes, dislikes and needs of individual editors play the major part in deciding an applicant's fate (Boyd Barrett 1970). In the print sector, a standardized training scheme only came about through outside pressure, when the 1947 Royal Commission on the Press reported that journalists needed to be highly skilled to fulfil their public accountability role (*The Royal Commission on the Press* 1949). The system which developed for print journalism of block release courses and pre-entry training run by colleges left responsibility for recruitment firmly in the hands of employers. This particular aspect, which is fundamental to the training debate, has never been questioned in the UK. Unlike other 'professions' such as law or medicine, a particular course of study is not a pre-condition of employment for either journalism or broadcast journalism. Thus, despite the attempts of the Institute of Journalists to introduce an examination for aspiring journalists, by not linking pre-entry courses directly to employment, employers have been able to tailor their recruitment to their organizational needs (Bainbridge 1984).

The success of validated courses is due in part to the close relationship between the teachers and employers. Indeed, courses are carefully controlled in a number of different ways to ensure that the student experience is as closely geared to a newsroom experience as possible. Tutors, when hired, are required to have extensive experience of the industry (BJTC 1999). This guarantees that, when the selection of students takes place, the selection criteria match those of the industry employer. Students are recruited to 'fit in' because those involved in the selection process are recent employees of the industry. Indeed, it is in the course tutors' interests to ensure that the students recruited are 'suited' to the industry as validation partly depends on employment outcomes. However, this rigorous process succeeds at the expense of diversity. Students who don't match the ideal profile may be excluded. This lack of diversity not only limits opportunities but it also gives a fragmented industry, with in some cases little in common and less choice over whom it employs. Moreover, the teaching methodology adopted by the courses, namely the recreation of a working environment, hampers any challenge to traditional professional paradigms. Regular and tight deadlines with assessment geared around professional practice criteria militate against much reflection on, discussion of, or experimentation with current working practices as carried out within the industry. Not only is professional socialization guaranteed but also journalistic practice is perpetuated.

But both the journalistic practice and the professional socialization reflect a 20-year old tradition, when both commercial and public sector broadcasters had largely similar outputs and differences were slight and only matters of style.[11] This approach is increasingly under pressure in a broadcast news industry which is fragmented and intensely competitive and in which individual companies are using new technology and delivery systems in ways which can change their output fundamentally. Increasingly, as interactivity becomes possible, the debate is about how much the journalist's job is changing (Yelvington 1999). Furthermore, whereas a core skills approach may still be relevant to the more traditional broadcasters, smaller companies may feel they do not need the broad range or complexity of skills which are being taught on validated courses. One consideration which makes the courses more of a training ground for the larger, traditional broadcast organizations is the cost factor. A recent survey said that most students expected to leave university with debts of £3,700 (Observer 1999). Postgraduate accredited courses attract no local authority grants and, whereas a new recruit at a small to medium-sized commercial radio station outside London can expect to earn around £11,500, the equivalent wage at a BBC regional bi-media centre would be £15,000 plus up to £4,000 unpredictability payments.[12] This discrepancy makes a job at the BBC a more desirable prospect for a student in debt. However, students who are able and prepared to pay for a course are likely to be from middle-class backgrounds, another factor affecting the diversity of entry and one which particularly concerns the BBC.[13]

More indications of how editors differ in their needs and preferences became evident though a series of informal interviews with editors in several of the different sectors.

As technology enables programmes to be made by fewer people, the demand for students to be able to master techniques previously handled by 'specialists', such as editing and camera work, is increasing the pressure on courses to teach those skills. Those students who possess such skills are in demand from newer broadcasters, such as ONDigital and Channel 5, who are keen to attract multi-skilled, multi-functional journalists. Such students are able to take advantage of flexible promotion systems which allow them to progress quickly. The 'Channel 5 effect', as it's been called, is already driving 'traditional' broadcasters down a similar route and the 'fast-track', multi-skilling route has been taken up by other independent broadcasters, enabling some individuals to pursue a programme idea to completion single-handedly (Pile 1999). However, there are some editors who feel that allowing journalists to fast-track through the system eventually leads to lower professional standards and does a disservice to journalism. They argue that there is insufficient time for courses to teach both highly specialized craft skills and the pure journalistic skills of investigation and research and have accused courses of colluding with companies by 'giving the industry what it wants but not training journalists'.[14]

In other cases, highly trained students find the skills they have learned at such cost to themselves are unnecessary or inappropriate. Work in many different news organizations is now largely processing, re-versioning or 'information sequencing' and the hopes of young journalists who are highly trained and want to report and present, are frustrated.[15] Likewise, whilst the ability to conduct a challenging, in-depth, live interview is prized by some news organizations, for others, it is an irrelevant skill.

Editors in some organizations complain that newly trained journalists are still wedded to 'old' ideas of news which are in conflict with audience desires and expectations. They say journalism should be reporting on what interests the audience, rather than what interests the professional journalist. This is a view which is influencing many news organizations to review their news agendas.[16]

An employer from an independent production company, said that he never recruited from training courses as he wanted non-standard people[17] and a commercial radio manager agreed that he preferred to train people himself.[18] One television editor complained that students from validated courses were identical with the same ideas and the same CVs.[19]

These contradictory views cannot fail to impact on the training courses. One experienced trainer confessed that it was impossible to know whether his programme was doing the 'right sort of training' and whether it was training students for the industry or for his own vision of what journalism should be.[20] It is clear that industry fragmentation and differing perceptions of the role of broadcast journalism in today's media have serious repercussions for training courses.

Conclusion

The difficulties and tensions within vocational training of broadcast journalists are neither new for vocational training nor confined to broadcast journalism. Other 'professions', such as nursing and teaching, also have to address both the contradictions of training in a higher education context and of training for employment in an uncertain and complex world (Thomson 1999). Unlike the health and education services, however, in the world of broadcast journalism, individual media companies and organizations are able to decide their own individual standards and what constitutes 'good practice' and professionalism in their own individual worlds. If industry standards have become a moving target, therefore, is it possible for training to serve its two most important customers – the students and the broadcast industry itself – and what can we learn from current training about broadcast news and the role of the journalist?

The research clearly suggests that editors not only recruit from many different sources but also value personal qualities over and above both skills and knowledge. Those qualities of curiosity, enthusiasm and quick-wittedness are associated with the need for today's journalists to adapt flexibly and quickly to new technology, new working practices and new definitions of professional practice. The diversity of entry also suggests that the traditional, industry-validated training courses cannot satisfy the different demands which need to be met.

These courses are bound by the core skills approach demanded by the Broadcast Journalism Training Council. While this approach is both highly professional and comprehensive, it also tightly regulates what skills are learned by students who may ultimately work for organizations which require different skills or have different standards and ideas or which actively want new recruits who have less knowledge about how journalism 'should' be practised.

Furthermore, while broadcast journalism is being driven by this complex mixture of new technology, competition and changing fashions, training courses and industry accreditation bodies, almost by definition, lag behind. This leaves editors, who are at the very cutting edge of the changes, to manage their recruitment in whatever way they can to answer their organizations' particular requirements.

Thus, a student with a general and broad education, no pre-conceived ideas about how 'news' is produced and whose skills are not limited to whatever equipment was available, may be just as valuable to some editors as a highly trained, multi-skilled journalist is to others. Contrary to the damning press reports about 'media courses', some commentators and editors believe that broad-based, non-vocational media studies (and, indeed, more general) courses are ideal environments for young people to learn about the broadcast industry and make their own critical assessments of it without confining themselves to a particular way of thinking or working (Phillips and Gabor 1996). This is not a point of view which is shared by the highly influential National Training Organisation, Skillset, which has linked the amount of practical training and industry involvement in courses to students' success in getting jobs

(Skillset 1995/96a). Their new Related Vocational Qualifications in production research and editing, which are currently being piloted by 19 education and training providers in England and Wales, are further attempts to link education to industry needs (*Skillset News* 1999).

But, whereas these RVQs may well ease confusion amongst students and employers as to what a course provides, they are unlikely to change radically the recruitment practices of employers who hire broadcast journalists. These employers cannot be seen as one homogenous group and, just as some may require the 'core skills' approach and others a student with a more general and less specific education, a third way is also emerging. The fragmentation of the industry has led some sectors or even individual organizations to take training into their own hands. A number of independent production companies, for example, concerned about production research training, have developed a training scheme tailored to their own specifications and designed to train researchers, not in general research methods but according to their own particular needs.[21] The new scheme, supported by Skillset, involves placements at several independent production companies. This training has grown out of a perceived lack of sector-specific training and may be a precursor of more sector-specific, or even employer-specific training, already obvious in other areas of industry. Textile and fashion courses within higher education have long done deals with specific employers which have not just ensured support but also continued sector relevance (Kingston 1998). There are some who believe that employer-specific courses could be set up with specially selected colleges or universities to offer opportunities to students to be trained in whatever skills are required by their particular organization.[22] By locking in to an organization's recruitment policy, a course could be sure of maintaining its relevance although the sheer unpredictability of the industry would make it unlikely that subsequent employment could be guaranteed.

The increase in outlets and occupations with a journalistic component and diverse ideas about broadcast journalism and the role of the broadcast journalist today mean that a 20-year cross-industry consensus on what is required by a broadcast journalist is breaking down. As the industry fragments, so too do the number of routes into broadcast journalism multiply. Increasingly students have to decide what area of broadcast journalism attracts them and seek out the most appropriate route towards it, whether it be an industry-validated course, a sector or organization-specific programme, a good general education or a one-year working holiday in Africa.

It was, however, ever thus. If, as Carr-Saunders and Wilson said nearly 70 years ago, the range of activities within journalism is so great that a connecting link is impossible to find, training can never be more than partially successful. Crucially, however, training can shed light on the values and priorities of broadcast news itself and the fact that the traditional, highly professional training routes into broadcast news are being by-passed by a significant proportion of employers suggests that some of these values and priorities may be changing. This could be an indication that parts of the broadcast news industry are becoming 'less professional', that the journalism is no longer at the service of the public, that it is, in fact, being dumbed-down. Conversely, it could indicate that journalism in the UK is being re-defined in order to serve a more diverse public in a way which is more effective and more relevant for the very varied audiences of the twenty-first century.

Notes

1 Author's interview with commercial radio news editor, September 1999.
2 Author's interview with BBC Managing Editor, July 1999.
3 Original research carried out 1997/1998. Questionnaires completed by 165 editors across BBC Radio and TV, Commercial Radio and TV. Response rate of 64.2 percent.
4 Author's interview with television news editor, July 1999.
5 Author's interview with Gerard Mansell, first chair of the Joint Advisory Committee for the Training of Radio Journalists (JCTRJ).
6 Author's interview with BJTC course trainers, July 1999.
7 Job specifications for lecturer posts.
8 The Research Assessment Exercise assesses the quality of research in colleges and universities. www.rae.ac.uk
9 Original research.
10 Author's interviews with BBC managers, July 1999.
11 Author's interview with Gerard Mansell.
12 Author's interviews with BBC and commercial radio editors, July 1999.
13 Author's interview with BBC manager, July 1999.
14–19 Author's interviews with commercial and public sector broadcast news editors, July 1999.
20 Author's interview with journalism course leader, July 1999.
21 Author's interview with independent producer, July 1999.
22 Author's interviews with editor in commercial radio and industry commentator.

References

Bainbridge, C. (1984) 'The formative years', in Bainbridge, C. (ed.) *One Hundred Years of Journalism – Social Aspects of the Press*, Macmillan Press, Hampshire, London.
Barnett, S. & Seymour, E. (1999) 'A shrinking iceberg, travelling south . . .', as quoted in *UK Press Gazette* 'Study confirms decline of serious TV current affairs', 29 October.
Boyd-Barrett, O. (1970) 'Journalism Recruitment and Training: Problems in Professionalisation', in Tunstall, J. (ed.), *Media Sociology*, Constable, London.
Broadcast Journalism Training Council (1999) *Course Guidelines*.
Bromley, M. (1997) 'The end of journalism? changes in workplace practices in the press and broadcasting in the 1990s', in Bromley, M. & O'Malley, T. (eds), *A Journalism Reader*, Routledge, London.

Bromley, M. & Purdey, H. (1998) *Journo-Morphosis* – 'Today's New Media and the Education of Tomorrow's "Cool" Journalists', in *Convergence* 1998, Vol. 4, No. 4.

Eyre, Richard, Chief Executive ITV (1999) in the 1999 James MacTaggart Memorial lecture, 27 August.

Carr-Saunders, A.M. & Wilson, P.A. (1933) *The Professions,* Clarendon Press, Oxford.

Chantler, P. & Harris, S. (1997) *Local Radio Journalism,* Focal Press, Oxford.

Commercial Radio Companies Association (1998) *An Introduction to Commercial Radio,* CRCA, London.

Corbett, B. (1977) 'Get it sorted', *The Journalist* (March/April).

Delano, A. & Henningham, J. (1995) *The News Breed – British Journalists in the 1990s,* London Institute.

Kingston, P. (1998) 'Tailor-made or off the peg', *Guardian* (13 October).

National Council for the Training of Journalists (leaflet) *A World of Challenge – Training as a Journalist for a Great Career,* NCTJ, Harlow.

National Union of Journalists (1998) *Careers in Journalism,* NUJ, London.

Observer (1999) 'Survey by NatWest' (26 January).

Parsons, T. (1968) 'Professions', *International Encyclopaedia of the Social Sciences,* New York, as quoted in Jackson, J.A. (ed.) (1970) *Professions and Professionalisation,* Cambridge University Press, London.

Phillips, A. & Gabor, I. (1996) 'The case for media degrees', *British Journalism Review,* Vol. 7, No. 3.

Pile, S. (1999) 'One woman, one camera – is this the future of TV?', *Daily Telegraph* (23 October).

The Royal Commission on the Press (1949) *Report* Cmd 7700, HMSO, London.

Shawcross, W. (1992) *Rupert Murdoch: Ringmaster of the Information Circus,* Chatto and Windus, London.

Skillset (1995/96a) *Media Courses Survey and Consultation,* London.

Skillset National Training Organisation for Broadcast, Film, Video and Multimedia (1995/96b) *Employment Patterns and Training Needs,* London.

Skillset News (1999) 'The bigger picture', issue 5, Autumn 1999.

Smith, Rt. Hon. C., Secretary of State for the Department for Culture, Media and Sport (1999) in a speech to the Royal Television Society in Cambridge, *Guardian* (20 September).

Sunday Telegraph (1996) (4 February).

Thomson, S. (1999) 'Kiss of life can't come too soon – the crisis facing nurse education', *Guardian Education* (6 July): iv.

The Times Educational Supplement (1996) (2 February).

Tunstall, J. (1971) *Journalists at Work,* Constable, London, as quoted in Franklin, B. (1997) *Newszak and News Media,* Arnold, London.

UCAS website www.ucas.co.uk

West, J. & Eedle, P. (1999) 'Out There News Agency', as quoted in *UK Press Gazette,* 'Making it big' (23 July).

Yelvington, S. (1999) Cox Interactive Media, Keynote address, NetMedia, City University, London.

CHAPTER 11

Public relations and broadcast news: An evolutionary approach

Brian McNair

Of the many forces shaping the development of broadcast news, the communicative skills and techniques associated with the term 'public relations' have been amongst the most controversial. In recent years one form of public relations in particular – 'spin' – and its purveyors – 'the people who live in the dark', as Clare Short famously described them[1] – have been centrally implicated in 'the death of news',[2] and the broader 'crisis' of political journalism identified by many critics, blamed for a variety of perceived threats to the integrity of the public sphere and the quality of political debate. Prominent targets in this unfolding critique have been such figures as Peter Mandelson and Alistair Campbell in the United Kingdom, and Dick Morris and George Stephanopoulous in the USA.

Spin, of course, is only the most recent name for a set of political communication practices – leaking, disinformation, lobbying, the staging of what Daniel Boorstin called in the 1960s 'pseudo-events' (1962) – which are at least as old as the mass media themselves, and which have tended to be viewed in the broader public domain with, at best, suspicion; at worst, contempt for the damage which they allegedly do to the normative workings of the media in a liberal democracy.

Public relations, as I will discuss it in this essay, incorporates spin as well as those older and less fashionable, but no less important communicative practices engaged in by political and corporate actors when they seek to influence various publics, be they share holders (in the case of business PR), governments (in the case of single issue pressure groups and lobbyists), or members of the electorate (political parties), to list three of the 'targets' of public relations professionals. Journalists and editors also form an important PR 'public', in so far as they are viewed as channels in the two-step influencing of the wider publics who read, listen to or watch their output. It is the perceived danger to a properly functioning public sphere of this, media-oriented activity which has generated the fiercest attacks on public relations in recent years, peaking in the late 1990s with what I have called elsewhere the 'demonisation of spin' (McNair 2000) which accompanied the progress of the Clinton administration in America, and the rise of New Labour in Britain. This essay explores the impact of public relations on the broadcast media, and assesses the arguments advanced by its many and vociferous critics in both the academic and journalistic worlds.

Journalism and public relations: an evolutionary model

Let me begin by suggesting that, despite the impression given by the acres of anti-PR media coverage – the demonology of spin – which characterized the 1990s in both Britain and the United States, it is misleading to think of journalists and public relations practitioners as innately hostile opposing camps, or to assume that the ascendancy of one group means the corruption and demeaning of the other, as if the journalist–PR relationship were a zero sum game, in which benefits to one side could be had only at the expense of the other. Although this is how the issue is often posed by critics from Habermas onwards (1989), it is more productive to consider the two categories of communication professional as inhabiting a constantly interactive, mutually adaptive state of inter-dependence, whereby changes affecting one group are closely connected with, and influenced by modifications in the work of the other.

The basic techniques of contemporary PR are not new to the modern era, as already noted. But the emergence of a profession of public relations, practised by recognized experts working independently as consultants or as members of in-house public relations teams, was undoubtedly a by-product of the development of the mass media from the late nineteenth century on. The expansion of the media, in the context of widening and eventually universal suffrage throughout the capitalist world, gave public opinion a key role for the first time in the history of human affairs. These processes created the conditions for the emergence of a professional group whose job it was to manage relations with that public (or publics) (McNair 1999b), including the management of relations with its media. On the assumption that journalism can influence opinions, shape public agendas, and even change attitudes and behaviours, the emergence of a profession of media management was an inevitability as soon as mass media became the dominant channel of political communication and public intercourse. As Walter Lippmann recognized in 1922:

> The enormous discretion as to what facts and what impressions shall be reported is steadily convincing every organised group of people that whether it wishes to secure publicity or avoid it, the exercise of discretion cannot be left to the reporter. It is safer to hire a press agent [as PR practitioners were then known] who stands between the group and the newspapers. (1954: 344)

Seventy-five years later, at the height of the late 1990s, media panic around spin doctors, Tony Blair's press secretary Alistair Campbell defined (and defended) his communicative work in terms which Lippmann would easily have understood:

> We live in the media age. There are more newspapers, magazines, television and radio stations than ever before. They all have space to fill, and they look to politics to fill a good deal of it. The political party that does not understand the needs of the media is doomed. Much of the work involves ensuring all outlets are spoken to, a consistent line is taken, and our central points communicated . . . We offer advice on media and political strategy; we brief journalists and MPs. Big deal.[3]

And as for political parties, so too for charities, environmental organizations, business lobbies, trade unions, churches, and every social actor, individual or institution, aiming to have an impact first on public opinion and then, through the impact of that opinion on decision makers and governors, the political process.

At the same time as 'press agents' took on the role of managing relationships between various social actors and the media in a political environment of growing complexity and volatility, the practice of public relations was becoming an increasingly important technical input to the media production process. As Alistair Campbell points out in the quote reproduced above, the proliferation of media outlets, and the constant acceleration of the speed of information flow between the social world and the media (processes which continue at an exponential rate with the development of internet and digital technologies) has presented journalists with a fundamental logistic problem – how to fill their columns and airtime? From the nineteenth century, the professional ideology of liberal journalism had stressed the importance of the objective sourcing of information (Schiller 1987; Schudson 1978; McNair 1999a). For the print media, and even more so for the broadcasters, fulfilling this requirement and thus securing the market's acceptance of their 'objectivity' became more difficult as production schedules shrank, editorial demands increased, and competition between media organizations intensified. In the expanded public sphere of the twentieth century, public relations became a convenient and crucial means of filling the media's 'news holes', as Jay Blumler describes them (1989), both in the readiness of its practitioners to supply the raw material from which the various forms of journalism were then constructed, and in making it easier for the media to process and make sense of a growing torrent of information in a world where truth and falsehood were fiercely contested. Lippmann again:

> Were reporting the simple recovery of obvious facts, the press agent would be little more than a clerk. But since, in respect to most of the big topics of news, the facts are not simple, and not at all obvious, but subject to choice and opinion, it is natural that everyone should wish to make his own choice of facts for the newspapers to print. The publicity [PR] man does that. And in doing it, he certainly saves the reporter much trouble, by presenting him with a clear picture of a situation out of which he might otherwise make neither head nor tail. (Ibid)

Jonathan Haslam, when director of communications at the Department of Education and Employment, argued from his own experience as a government information officer that 'journalists rely on [us] to deal in facts, to explain policy, and to ensure that credibility is never put at issue'.[4]

In the competitive market place of news-as-commodity, moreover, media organizations acquired a reliance, not just for clarity and sense in their efforts to cover the complex social world, but for exclusivity and distinctiveness in their reportage – for 'scoops', and for a particular angle and 'spin' on their stories which would set them apart from those of their commercial rivals. These qualities too were provided by PR practitioners, who became convenient sources of the 'real' (and exclusive) stories behind the apparent surface of things.

Thus, the journalists of the fourth estate came in the twentieth century to depend, to a greater or lesser degree, on the PR men and women of the 'fifth estate'. The latter, consequently, grew in number and importance as the market for their services expanded. By the turn of the millenium, every political and government organization, every business and public service institution, every celebrity of screen, stage or sports field, was a routine user of public relations in their dealings with the media. One writer estimates that in the United States, PR practitioners had, by the late 1990s, come to outnumber journalists by some 150,000 to 130,000. In the UK, where the profession was somewhat less developed, there were some 2,700 PR companies and 6,500 in-house PR departments, employing about 25,000 people (Michie 1998).

Public relations and the news: some positives

Before considering some of the critical concerns which the interdependence of journalists and PR practitioners has provoked, we should not underestimate the positive implications of this transformed communicative environment on all of those organizations and individuals who seek access to the media on terms which, if not necessarily always favourable, at least amount from their perspective to a politically necessary presence in the public sphere. The critical media studies tradition has traditionally, and not without good cause, highlighted the structural imbalances underpinning mainstream media production, and especially the output of journalists in the broadcast media. From the 1970s onwards, critical scholarly work on such questions as news 'bias', or on the privileged access of elites to those spaces where news agendas and interpretive frameworks are primarily defined (Chomsky 1988), has argued that media output tends to reflect the political and economic hierarchies characteristic of a given society, and that structuring devices such as objectivity and (in the case of British broadcasting in particular), impartiality, merely serve to legitimize in-built patterns of discursive and ideological domination (GUMG 1980).

The growing dependence of the news media on, and their logistically driven responsiveness to sources has undermined this structural dominance, allowing a more fluid and open symbolic field to take shape within the mainstream media. In this emerging environment, the historic exclusions of, and biases against, subordinate or marginalized groups are much less automatic than was once the case. Armed with a knowledge of how the media work; of what kinds of stories, and what verbal and visual strategies fit best into journalistic grammars, organizations like Greenpeace, Amnesty International, and the Countryside Alliance have demonstrated a capacity to shape the public agenda through their presence in the news, often in opposition to the better-resourced source strategies of the political and economic elites with whom they are engaging in their campaigns. The routine production needs of the media have rewarded the entrepreneurial communicative skills of resource-poor groups, as well as the PR-rich and politico-economically powerful.

In the 'battle for Seattle', for example, a loose but media-wise coalition of anarchists, environmentalists, and developmental activists organized street demonstrations which, by design and by accident (in so far as heavy-handed police responses gave the demonstrations more newsworthiness than might otherwise have been the case) seriously undermined the business of the World Trade Organisation's December 1999 summit, and forced onto the global media an alternative agenda to that preferred by the pro-free trade WTO. In 1995, the Greenpeace organization successfully campaigned against the Shell corporation's attempts to dispose of the disused Brent Spar oil rig in the North Sea. Carefully manufactured media images of Greenpeace activists' occupation of the rig fed a continent-wide campaign of protest, and seriously damaged Shell's desired reputation as an environmentally-friendly oil company (McNair 1998).

The substantive issue of who was right and who was wrong in the Seattle or Brent Spar cases is less important for our discussion than the fact that in both, 'subordinate' source strategies determined a broadcast news coverage which effectively subverted 'dominant' ideas and agendas (i.e., those of the WTO governments, and of the oil industry respectively).

Since the 1960s, terrorist organizations too, have exploited the broadcast media's ever-growing demand, not just for news stories, but for exciting and dramatic visuals to accompany those stories. Baudrillard (1983) has referred to 'a Theatre of Cruelty' – by which he means the staging of violent tele-visual 'spectaculars' such as bombings, assassinations, and hi-jackings intended to capture the broadcast media's attention and put the responsible organization's demands on the public agenda.[5] One does not have to agree with the goals or values of organizations like the IRA or ETA to appreciate the facility with which they have influenced, through their exploitation of the broadcast media's hunger for exciting visual material, the development of political processes in Northern Ireland and Spain respectively.

In the late 1990s, the IRA and its political wing, Sinn Fein, distanced themselves from the 'Theatre of Cruelty' and became more reliant on conventional, non-violent public relations instruments like news conferences, broadcast interviews, lobbying, and photo-opportunities. These, like the bombings and murders of the pre-Good Friday period, reflected the republicans' recognition of the importance to their cause of capturing and controlling the media agenda – albeit as constitutional politicians rather than armed paramilitaries – and showed once again that effective public relations is not the monopoly of big government or big business.

Half a century ago, Harold Lasswell observed that 'skill, like wealth or prestige or position, is a basis of power in society, and changes in the skills used in political action will have discoverable consequences for the distribution of power and influence' (from Lasswell and Kaplan 1950, quoted in Bloom 1973). The development of the media–source relationship in the late twentieth century has made *communicative* skill an increasingly important factor in political and ideological competition, alongside the more familiar benefits accruing to the possession of wealth, status and institutional power. The consequences of this for 'the distribution of power and influence' within the advanced capitalist societies of the new century remain to be 'discovered', in theoretical and empirical terms. There is already considerable evidence, however, to suggest that they will tend to be pro-democratic in their subversion of the structural communicative biases which have tended to favour established political and economic elites. The widespread adoption, by dominant and subordinate actors alike, of the communicative skills which comprise public relations, in an environment of enhanced media dependency on sources, creates a more dynamic and 'chaotic' public sphere than that which features in traditional materialist sociologies of the media (McNair 1998). It can be expected to enhance its democratic qualities in so far as it contributes to 'a change of focus from the rhetoric of the elite speaker to the rhetoric of the emerging or subaltern voice' (King 1992: 1).

Public relations and the crisis of broadcast news

There is a downside to all this, of course, and the rise of public relations has not proceeded without adverse critical commentary from a wide spectrum of academic and journalistic opinion. This alleges the corruption of journalistic independence and quality by public relations, as the reporter's traditional tasks of investigation and disinterested news gathering have gradually been replaced by the relatively inexpensive, but highly motivated offerings of PR men and women, whether working for governments and political parties, pop stars and media celebrities, or 'Reclaim the Streets' activists. The convenience of source-generated material, it is argued, has bred journalistic laziness, and a reluctance to spend the time and money necessary to construct authentically independent or objective accounts of events and issues. The news media are argued to have been seduced by the false realities and pseudo-events of the PR repertoire, allowing news to be transformed into a form of promotional culture.

In other work, I have discussed the example of 'Branson's balloon', and the success of the Virgin boss in gaining headline coverage on ITN's flagship news bulletin for his adventuring exploits (McNair 1998). Mr Branson may be a very nice man, and an inspirational entrepreneur to many but, the critics would argue, was the story of his (failed) January 1997 attempt to fly around the world in a balloon really the stuff of headlines on *News at Ten*? Was it really 'news' at all, as opposed to advertising for Branson and his company, pursuing at that time, as ever, commercial expansion and diversification across the globe? Self-evidently, the critics would say, it was the latter, wholly predictable and entirely in keeping with the Virgin boss's penchant for publicity and 'free media' – i.e. media coverage which performs the commercial functions of advertising in enhancing brand recognition and customer goodwill, whilst not having to be paid for because it is accepted by the media as 'news'. The story's prominent appearance on a flagship British TV news bulletin can be advanced as an excellent example of the extent to which broadcast media outlets have become the willing vehicles for PR 'puffery' – stories which are principally promotional rather than informative in the sense usually associated with quality journalism.

Critical attention has also highlighted the increased use of video releases by many organizations, who calculate that by supplying well-produced (if heavily slanted) packages of information to story-hungry broadcasters, they will increase their chances of being able to influence the news agenda. Whether the video release emanates from a philanthropically minded charity, a politically correct pressure group or a self-interested capitalist, the end result is the same – the undermining of journalistic independence and integrity. Some organizations, like the BBC and Sky News, have a policy of not using video releases, or at least labelling them as such on screen; signalling to the viewer that particular footage originates with an external non-journalistic source. In many instances, however, the material is integrated seamlessly into a broadcast news package, passed off as the original (and thus trustworthy) product of journalistic news-gathering work.

Criticisms of public relations are most acute in relation to broadcast coverage of politics, where the negative effects are said to threaten the quality of democracy itself. The rise of 'soundbite culture', for example, in which broadcasters are fed, and willingly pass on in their bulletins, carefully honed packets of persuasive-sounding rhetoric, has been noted with alarm in both the United States (Hart 1987) and the United Kingdom (Franklin 1994). Critics have noted the ease with which broadcasters collude in the staged photo-opportunities which make dramatic pictures but reveal nothing of policy; with the orchestrated feel-good rallies which have replaced the traditional party conferences; and with the informal, behind-the-scenes leaking and lobbying practices through which spin doctors and communication directors seek to drive the political news agenda and shape the journalistic interpretation of a story. Journalist Peter Riddell notes 'the specific Blairite innovation' of 'using specially staged events, like appearing at a hospital or school to provide a favourable, and non-adversarial backdrop to a [policy] announcement' (1999: 30). The political editor of Sky News observes with admiration that 'they [the New Labour communication specialists] are good. They are well aware of what each news organisation is looking for, and they are good at servicing them. They are excellent at managing deadlines'.[6]

It is of course the very professionalism and 'excellence' of contemporary PR practitioners that has encouraged the critical backlash against their activities, and fuelled the 'demonology of spin' referred to above. As Sky's political editor concedes, 'there is a certain amount of frustration amongst broadcasters. They do feel that they are being managed very tightly'.

Underpinning such frustrations is the journalists' sense that, while some PR activity may be a welcome input to an increasingly pressured news production process, there has been a decidedly unwelcome shift in the balance of power existing between the 'fourth' and 'fifth' estates; that PR practitioners in their various guises have become rather too big for their boots, and have moved from being mere suppliers of scarce information to dictators of how that information is used. 'Labour's media minders cruise the lobbies these days like celebrities', complained one journalist with obvious distaste in 1997,[7] not long after the party's general election victory – a victory, of course, in which the role of public relations and spin was viewed by most observers as pivotal. Such comments, and there have been many in similarly hostile vein, reveal the extent to which journalists in the late 1990s came to perceive that public relations was usurping their status and position in qualitatively new ways. And indeed, there *have* been some notorious instances of PR practitioners attempting to intimidate broadcasters. According to one BBC news presenter interviewed by the author:

> The [Charlie] Whelans[8] of this world do that [intimidate journalists] all the time. That is their stock-in-trade. At the Labour conference he came up to me and said, 'If you go ahead with what you are planning to do, I'll fucking have you'. That's the way he works. 'It's not a threat', he said! I said, 'Oh, fine'.

According to another BBC presenter:

> They shout down the phone. They get quite bullish about it, particularly the Labour Party during the [1997 general election] campaign. Alistair Campbell used to come on, and Mandelson, roaring and shouting and very upset.

Scottish Television's fly-on-the-wall documentary, 'We Are the Treasury', broadcast by ITV in September/October 1997, showed Whelan using his considerable persuasive powers to browbeat various unnamed journalists into adopting his [Whelan's] preferred 'spin' on a particular story then in the news. We also saw him manipulating media in such a way as to gain coverage of a story which he knew would frame his then boss, Gordon Brown in a positive light. This he did without embarassment or apology, accepting such tactics as a legitimate part of his work for the Labour Chancellor.

Despite the frustrations felt by individual journalists, their ability to resist such methods is undermined by their dependence on such as Whelan and Campbell for access to those 'sexy' political stories which are both new and exclusive: a policy announcement; an interview with a senior politician; a reliable steer on what's really happening to a particular minister's career. According to one broadcast journalist, 'you get given stories. You get given ministers, prime ministers, anything you want, provided you are playing the game. When you stop playing the game, you don't get that'. Print journalist and scourge of the spinners, Anthony Bevins, makes a similar point:

> One of the problems of the interface between political reporting and the [political] machine is source pressure. If you upset a source, if you cross a source, you'll be punished for it. If you do as you're told, act like a patsy and take stories on trust, albeit untrue, then you're rewarded. It's a corruption of journalism.

Of course, New Labour, in opposition or in government, is not the first political organization to have exerted what some feel to have been undue influence on the broadcasters. Michael Schudson records that the Nixon administration 'sought to intimidate uncooperative newscasters, while the White House office of telecommunications policy prodded local affiliates to pressure the networks to report on Nixon more favourably' (1995: 155). H.R. Haldeman was doing for Nixon in the 1960s and early 1970s what Campbell, Mandelson, Whelan and the rest did for the Labour leadership in the 1990s. On this basis, Michael Brunson of ITN denies that the 'hired hands' of New Labour (as he calls them), or indeed those of any other party, are doing anything except the old-fashioned work of promotion, presentation and packaging undertaken by press and publicity agents throughout the twentieth century, albeit with more tenacity and bravado than was demonstrated by parties and organizations in the decades before this kind of lobbying activity came to be known as 'spin':

> These people have got a job to do and they do it very well indeed. [Their job] is to make certain not only that they get the message across but that it gets across accurately. What is wrong with calling in journalists, phoning up people, and saying 'This is what we are about, this is what we are trying to do, and this is where we think you have got it wrong?' I accept that, and frankly, if you think they have gone too far, you simply say 'Leave off!'

Except that competitive pressures on individual journalists and their organizations to maintain good relations with authoritative political sources (and the political actors on whose behalf they are spinning) may make them reluctant to engage in direct rejection of the spin doctors' advances, lest they be left out of the loop when the next story comes along.

There are alternatives to 'leave off!', however, in the struggle between journalists and their PR rivals for definition of events and issues in the public sphere. In the course of the process of adaptation and counter-adaptation referred to at the beginning of this essay, a number of reportorial, analytical and presentational strategies have been developed by the broadcasters which can be viewed both as responses to, and defences against, the rise of public relations and its perceived effect on their ability to report without fear or favour. Ironically – and although, as I will argue in the remainder of this essay, these approaches can be defended as a means of protecting the interests of the public against the manipulations and seductions of the public relations professionals – some at least of them have been included in the broader academic and journalistic critiques of PR's degenerative impact on the public sphere. They have been seen as part of the problem of PR, rather than the solution to it.

Spin and counter-spin

Deconstructing the process

The rise of public relations has, for example, been paralleled by the development of a new sub-genre of political journalism, concerned with what, for simplicity's sake, we can describe as *process*. Process journalism, for Michael Schudson, is characterized by 'an emphasis on strategy and tactics, political technique rather than policy outcome, the mechanical rather than the ideological' (1995: 10). For many critics – though not Schudson himself, who wishes 'to dispel the retrospective wishful thinking that beclouds too much contemporary political and cultural analysis' (ibid: 191) – the shift of focus embodied in process journalism represents another PR-driven corruption of the normative ideal of the fourth estate, in so far as it marginalizes coverage of the serious issues of politics in favour of a concern with trivial questions of performance, style, and image – all, of course, the responsibility of various types of public relations professional. Broadcast journalism (and print too), when it is not acting as a compliant vehicle for the reproduction of political sound-bites, photo-opportunities, and other pseudo-events, is said to be engrossed in the obsessive contemplation of the processes whereby political actors rise and fall, and the relationship between these changing fortunes and the political promotional techniques employed. In so doing, argue the critics, journalists cede ground to PR and endorse its reduction of the serious business of politics to a game in which the competition and the manner of winning (or losing) are given greater prominence in news content than the substantial issues which divide parties and candidates from each other, and the rational discussion of which give democracy its only point.

Part of this process has been the growth of interpretive, analytical journalism, often denounced as a poor substitute for the reportage of facts or, as it is sometimes put, 'straight reportage'. Journalists are accused of spending more and more time on analyzing and commenting on the frequently arcane sub-surface meanings of political action (including its promotional aspects), and not enough on the basic rights and wrongs of the policies being communicated. The broadcasters become reviewers of political performance and rhetoric, rather than independent, objective analysts and scrutinizers of policy and action.

If there is some substance to this argument, it is at least partly because one consequence of the rise of public relations has been the growth of media monitoring; a practice now engaged in by all major political parties as they seek to ensure 'fair and balanced' coverage of their activities in what they regard as the most important of all the media. Broadcasting is seen to be important because of its presumed impartiality. But this ethic of impartiality, closely policed as it is, militates against the journalistic analysis of party policy, and encourages instead evaluation of the processes of policy development, packaging and presentation. Reviewing performance and process distances the journalist from subjective judgments on policy, and thus carries far less risk of attracting potentially damaging accusations of 'bias'. Robin Oakley or Michael Brunson can say more or less what they like about William Hague's verbal performance during question time in the House of Commons, or what the election of Michael Portillo as MP for Kensington means for the future leadership of the Conservative Party, but must tread extremely carefully in passing on an opinion about Tory policy on Europe. In this sense, process journalism is an intelligible adaptation by the broadcasters to a political environment in which their statements and interpretations are watched and weighed up more closely than in the past; a necessary evil, some will say, to be regretted by the advocates of a quality public sphere, for whom 'rational', policy-oriented discourse is all.

A more whole-heartedly positive reading of process journalism is also possible, however. This sees it not as a surrender to the trivializations and manufactured surfaces of PR, but a means of second-guessing them, and an important sense-making complement to the more policy-oriented coverage possible in the traditionally partisan print media. This view accepts what is self-evident and irreversible – that politics is in contemporary conditions a highly promotional activity, and proceeds from that recognition to suggest that journalists are perfectly entitled to – indeed, democratically obliged to – analyze and dissect it on those terms; that process journalism is a valuable deconstructive technique, which alerts the audience to the constructed nature of the political processes they are witnessing through their media. Through the journalistic dissection of political process the audience are made aware of the potential difference between policy rhetoric and governmental action; between performance style and policy substance; between glossy, rehearsed, PR-honed appearance and harsh political reality.

On 30 September 1996, for example, the BBC's *Panorama* current affairs strand devoted an edition to the public relations activities of all three major parties, with an emphasis on New Labour. The programme appeared at a time when the BBC was coming under increasing pre-election pressure from spinners on all sides, including published newspaper pieces by Alistair Campbell and Peter Mandelson attacking the media's obsession with spin and defending their own role in the political process (see above). It can thus be seen as a pre-emptive strike across the parties' PR bows, warning them not to overdo the shouting, the rude phone calls, and the threats in the election campaign to come. But beyond its role as a statement of defiance from the main public service broadcaster to those ascending politicians who might be tempted to try it on with them, the programme also contained a valuable lesson about political public relations for the audience. If the viewers of *Panorama* did not know before the programme's transmission what 'spin' was, and why it was so threatening to the impartiality of the broadcasters and the quality of British political debate in the late 1990s, they certainly knew afterward, and could go on to make appropriately contextualized judg- ments about Labour, Tory and Liberal Democratic policies.

The confrontational interview

A similar appeal can be made on behalf of another oft-criticized develop- ment in broadcast journalism. The evolution of the broadcast political interview towards the aggressive, confrontational style characterized by the American commentator James Fallows as *hyperadversarialism* (1996) is, like the journalism of process, at least in part a response to the perception of political public relations as a threat to the journalist's professionalism and public role. This has not, however, prevented criti- cism of the form as a commercially driven distortion of the legitimate adversarialism of the journalist in a liberal democracy, and the label- ling of its best-known practitioners as excessively rude, disrespectful, and obfuscatory. In the figures of Jeremy Paxman, John Humphrys and others, argue the critics, we see the inappropriate elevation of the journalist-as-star, and the promotion of his (and often her) confronta- tional abilities over the needs of the citizenry to find out what their politicians think. As columnist Bruce Anderson puts it, 'it [the political interview] just becomes a rough house . . . it's theatre not information'. Even Sir John Birt, when still director general of the BBC, was moved to criticize 'overbearing interviewers who sneer disdainfully at their interviewees',[9] a statement generally assumed to have been directed at the star interviewers in his own organization.

It is true that the development of the interview form since its first appearance in the late nineteenth century has been a product of the commercial needs of the media for distinctive journalistic commodities (Silvester 1993), and that the development of the adversarial broadcast interview in particular has been encouraged by competition between channels to establish *their* interviewers as the most effective and entertain- ing. In this process, led by Robin Day and ITN in the 1950s, adversarial- ism replaced deference as the preferred brand, with most subsequent innovations in interviewing style representing variations on that theme. It is true also that these competitive pressures can lead to excess, in the sense that political interviewees can sometimes be prevented from making their point calmly and clearly. Satirist Rory Bremner's TV shows play on this with his impersonations of Jeremy Paxman, which barely exaggerate the savagery and humiliating wit of the broadcaster's approach to his political guests.

But the confrontational interview is more than a form of political infotainment. On the contrary, it reflects the interviewer's awareness that what he or she is getting from the politician is very likely to be calculated, scripted and rehearsed by the media advisors (who were also satirized during the 1999 run of the Bremner show, as it happens). The political interview, believe its best-known practitioners, *needs* to be confrontational in order to penetrate the presentational rhetoric of the politician, and to expose the shortcomings of that rhetoric to the audience. Paxman, Humphrys, Snow, Mcgregor, or Wark may not always succeed in doing so, but that doesn't mean they shouldn't try. Like process journalism, and without excusing the excesses of presenter-vanity which occasionally shine through – or indeed the inadequacies in the performances of some interviewers, who may be good at being rude but not so effective in eliciting useful information from the politicians – the interview is an important broadcast vehicle for the deconstruction of political public relations. When it works as it should, it adds to rather than detracts from the quality of public debate, and allows broadcasting to play a significant part in the critical scrutinizing of political elites.

Conclusion

The relationship between broadcasting and public relations is frequently uncomfortable and tense, verging at times on the openly hostile. Academics, too, have identified the closeness of their relationship as a factor in the on-going crisis of the public sphere, and its alleged decline into infotainment and promotionalism. I have presented an alternative view in this essay, suggesting instead that the skills associated with public relations have evolved naturally to become a permanent component part of the contemporary media and political environments, as much part of the infrastructure of media production as the cameras, computers, and cables which journalists use.

Secondly, I have argued that those skills are available for use not just by political and other elites, but by what materialist media sociology has tended to call 'subordinate' social groupings, who can use them to intervene, through the access which they may allow to the media, in the construction of the mainstream news agenda and the competition for definition of issues.

Finally, I have argued that the perceived threats to journalistic quality posed by the rise of public relations – and some of those have been discussed – have produced various forms of 'counter-spin' which, though often criticized by scholars and cultural commentators as negative developments, reinforce the public sphere by exposing PR's role within it. Most of this deconstructive output has focused on political PR and spin, but there has also been substantial critical media coverage of celebrity PR and other categories of image management in both broadcast and print media in recent years. Public relations has become a key factor in the production of broadcast media, but also a recurring subject of broadcast journalism, as well as a theme of TV drama and cinema in both Britain and the USA. The cultural tensions and dangers caused by the rise of public relations should not be drifted out of the analytical frame, then, but neither should we underestimate the capacity of the media to respond to and mitigate those dangers, and to absorb PR into the fabric of the modern (or post modern) public sphere, where it can be recognized and understood for what it is.

Notes

1 From her interview with Steve Richards, published in the *New States-man*, 9 August 1996.
2 Cohen, N., 'The death of news', *New Statesman*, 22 May 1998.
3 Campbell, A., 'Auntie's spinners', *The Sunday Times*, 22 September 1996.
4 Haslam, J., 'Briefer bites back', *Independent*, 23 October 1997.
5 These 'ritual' forms of violence, he argues, 'oppose to the political or historical model or order the purest symbolic form of challenge' (1983: 114).
6 Here and elsewhere in this essay, unless otherwise indicated, state-ments by broadcasters were obtained by the author in the course of interviews conducted in 1997–8 as part of the ESRC-funded *Political Communication and Democracy* project (award number L126251022).
7 McWhirter, I., 'Running with the spin', *Independent*, 21 October 1997.
8 The interview from which this quote is extracted was undertaken by the author before Charlie Whelan was forced to resign in December 1998.
9 From the BBC-supplied text of a speech delivered by Birt in Dublin on 5 February 1995.

References

Baudrillard, J. (1983) *In the Shadow of the Silent Majorities . . . or the End of the Social*, Semiotext, New York.
Bloom, M.H. (1973) *Public Relations and Presidential Campaigns*, Thomas Crowell, New York.
Blumler, J. (1989) 'Elections, the media and the modern publicity pro-cess', in Ferguson, M. (ed.), *Public Communication: the New Impera-tives*, London, Sage: 101–13.
Boorstin, D. (1962) *The Image*, Weidenfeld and Nicolson, London.
Chomsky, N. (1988) *Manufacturing Consent*, Pantheon, New York.
Fallows, J. (1996) *Breaking the News*, Pantheon, New York.
Franklin, B. (1994) *Packaging Politics*, Arnold, London.
Glasgow University Media Group (1980) *More Bad News*, Routledge, London.
Habermas, J. (1989) *The Structural Transformation of the Public Sphere*, Polity Press, Cambridge.
Hart, R.P. (1987) *The Sound of Leadership: Presidential Communication in the Modern Age*, University of Chicago Press, Chicago.
King, A. (ed.) (1992) *Postmodern Political Communication*, Praeger, London.
Lasswell, H. & Kaplan, A. (1950) *Power and Society*, Yale University Press, New Haven.
Lippmann, W. (1954) *Public Opinion*, Macmillan, New York.
McNair, B. (1998) *The Sociology of Journalism*, Arnold, London.
McNair, B. (1999a) *News and Journalism in the UK*, 3rd edn, Routledge, London.

McNair, B. (1999b) *An Introduction to Political Communication*, 2nd edn, Routledge, London.

McNair, B. (2000) *Journalism and Democracy*, Routledge, London.

Michie, D. (1998) *The Invisible Persuaders*, Bantam Press, London.

Riddell, P. (1999) 'A shift of power – and influence', *British Journalism Review*, vol. 10, no. 3: 26–33.

Schiller, D. (1987) *Objectivity and the News*, University of Pennsylvania Press, Philadelphia.

Schudson, M. (1995) *Discovering the News*, Basic Books, New York.

Schudson, M. (1978) *The Power of News*, Harvard University Press, Cambridge, Mass.

Silvester, C. (1993) (ed.) *The Penguin Book of Interviews*, Viking, London.

PART IV

Publics, protests and participation

establishment of the new ITV franchises post-1992 has been very much the fulfilment of the commercial wishes of the larger ITV companies.[1]

However, the 1990 Broadcasting Act did limit the stake which national newspapers could have in ITV franchises to 20 percent and restricted takeovers between ITV companies, allowing any of the nine biggest to buy one of the six small companies, and no more. This led to the creation of two separate lobbying efforts within the media industry to change the ownership rules. The first, and most immediately successful, was by Carlton Communications and Granada Television, who lobbied the National Heritage Minister, Peter Brooke, for rule changes so that they could each take over another big franchise without competition from newspaper groups. Carlton at the time had a 20 percent stake in Central TV (which bid a meagre £2,000 to regain its franchise under the ludicrous blind-bid auction required under the 1990 Act), and Granada had a 20 percent stake in London Weekend Television (LWT). In November 1993, Peter Brooke gave them exactly what they wanted, and less than a week after his announcement Central merged with Carlton in a £758 million deal, and in early December Granada started a bitter and ultimately successful struggle for control of LWT with a bid of £600 million.

Very few critical voices were reported in the media on the impact and consequences of such rule changes. Much was made of the industry defence for these mergers, that only a much larger UK-based television industry could be internationally competitive, and prevent takeovers by European media companies. But there was opposition and concern from the ITC, whose chief executive, David Glencross, rejected arguments that a change in ownership rules was needed to help ITV compete in international markets. 'The strength of British television has always lain in the emphasis on producing programmes for a domestic market', he said. 'The export performance of British television has never been commensurate with the prestige, popularity and quality of British programmes. These are programmes made for British viewers and changes in ownership will do nothing to resolve this dilemma.'[2]

The other concerted, and much more protracted, lobbying focus was an unholy alliance of Associated Newspapers, Pearson, Guardian Media Group and the *Telegraph* who established the British Media Industry Group (BMIG) in the summer of 1993 to press for an end to restrictions on cross-media ownership. In *PR Week* (20 August 1993) there was the announcement that BMIG had hired a public affairs consultancy, Market Access International, to build political support for their objectives. The successful culmination of this lobbying was to be the Broadcasting Act of 1996, which lifted controls on newspapers owning ITV and other commercial television stations, and vice versa. One provision was due to the dominance of Rupert Murdoch's News International; it meant that newspaper groups with over 20 percent of newspapers by circulation were excluded from this cross-media rule change. Another media group, Mirror Group Newspapers (MGN), which had a stake of 20 percent in Scottish Television, was also blocked from expansion by this ceiling.

The activities of the BMIG provide a telling example of the use of media power to shape favourable legislation. This was achieved through discreet lobbying, high-profile conferences aimed at opinion formers, and a stream of articles and reports promoting the case for abandoning media ownership restrictions. Sir David English, chief executive of Associated Newspapers, in a speech made in July 1996, just as the Broadcasting Bill was in its final stages, described his role in BMIG. Dismissing the 1990 Broadcasting Act, which was 'obsessed with the so-called dangers of cross-media ownership. . . . phantom fears in somewhat disturbed political minds', he outlined the case for jettisoning such obsolete restrictions in the multimedia age: 'This was the gist of our case to the Governemn and back benchers of all parties. I was always involved in politics but, in three years of lobbying, I got to know and talk to more politicians than I had in all the 23 years I had been a national newspaper editor. Lobbying turned out to be a full-time occupation in addition to my day job. Parties, dinners, receptions, the rubber chicken circuit. But we all have to make sacrifices on behalf of our companies!' (English 1996)

Since the 1996 Act, the pressure to further consolidate the original fifteen ITV franchises has continued apace. The present structure consists of the the 'big three' – Michael Green's Carlton Communications (Carlton, Central and Westcountry); Gerry Robinson's Granada (Granada, LWT and Yorkshire Tyne-Tees), and Lord Hollick's United News and Media (Meridian, Anglia and HTV). The Scottish Media Group, the other large group, owns Scottish Television and Grampian, as well as press interests in Scotland. At different times it has also been linked to takeovers of the Border and Ulster ITV franchises. The Act, however, placed a 15 percent ceiling on a single company's control of TV audience share; Carlton and Granada are just below the ceiling, and United News and Media behind them. However it is clear that there is now an insistent lobby for a single ITV company. This began shortly after the May 1997 landslide victory of the Labour government, in which Gerry Robinson, a long-time Conservative voter, switched with a good deal of publicity, to support New Labour. A profile of him in the *Independent on Sunday*, 15 June 1997, quoted one analyst as saying, 'His footwork was neat in terms of positioning himself next to the government. He has manoeuvred himself into being one of Labour's businessmen, so he'll be privy to what they are thinking.' The profile writer, Dana Rubin, added, 'That insider status will come in handy in the fight for digital broadcasting licence, and in the manoeuvres for legislation that would allow ITV companies to make further bids.' Since then Gerry Robinson has been appointed chairman of the Arts Council by Chris Smith, the Culture Minister whose departmental remit includes broadcasting, the arts, film and sport.

The arguments for a single ITV structure were publicly rehearsed at the 1997 Edinburgh International Television Festival, a couple of months after Gerry Robinson floated his idea for a single ITV structure under one management. Anthony Fry, the head of global media at investment bank BZW, speaking in a session, *ITV plc*, on 24 August, put the case bluntly by asserting that if the government 'pursues competition policy which considers only a narrow domestic agenda, it will not only condemn Channel 3 to a perhaps not-so-slow decline, but it will also ensure that

Britain has no serious commercial companies able to compete globally'. He argued that if ITV was to be turned into a single company it would be worth up to £2.5 billion more than the combined value of the ITV companies, but 'without rapid consolidation of ownership and operation, Channel 3 faces marginalisation domestically, let alone internationally.'

By 1999, an industry consensus had emerged. It is exemplified in the report, *Building a Global Audience*, produced by David Graham and Associates, with the support of the commercial television industry (companies like Carlton, Granada and Pearson), and in articles in magazines like *The Economist* and *Broadcast*.[3] In essence it is a restatement of the arguments used for previous changes in media ownership and regulation which start off from the premise that the UK television industry is too tiny and over-regulated, dominated by a public service broadcasting ethos, and not able to make programmes for global audiences because it is concerned with appealing to domestic audiences. Within the overall structure, the pervasiveness of the BBC is criticized because, whether it is radio, television or the Internet, the state-funded BBC competes unfairly with privately funded competitors. It was *The Economist* which presented the view for a pure, commercial television future most starkly. Arguing that 'the rich global companies have the resources to make the interesting programmes as well as the rubbish', it suggested that 'if the government wants British media companies to be in that league, it needs to make room for them to grow. ITV should be unbound, and the BBC should be forced to shrink. It could reduce its range of output, and concentrate on making classy stuff; it could become a subscription service, which would have the added advantage that it was no longer dependent on taxation; it could be privatised and compete, unfettered. Either way, a creative solution needs to be found.' (*The Economist* 1998: 19).

What is clear is that the media companies are in a strong position, through their access to the key departments (the Department of Trade and Industry, DTI, and the Department for Culture, Media and Sport, DCMS) and their broader political contacts with the government, to dominate the arguments about media ownership and regulation as the detail of another Broadcasting Act is discussed.

Media watchdogs and pressure groups

This brief analysis of recent US and UK experiences suggests broadcasting policy has largely been determined by media groups who have, for commercial reasons, successfully achieved favourable legislation. But this process has not been uncontested. Public interest organizations and pressure groups have also attempted to influence legislation and policy debates. In contrast with media industry lobbyists, these groups have sought to highlight more broadly social, cultural and democratic concerns to argue for diversity in media ownership and in framing principles for media reform. The results of their different efforts have been mixed, but the issues and arguments they raise have greater relevance

in the emerging era of global media. Groups which speak on behalf of citizens' interests, or viewers and listeners, raise basic questions about the role and purpose of broadcasting in society, and for this reason alone are important alternative voices to the heavily promoted campaigns by the commercial media which dress the technological explosion of new channels with the allure and promise of consumer choice.

United States

In the US there is a multiplicity of publications, media literacy organizations, media watchdog and advocacy groups or groups concerned with media policy. The excellent Open Media Pamphlet series includes *The Progressive Guide to Alternative Media and Activism* by Project Censored, published in 1999, which contains comprehensive listings.[4] I want to focus on the work of two organizations, which represent different media policy concerns and work in different ways to promote them.

Fair and Accurate Reporting (FAIR)

FAIR was launched in 1986 and published the first edition of its magazine *Extra!* in June 1987. Jeff Cohen, executive director of FAIR, outlined the aims in that first issue as 'a media watch organisation offering constructive criticism in an effort to correct media imbalance. We advocate for media access on behalf of those constituencies in our society that do not have the wealth to purchase their own TV stations or daily newspapers'. The Reagan administration had been in office for six years, and Cohen described a society where 'the major media were bending distinctly rightward', media takeovers meant 'big media businesses were being absorbed by even bigger ones', and 'well-financed rightwing groups like the misnamed Accuracy in Media (AIM) were harassing journalists who uncovered unpleasant truths'.

FAIR wanted to expose and challenge media bias, and the pattern of media exclusion. It identified, too, the villain – 'not a person or a group, but a historical trend: the increasing concentration of the American media in fewer and fewer corporate hands'. As the organization became established *Extra!*, beginning with the May/June 1989 issue, carried a statement: 'FAIR is the national media watch group offering well-documented criticism in an effort to correct bias and imbalance. FAIR focuses public awareness on the narrow corporate ownership of the press, the media's persistent Cold War assumptions and their insensitivity to women, labour, minorities and other public interest constituencies. FAIR seeks to invigorate the First Amendment by advocating for greater media pluralism and the inclusion of public interest voices in national debates.'

The *Extra!* file contains some memorable and informative issues – it has tracked the relentless trend of media concentration, media coverage during the Gulf War, pressures on the shrunken public service broadcaster, PBS, and a range of issues on media distortions. In addition it produces *Counterspin*, FAIR's radio programme, which is broadcast over more than 100 stations, and has a number of local media activist contacts. It has also actively supported other broad-based coalition movements for media reform like the Media and Democracy Conferences, and the establishment of the Cultural Environmental Movement (CEM).

Media reform became a concern in the mid-1980s in the US because of the increasing pace of media mergers. Ben Bagdikian, in the preface to the fifth edition of *The Media Monopoly*, neatly summed up the sheer scale of changes: 'At the time of the first edition of this book, in 1983, the biggest media merger in history was a \$340-million matter, when the Gannett Company, a newspaper chain, bought Combined Communications Corporation, an owner of billboards, newspapers and broadcast stations. In 1996, when Disney merged with ABC/Cap Cities, it was a \$19-billion deal – 56 times larger. This union produced a conglomerate that is powerful in every major mass medium: newspapers, magazines, books, radio, broadcast television, cable systems and programming, movies, recordings, video cassettes, and, through alliances and joint ventures, growing control of the golden wires into the American home – telephone and cable.' (Bagdikian 1997a: xiii)

FAIR's concerns grew out of these sorts of changes in media ownership. Rachel Coen, communications director of FAIR, argues that its work 'has been a major factor in alerting the public to the fact that ownership of the mainstream media is becoming concentrated in fewer and fewer corporate hands and the media cannot be seen as transparent conduits of information – news reports must be read with an awareness of the constraints placed upon reporters by their parent corporations'. In addition it has helped to 'transform the national debate over media issues, and inspired the establishment of media activism groups all over the country'. She also identifies 'more quantifiable victories' achieved through influencing the media, such as raising awareness about the racist radio talk show host, Bob Grant, and getting Disney to reconsider whether it was serving the public interest. But ultimately she acknowledges that the difficulties the organization faces in promoting its goal of a truly democratic and diverse media are two-fold. One is political, and to do with the passage of damaging laws, like the deregulation of the telecommunications industry, and the other is to do with the idea promoted by conservative and right-wing groups that the media is a bastion of liberal power.

However, FAIR is clear that its central goal will not be realized until 'substantial structural reforms have been enacted to break up the dominant media conglomerates, establish independent public broadcasting and promote strong, non-profit alternative sources of information'.[5]

The Center for Media Education (CME)

In contrast with FAIR, the CME has a narrower, but still very important, set of objectives. The CME was founded in 1991 to carry on the work of Action for Children's Television, and its primary focus remains on children. It is a non-profit organization which has built links at national and state levels with education, library and child advocacy organizations.

One of its first activities in 1992 was to spearhead a 'Campaign for Kid's TV' which drew together 80 child advocacy, education and parents' groups. It was a successful campaign which resulted in the Federal Communication Commission (FCC) decision to require TV stations to transmit a minimum of three hours of educational children's programmes per week. This was considered a major victory, and the FCC decision strengthened rules which TV stations had sought to evade under a 1990 law. TV stations had responded to the law by passing off cartoons such as *The Jetsons* and *The Flintstones* as 'educational' and scheduling programmes within narrow early morning time-slots.

The CME hoped to see 'a flowering of quality educational programmes for children in the commercial marketplace'. However it also made clear that the coalition which had successfully won the stronger rules intended to 'mobilize our constituencies all around the country to monitor the TV programming on their local stations, to challenge broadcasters to make good on their commitment to children, and to notify the FCC of failures to do so'. (CME 1996b)

The CME has also taken important initiatives on digital media and the Internet, both co-founding the Telecommunications Policy Roundtable, which drew together over 200 groups involved in policy debates on the information superhighway, and also through its Action for Children in Cyberspace project. A good example of its work in the latter area was a March 1996 report, *Web of Deception: Threats to Children from Online Marketing*, an exposé of manipulative World Wide Web advertising targetted at children. What the well-researched document revealed was an invasion of children's privacy as marketers devised techniques to collect data and to compile individual profiles of children. Also, it identified online advertising practices where advertising and content are 'seamlessly interwoven in new online *infomercials* for children'. It also cited the way advertising agencies like Saatchi & Saatchi were setting up special units to study children online and to develop sophisticated marketing strategies to target them. (CME 1996a)

A specific piece of legislation was passed by Congress on October 21, 1998, the Children's Online Privacy Protection Act, which authorized the Federal Trade Commission to develop rules for regulating data collection on commercial Web sites targeted at children. The FTC has been in discussion with a range of organizations to agree the rules, and the CME has been active in resisting corporate lobbying for a weak and delayed application of the law, and to ensure effective regulation.

A final example of CME's work is its concern with the consolidation of the cable industry, telephony and Internet services under the AT&T umbrella. With other organizations, CME expressed its worries about the declared policy of 'watchful waiting' by the FCC chairman, William Kennard. The case presented by the CME is that 'the Internet is being fundamentally reconfigured to serve the cable industry's monopoly business model' and cites the development of sophisticated network controls which discriminate against unaffiliated content. 'These network controls allow operators to police and limit particular kinds of network traffic based on policy decisions as to what priority different types of packets should receive,' a letter to William Kennard argues. It concludes by urging that the FCC should conduct a full public enquiry because the FCC policy of 'watchful waiting' will 'allow the future of the Internet to be placed at the service of the cable industry. To allow cable to proceed unfettered simply ignores the industry's well-documented history of thwarting competition, program access, and innovation'. (CME 1999)

United Kingdom

The first and most obvious contrast between media pressure groups in the two countries is that, compared with the range and variety of groups in the US, in the UK there are far fewer and they lack the more extensive staff and resources which characterize groups like FAIR and CME. A partial explanation for this disparity could be the fact that the UK has had an extensive period when the structures and programming concerns have been overlaid with the ethos of public service broadcasting, and audiences have been broadly content with the range and choice of programming.

This, of course, has not meant that some sections of society have not been moved to protest and complain about television programmes. The National Viewers' and Listeners' Association (NVLA) grew out of the Clean Up TV Campaign founded by Mary Whitehouse in Birmingham in 1964, and has been concerned about the portrayals of sex and violence on television. It certainly had the ear of some Conservative politicians and an active presence in different church and women's organizations. The NVLA also claims that its activity was influential in the creation of the Broadcasting Standards Council (BSC) in 1988. The BSC's remit was to research and report on issues of taste and decency, but it was merged, as a result of the 1996 Broadcasting Act, with the Broadcasting Complaints Commission to form the Broadcasting Standards Commission.

One group which has had a strange gestation is the Campaign for Quality Television (CQT), originally set up by staff working at the ITV company, Granada, but drawing on wider industry support, including, amongst others, actor John Cleese and comedian Rowan Atkinson. Its aim was to work to amend what it saw as some of the more damaging proposals of the Conservative Broadcasting Bill which was being discussed in Parliament. It had some success with this, and won the ear of the minister, David Mellor, responsible for shaping the legislation in its final stages. With the passing of the 1990 Broadcasting Act the Campaign was dormant, but in 1996 it was relaunched. This time it had no connection with the ITV companies; indeed its chair was Ray Fitzwalter, former head of current affairs at Granada, and an independent television producer, who was concerned about the diminution in diversity and range of programming on ITV.

It has published three pamphlets on UK broadcasting. *Serious Documentaries on Television* provided the statistics to demonstrate the dwindling commitment of ITV to commission and transmit document-aries which dealt with controversial or topical national or international issues. (CQT 1998a) *The Purposes of Broadcasting* took a broader view of the future direction of broadcasting policy, and the principles which could inform and shape it. It was written partly in response to a joint DTI/DCMS green paper, *Regulating Communications* (1999), and argues that broadcasting 'is the lynchpin, and a vital determinant of, our demo-cratic culture' and especially in the new multi-channel industry, the public service tradition needs to be reasserted (CQT 1998b: 3).

In October 1999, another report, *A Shrinking Iceberg Heading South* (CQT 1999), analyzed trends in current affairs and drama over the past 20 years. The report received extensive publicity for its claim, based on interviews with 30 programme makers and commissioning editors, that many in the television industry are deeply depressed by the growing 'Disneyfication' of TV culture, in which glossy, safe and formulaic ratings winners are squeezing out more challenging and stimulating programmes. The report also compared the output of peaktime current affairs and drama output in 1978, 1988 and 1998 and identified a rapid decline. However, in contrast with the broad support the television industry gave to the work of the CQT around the 1990 Broadcasting Bill, its responses to the three CQT publications have been defensive or dismissive, in part because they provide uncomfortable challenges to, and critiques of, the current policy concerns which shape the direction of UK broadcasting.

Campaign for Press and Broadcasting Freedom (CPBF)

The election of a Labour government in May 1997 might have seemed an opportune time for an organization like the CPBF to see some of the aims which it had promoted since its establishment in 1979 translated into real policies. After all, throughout the 1980s and 1990s it had worked closely with Labour shadow ministers on media policy issues, included a number of Labour MPs amongst its members and supporters, and indeed the document *Arts and Media: Our Cultural Frame*, published in September 1991, in the section 'Freeing the Media', had a clear commit-ment 'to tackle the issue of cross-media ownership. We are particularly concerned about the cross ownership of newpapers and television and will refer this issue to our strengthened Monopolies and Mergers Com-mission'.[6] In fact, the policies promulgated by Labour changed so rapidly after the 1992 election defeat that the CPBF has found itself very much in a critical and adversarial relationship with many of Labour's policy proposals since then.

The CPBF's key policy concerns for broadcasting emerged and de-veloped from 1982 onwards when the name changed from the Campaign for Press Freedom. The organization worked energetically in the late 1980s and early 1990s to defend public service broadcasting against the twin thrusts of deregulation of the commercial television sector, and the threatened commercialization of the BBC. In mid-1988 the CPBF published *Switching Channels: The Debate over the Future of Broadcasting* by Tom O'Malley which analyzed the new forces which wanted to restructure broadcasting in the UK. The people 'with the money and influence necessary to shape public and political opinion would rather see broadcasting run as a privately owned and under-regulated industry like the national press', he argued. In opposition to the free market approach, the CPBF wanted 'more diversity and democracy within a public service framework. We have the advantage of wanting to extend the principles of a system that works. The government and the lobbyists want to make changes which we know will destroy the best elements of the current system and put worse in its place.' (O'Malley 1988: 2, 50)

The CPBF's work involved joint activity with the media unions, BETA, ACTT and NUJ and close liaison with Labour MPs as the Bill was debated in Parliament. From the 1988 Broadcasting White Paper, *Broadcasting in the 90s: Competition, Choice and Quality*, through the passage of the Bill to the 1990 Act, apart from the Parliamentary activity, there was also a focus on public meetings and a concerted attempt to mobilize public opinion against the proposed changes.

After the 1992 general election, the main focus of the CPBF's broadcasting work shifted to researching and analyzing the lobbying activities by the BMIG for an end to restrictions on cross-media ownership, and to challenge the assumptions behind the largely technology-driven arguments that convergence, the development of the information superhighway, and the 'multi-media revolution' meant an end to such outdated concerns as regulation, media ownership restrictions and public service obligations on broadcasting. The CPBF was active on a number of fronts, including the joint publication of *Britain's Media: How They Are Related* with a media ownership map in 1994; organizing a very successful conference, *Media Versus the People* in March 1995, followed by the publication of a media manifesto which was launched at another successful conference, *Media and Democracy: The Real Share Issue* in May 1996. The media manifesto, *21st Century Media: Shaping the Democratic Vision*, was very much an intervention in a rapidly changing political landscape.

Labour changed direction sharply on media policy after Tony Blair became the Labour leader. The most public and symbolic moment was, of course, the trip by Tony Blair to Hayman Island to speak at a News Corporation management conference in July 1995, but also during the passage of the 1996 Broadcasting Bill, it was National Heritage Minister Virginia Bottomley who was put in the strange position of defending limits on cross media ownership against her Labour counterpart, Jack Cunningham. Another member of the Labour national heritage team, Lewis Moonie, asserted, 'Cross-media ownership is a good thing. The whole point is to ensure the creation of bigger companies that can compete abroad.' (*Financial Times*, 17 April 1996).

Since the 1997 general election, the CPBF has responded to a range of government documents on broadcasting issues from the Department for Culture, Media and Sport (*Regulating Communications: Approaching Communications in the Information Age* CM 4022, July 1988; *Building a Global Audience*, April 1999; *The Future Funding of the BBC*, July 1999) but it has also raised its disquiet at the way policy-making is often driven by small groups hastily investigating aspects of media policy. The organization has called for a public inquiry, arguing that since 1979 'changes in the media industries have occurred with only the minimal debate and public scrutiny' whereas 'mass communication policy should be formed in the context of a sustained, periodic process of public inquiry and consultation' (*Free Press*, November/December 1998: 8).

Conclusion

Groups arguing for media reform in the US and the UK face a simple dilemma. In the era of cross-media ownership and global media conglomerates it is unlikely that the policies media reformers espouse will get more than perfunctory attention in the mainstream media. After all, the dominant commercial and corporate concerns in the media industry sit uneasily with a different, and conflicting, set of concerns about the democratic and cultural role of the media. It is not even that there is a state of peaceful coexistence between the two positions, but rather a relentless war of attrition. For example, in the USA, the tiny beachhead of PSB has been under assault since the Nixon administration sought to veto all federal funding for public television in 1972, and whilst it survives, recent critiques of the organization suggest it is 'more market-savvy and commercially oriented than ever before' and identify 'the melding of commercial and public service priorities . . . a logical result of the increasing, now dominant use of public broadcasting as a marketing and promotional outlet' (Ledbetter 1997: 15; *Extra!*, September/October 1999: 11).

And in the UK, the adoption by the Labour government of market orientated policies before and after the May 1997 general election has meant that government documents emphasize the broadcasting audience as 'consumers' and the need for future policy to 'foster competitive markets', to build on its 'competitive strengths' in the broadcasting, telecommunications and information technology industries 'to remain a world leader in the provision of communication services' (DTI/DCMS 1999: 4).

Within these changed priorities about the role and purpose of broadcasting, it becomes more difficult for media reform and pressure groups to insist on the importance of a public service dimension in broadcasting, or to raise issues about the threats to diversity and plurality from growing cross-media concentration of ownership. But it is clear that in spite of the difficulties and differing conditions in the USA and the UK the groups discussed (and others which space precluded) continue to work and inject alternative perspectives into debates on the formulation of media policy. It is also the case that changes in the broadcast media, and the development of new media like the Internet, will continue to generate new policy concerns and stimulate activity. We can be sure that in the future, with all the disparities in terms of wealth and power between the lobbying efforts by media companies and those of media advocacy and pressure groups, there is fertile ground to continue to nurture the long-standing concerns about media democracy, pluralism, access and accountability which have sustained the work of these groups in the past.

Notes

1 Two useful works on this period of change in UK broadcasting are O'Malley (1994) and Goodwin (1998). A much more detailed account with a specific focus on ITV and the IBA is in Bonner (1998).
2 Georgina Henry (1993) 'Uncertainty at ITV rule changes,' *Guardian*, 4 December.
3 *Building a Global Audience: British Television in Overseas Markets*, David Grahame and Associates. Published by the Broadcasting Policy Division of the Department for Media, Culture and Sport, April 1999. For examples of the case for radical restructuring of UK television see Barry Cox, *Broadcast*, p.13, 25 June 1999; Mathew Horsman, 'Off message', *Broadcast* p.15, 30 July 1999; 'Britain's Media Giants', *The Economist*, 12 December 1998.
4 The Open Media Pamphlet series is published by Seven Stories Press, which also publishes the excellent annual *Project Censored: The News That Didn't Make The News*. This publicizes, along with a mass of other material, the top 25 stories which a panel of judges consider to be important news stories marginalized by the mainstream media. The project director, Peter Phillips, argues in the Spring 1999 issue of *Censored Alert!*, the newsletter of Project Censored, 'The U.S. media has lost its diversity and its ability to present different points of view. Instead there is a homogeneity of news and a regurgitation of the same news stories on every channel and headline. Our corporate media outlets in the country spent hundreds of hours and yards of newsprint to cover Bill Clinton's sexual escapades and ignored many important news stories in the process. This amounts to structural censorship of the news.'
5 Email correspondence with Rachel Coen. FAIR's website is: http://www.fair.org. The Center for Media Education's website is: http://www.cme.org/cme
6 The quote is from p.50, and other commitments include the defence of public service broadcasting, and ministerial intervention 'to ensure that franchise commitments on the quality and range of programmes are delivered'. The 1992 Labour election manifesto also pledged 'an urgent enquiry by the MMC into the concentration of media ownership'.

References

Bagdikian, B. (1997a) The Media Monopoly, 5th edn, Beacon Press, Boston.

Bagdikian, B. (1997b) 'Comment', in Hazen, D. & Winokur, J. (eds), We the Media: A Citizens' Guide to Fighting for Media Democracy, The New Press, New York.

Blanchard, S. (1982) 'Where do new channels come from?', in Blanchard, S. & Morley, D. (eds), What's This Channel Four?, Comedia, London.

Bonner, P. (1998) Independent Televison in Britain, Vol 5, Macmillan, London.

Campaign for Press and Broadcasting Freedom (1996) 21st Century Media: Shaping the Democratic Vision, CPBF, London.

Campaign for Quality Television (1998a) The Purposes of Broadcasting.

Campaign for Quality Television (1998b) Serious Documentaries on Television.

Campaign for Quality Television (1999) A Shrinking Iceberg Travelling South: Changing Trends in British Television.

CME (1996a) Web of Deception: Threats to Children from Online Marketing.

CME (1996b) Press Statement, 'Stronger children's television rules at last!'

CME (1999) Letter to F.C.C. Chairman, William Kennard.

Department for Culture, Media and Sport (1999) The Future Funding of the BBC, DCMS, London.

Department for Culture, Media and Sport/DTI (1998) Regulating Communications: Approaching Convergence in the Information Age, Cmnd 4022, HMSO, London.

The Economist (1998) 'Britain's media giants' (12 December).

The Economist (1999) 'The battle for the last mile' (1 May).

English, D. (1996) 'Cross-media ownership: how can radio develop?' Speech to Radio Festival (17 July).

Extra! (1999) William Hoynes, 'The cost of survival' (September/October), FAIR, New York.

Financial Times (1996) James Harding, 'Bottomley attacks Labour's media move' (17 April).

Free Press (1998) 'Open Letter to the Secretary of State, Media, Culture and Sport' (November–December), Campaign for Press and Broadcasting Freedom, London.

Goodwin, P. (1998) Television Under the Tories: Broadcasting Policy 1979–1997, BFI, London.

Home Office (1996) Broadcasting in the 90s: Competition, Choice and Quality, Cmnd 517, HMSO, London.

Ledbetter, J. (1997) Made Possible by . . . The Death of Public Broadcasting in the United States, Verso, New York.

Lowenthal, M. (1997) 'Censoring the telecoms debate', in Censored 97, Seven Stories Press, New York.

McChesney, R.W. (1993) Telecommunications, Mass Media, & Democracy: The Battle for the Control of U.S. Broadcasting, 1928–1935, Oxford University Press, New York.

McChesney, R.W. (1998) 'This communication revolution is brought to you by U.S. media at the dawn of the 21st century', in *Censored 98*, Seven Stories Press, New York.

The Nation (1998) Special issue: 'Who Controls TV?' (8 June).

O'Malley (1988) *Switching Channels: The Debate Over the Future of Broadcasting*, CPBF, London.

O'Malley, T. (1994) *Closedown? The BBC and Government Broadcasting Policy, 1979–1992*, Pluto Press, London.

PR Week (1993) 'Media groups hire lobbyists' (August 20).

Sendall, B. (1982) *Independent Television in Britain, Vol 1, Origin and Foundation, 1946–62*, Macmillan, London.

Williams, G. (1994) *Britain's Media: How They Are Related*, CPBF, London.

Wilson, H.H. (1961) *Pressure Group: The Campaign for Commercial Television*, Secker and Warburg, London.

CHAPTER 13

What have you done for us lately? Public service broadcasting and its audiences

Anne Dunn

Abstract: The paper poses the following questions, using radio news as its focus:

1. How is the Australian Broadcasting Corporation(ABC) responding to the historical dilemma of public service broadcasting – that it should be popular in its appeal, yet elitist in its content and values – since postmodernist and cultural studies' approaches to media challenge the distinctions between 'high' and 'low' culture?

2. How are public broadcasters to conceive of and address their audiences in view of the fact that digital technology offers a multiplicity of services whose convergence blurs the boundaries between one 'broadcast medium' and another? The paper suggests that answers to these questions can be found by looking at the historical development of the ABC's radio networks and at the use of radio content on its World Wide Web site. Like the BBC, the ABC began by creating separate populist local networks and 'highbrow' national networks. It was assumed that audiences would assign themselves to one or other end of the cultural spectrum thus set up for them. While these distinct networks continue to exist, the recently established 24-hour NewsRadio network and the ABC's World Wide Web site make much less obvious assumptions about the audience's cultural preferences and competencies. The paper concludes that the use of radio content on the ABC's World Wide Web site is in turn influencing radio. The traditional one-to-many transmission model of radio is changing, to one which is more interactive, 'multimedia' and creative of 'virtual' communities. The paper presents a model which contrasts the traditional form of radio news with an emergent form of radio news (as it appears in NewsRadio and the WWW), and predicts the appearance of a new pattern for public sector broadcasting.

In June 1999, the Australian federal Department of Communication, Information Technology and the Arts organized a two day forum in Canberra about digital broadcasting. Some time on the second day, a question from the floor drew our attention to the emphasis of the forum on technological and regulatory issues and the conspicuous neglect of public interest issues. The speaker was arguing that if 'the market' is the *only* arbiter, the public broadcasters – in Australia, the Australian Broadcasting Corporation and the much smaller Special Broadcasting Service – will not survive. A session called 'Convergence and Digital Television' had no representative from the ABC on its panel; yet the ABC's plans for digital services in television were at that time conspicuously different from those presented at this session by the commercial broadcasters. The key difference of course is that the audience for the commercial broadcasters is and must be made up of consumers, while the audience for the ABC is and is required to be conceived of as Australians – citizens. And it's for this reason that this chapter is intended to buck the trend of much of what has recently been published about the future for public broadcasting (Steemers 1998) and be optimistic about the opportunities presented by the always complex interplay between social and technological change we're a part of at the moment. But first – a bit of history.

There is a dilemma at the heart of the Australian Broadcasting Corporation and its relationship with its audience, a dilemma which is known to be shared to some degree with all public service broadcasting. On the one hand, the ethos of publicly funded broadcasting is not only that its services should be universally available but also that its content should be sufficiently diverse and broad to provide something for all interests and tastes. On the other hand, traditionally there is what Michael Tracey has called a 'paternalistic or patrician' relationship with the audience (Tracey 1998: 49), often expressed in the extent to which public service broadcasters are obliged to maintain and foster 'quality' programming, and national and cultural identity. In other words, there is an implied 'custodian' within the concept of public broadcasting: 'The language is of standards, quality, excellence, range. The logic is of social enrichment, that in however indefinable a manner this society is *better* for having programmes produced from within the framework of those social arrangements termed public service broadcasting, compared to those programmes produced within an environment in which commerce or politics prevail.' (Tracey 1998: 25).

For the ABC, the dilemma is to be found in the heart of the Act of Parliament which governs it, Sections 6(1) and 6(2), called the Charter of the Corporation. The Charter enjoins the ABC 'to provide . . . innovative and comprehensive broadcasting services of a high standard . . . and . . . programmes that contribute to a sense of national identity and . . . reflect the cultural diversity of, the Australian community . . .' Its functions also include 'to transmit . . . programmes of news, current affairs, entertainment and cultural enrichment that will [among other things] . . . encourage and promote the musical, dramatic and other performing arts in Australia' (ABC 1998).

Thus, the ABC was simultaneously asked to be the guardian of 'high culture' in broadcasting in Australia and to be reflective of a diverse nation, offering something for everyone. This presented the ABC with an apparently unresolvable contradiction that it should be popular in its appeal, accessible to all, yet elitist in its content and values. This tension has continued to dog the ABC since its creation.

Initially the ABC responded much as the BBC had before it, by developing separate radio networks, from populist local stations to 'highbrow' national networks. It was assumed that audiences would assign themselves to the cultural spectrum thus set up for them, according to their tastes and needs. The ABC Radio 1 network played a range of popular music styles and talk programmes in a flow format, with regular, mainly short news bulletins. The Radio 2 network carried predominantly classical music, including concert broadcasts, radio plays, serious discussion programmes, schools and other educational material, including the children's programmes, using a 'block' format rather than the 'flow' which was quickly the more characteristic radio form, exclusively so in commercial radio. Radio 2 also ran more, longer news bulletins and the first of the daily national current affairs programmes, *'PM'*. Radio 3 was the non-metropolitan network, often the only radio available to isolated Australians in rural areas, and it broadcast a hybrid of Radio 1 and Radio 2 programmes, with specialist rural programmes such as *The Country Hour*, and regional news bulletins.

This network structure was last consolidated in the mid-1980s. What's interesting about the restructure that took place then was that it consciously isolated the 'cultural custodianship' role of the ABC into what had been Radio 2 and which now is called Radio National. Radio 1 became Metro Radio, and in the language of the report which described the proposed restructure in most detail, was actively to compete for audiences with its commercial talk radio equivalents in each of Australia's major population centres – nine in all. This meant that it was also identified as the home of local news and – anomalously – the national current affairs programmes. Metro stations were badged as 'information radio'. Regional radio – Radio 3 – became more locally focused as satellite technology and the opening of new transmitters enabled more and more Australians to receive Radio National and the stereo music and performance network, ABC Classic FM. The effect of this was to remove from Radio 3 those 'high culture' programmes its listeners had been hearing as part of the old hybrid programming.

By the end of the 1970s, a radio network specifically aimed at young Australians, Triple J, had begun, initially in Sydney, then networked around the country and in the last decade it has started up in about 20 regional centres. Triple J has been a great success for the ABC, at times presenting a serious threat to commercial youth music stations, especially in smaller markets. One of the most significant elements in Triple J's initial success was that it never identified itself on air or in its publicity as an ABC station. The ABC was too much identified with the establishment, and with older listeners, to have attracted young listeners in the 1970s in the way 2-double-jay – its original call sign – was able to.

One of the most controversial features of the original 2-double-jay – at least, inside the ABC – was its news service. Traditionally, the values associated with 'good' journalism have accorded well with those of public sector broadcasting: it is assumed that accurate, independent and objectively presented news and information are essential. The result in both the ABC and the BBC has been news services of which both broadcasters are rightly proud. However, the way this news ethos has been translated into radio practice has historically reinforced the 'paternalistic or patrician' relationship of the ABC with its audience.

Major bulletins of ABC Radio news – the flagship breakfast bulletins on Metro Radio and Radio National, for example – are introduced by a pompous musical theme called 'the Majestic Fanfare', which is instantly recognizable to almost every Australian. This sets the scene for the delivery of news 'from on high' as one analysis has put it (Van Leeuwin 1989); an effect reinforced by the usually authoritative and portentous delivery of the newsreader, usually also in what is called 'cultivated Australian' speech – that is, the accents of the educated middle class. Triple J changed all that. Its young journalists, working outside the newsroom and inside the radio station itself, wrote and read their bulletins, in the accents of young urban Australia and using its vocabulary – often provocatively so, in the early 1970s, referring to 'bucks' not dollars, and in one memorable example, to the police as 'pigs' in an item about a street march. Even today, although its news service has been corralled back into the newsroom, it uses an electronically generated news theme which is a satirical distortion of 'the Majestic Fanfare'. Despite the care with which it created an identity separate from that of the ABC, Triple J has in practice embraced the public broadcasting mission to educate its audience as citizens (Dunn 1997), not only through news bulletins but also through discussion, talk-back and documentary material.

Apart from Triple J, the other major factor which changed radio news delivery on the ABC was technology. By the beginning of the 1990s the news department was using two computer-based digital technologies: the networked system for handling news text, Basys, and an ABC-developed system called D-Cart, which enabled multiple users to record, edit and replay the same piece of audio material. D-Cart in particular not only revolutionized work practices in ABC Radio newsrooms around the country (see Dunn 1993) but also enabled the development of a new capital city based network, NewsRadio.

D-Cart and Basys together enabled the tailoring of news bulletins for the different networks for the first time. My research shows that the major breakfast bulletins on Metro Radio and Radio National in the early 1990s differed in story order, writing style and overall sound in ways that reflected news producers' beliefs about the audiences. The audience for Radio National was assumed to be interested in news, especially national and international stories. The Metro Radio audience was pictured as – and I quote one of the ABC Radio news producers I interviewed – 'harder to hold for news', more interested in parochial stories, as having a much shorter attention span and needing to be as much entertained by the sound of the news as informed by it. So, for example, when the story was felt to warrant it, the Metro breakfast bulletin would begin with some dramatic grab of audio immediately after the news theme, upon which the newsreader would then urgently come in, delivering the rest of the headlines. By contrast, the Radio National breakfast bulletin occasionally didn't have headlines at all;

an omission which never occurred on Metro Radio in six months of bulletins collected. Often the story order was markedly different in the two bulletins, with Radio National giving higher priority not only to international news but also to social issues news; stories about aboriginal people, for example. In other words, some subtle but discernible assumptions were being made about the audiences' cultural preferences and competencies. These differences notwithstanding, the central assumption – that radio news is something produced on behalf of the audience but not directly involving it – remained the same for both networks. By and large, news on the ABC's radio networks continues to be as Michael Schudson described it: 'a more important forum for communication among elites . . . than with the general population' (Schudson 1996: 156).

The other impact of D-Cart and Basys was that they enabled, as I said, the development of a new network, NewsRadio. NewsRadio may have been enabled by the new digital audio technology but it was originally conceived as a solution to the problem of Parliamentary broadcasts. Under its Act, the ABC is obliged to broadcast the proceedings of the Federal Parliament when it is sitting. These had originally been heard on Radio 1, but after the establishment of Metro Radio they were shifted to Radio National. Apart from their limited audience appeal, parliamentary proceedings had to be broadcast live, which across Australia's different time zones meant they could interrupt normal programming in Perth, for example, from as early as 5am, to as late as 11pm in the eastern States. As the general manager of the time put it to me, it was a 'programming nightmare'. In 1993, the ABC persuaded the Parliament to let the corporation move parliamentary broadcasts onto a network of eight standby transmitters, which were otherwise unused for most of the year, and which covered all Australia's major population centres. In those periods of the year that Parliament is not sitting, the network becomes NewsRadio, a 24-hour service of rolling news, current affairs, sport and information which has grown steadily in terms of audience size since its beginning.

The new technology made NewsRadio cost-effective; the ABC could not have contemplated it otherwise (and looked with envious disbelief at the budget given to BBC Radio 5). The digital audio and networked text-based news systems allow a small number of journalists to 'quarry' the enormous amount of information that pours in from the ABC's large number of news and current affairs journalists both around Australia and in the overseas bureaux, as well as from the various news agencies to which the ABC subscribes.

Less than five years after NewsRadio began, the ABC established ABC Online, a large and still-growing World Wide Web site. Increasingly, material produced for broadcast is linked using automated electronic publishing systems to the online service. And the knowledge that their material will be used on the Internet is in turn affecting radio producers; not so much in content as in presentation and in their relationship with their audiences. In particular, a new medium which is established with younger people, is exposing them to content which for decades has been housed in the network assigned the 'high' end of the cultural spectrum and with an audience aged predominantly in their fifties: Radio National. And this new audience is not prepared to accept anything 'from on high' but takes for granted its right to participate.

NewsRadio and the ABC website are what I would describe as far more democratic and inclusive in their definition and presentation of 'news'. NewsRadio is presented in a bright flow format of rolling news updates, which encompass international, national and regional or state-based stories. As a result, as a listener you often hear far more about what is going on in other parts of Australia than the bit you happen to live in than if you listened only to Radio National or your local Metro Radio service. The news updates flow smoothly into current affairs and other forms of reportage, without such a decisive partitioning of 'news' from 'not news' programming. Now this is quite significant change in the definition of radio news. About eight years ago, working as a net-work manager, I attempted to have the breakfast news bulletins begin without the ubiquitous 'Majestic Fanfare', but with a simple verbal handover – as of course happens on Radio 4's *Today* programme. The response of news editors and senior producers made it quite clear that it was of great importance to them that The News be audibly distin-guished from the non-news sound around it (Dunn 1998). Now obvi-ously NewsRadio is a station whose title announces it is a news station. But what it broadcasts goes well beyond the narrow definition of news – introduced with a fanfare and confined within a bulletin of fixed duration – that has characterized ABC Radio for over 50 years.

ABC News Online is one part of what is a very large and many-roomed website. The ABC website is one of the 3 most-visited sites in Australia, where a majority of adults has access to the web, if you include access at work. The content of the online news comes predom-inantly from radio, and if you have the right software, it is possible to play audio from the stories. Incidentally, although video is available, the ABC made a deliberate decision to enable people with the least sophisticated levels of access to be able to call up text alone and de-signed its site accordingly. It is also possible to click on the hyperlinks within the text and go to further reference material which may not only give you some insight into the source of the story (a published scientific report, for example) but also enable you to explore that story further, through links to other related sites or to the news archive.

Online news has the potential to make the audience part of the news experience and the ABC is beginning to exploit this potential in a number of ways. For example, every week – because I signed up for it – I receive by email a summary in advance of the content and key guests on a radio programme called *The Media Report* and this summary will also point me to any other Radio National programmes which feature items about the media that week. Now this in itself is not new – such pull and push techniques have been around for a while. But it represents a very big change for traditional concepts of the relationship between journalists and the audience, and a very big change in the relationship between the national public broadcaster and its audience. I am a potential participant in *The Media Report* rather than a passive recipient of its content; and moreover feel I am part of a community of like-minded listeners.

Nearly 20 years ago, Herbert Gans (1979) wrote about journalists' apparent lack of interest in their audiences. In his study of BBC news, Philip Schlesinger (1978) observed the same phenomenon. Both he and Gans concluded that professional journalists felt it was necessary and important to be at a distance from the receivers of the news, in order to retain those key values of independence and objectivity. Now journalists are encountering their audiences in ways they've seldom experienced – especially radio news journalists. Moreover, they are having to invite their audience, non-journalists, to participate in news generation and creation.

In July this year, the first of the ABC's 'community publishing sites' was launched in the state of Victoria, in a regional area in the south east, called Gippsland. This is a project initiated by the ABC in the lead up to the centenary of Federation in 2001. It's designed to encourage 'individuals, families and communities across Australia to publish their own stories, images and information on the Internet' – I quote from the ABC staff magazine, *Wavelength* (ABC July 1999: 1). This project was launched by the local radio programme manager. Its producer is a senior radio journalist. Each site will offer visitors access to a self-publishing tool for information about their own region. So people will be making their own news.

Another example is the annual competition to give a voice to rural youth, called *Heywire*. People aged 16–22 who live in regional Australia are invited to contribute a 3-minute radio documentary about their lives. The winning entries from each of 40 regional locations are produced for broadcast by ABC staff. The winners also attend a special forum in Canberra on goal-setting, communication, leadership and teamwork skills. An open forum on regional life is also conducted online, through the *Heywire* website. Each year's forum and the winning entries are archived on the site.

When NewsRadio began, journalists and other radio programme makers had to take account of the fact that their material would be quarried and re-used by the new service. Many of them preferred to edit their material in two forms, one specifically for NewsRadio, rather than entrust the long form to the hasty 'chopping' of NewsRadio's handful of journalists. Now it is the website which is audibly influencing radio. Not only in the reiteration of internet addresses and the inclusion of material provided by listeners, but also in a more open acknowledgment of the sources of information, of what has been excluded (and how you can find that) as well as of what has been included. For example, the Australian broadcasting regulator – the Australian Broadcasting Authority – has recently been investigating the case of two high-profile commercial radio talkback hosts being paid large sums of money by several organizations to make favourable editorial comment about them. The so-called 'cash for comment' story has of course been exhaustively covered by all the media in Australia, particularly in Sydney where the two men in question work. *The Media*

Report – the programme I mentioned before – has devoted a couple of programmes to the hearings. If you take up the invitation of the presenter to go to the programme's website – or indeed if you listen to it through the website – you'll find well over a dozen hyperlinks to other sources of information and comment, including to the ABA hearings themselves.

Conclusion

The nature of journalism has been in transition for some years. Radio journalism goes well beyond the provision of news bulletins. The traditional form of radio news – announced as distinct from other sound and presented within a narrow range of traditional formats – lingers on, but a new form is emerging. The emergent form of radio news is interactive, customizable, hypertextualized and multimedia. These characteristics present challenges to traditional journalistic values – jealously preserved inside the national public broadcasters – of accuracy, independence and objectivity – as well as to the practices which together have defined professionalism in news journalism. Equally, these characteristics represent a more democratic and inclusive relationship between the national public broadcaster and its audience.

At a time when the increasing privatization of public life and fragmentation of audiences has called the relevance of public broadcasters into question, but at the same time there is a growing unease with 'leaving the market to decide', the digital world including the Internet offers an opportunity. There is much more that could be said, but here I've tried to indicate the new relationship that is emerging between the ABC and its audiences and argue that it is of a kind which could see a revival in commitment to the role of public broadcasting as one of service to the public, in which public interest is paramount.

References

ABC (1998) *Australian Broadcasting Corporation Annual Report 1997–98*, ABC, Sydney, NSW.

ABC (1999) *Wavelength*, Staff Magazine (July), ABC, Sydney, NSW.

Dunn, A. (1993) 'Towards the tapeless newsroom: The development of D-Cart'. *Media Information Australia*, 67: 77–82.

Dunn, A. (1998) 'The music of the news', in Breen, M. (ed.), *Journalism Theory & Practice*, Macleay Press, Sydney, NSW.

Dunn, A. (1997) 'The role of ABC radio in the creation of citizenship models'. *Culture and Policy*, 8(2): 91–103.

Gans, H. (1979) *Deciding What's News*, Vintage Books, New York.

Schlesinger, P. (1978) *Putting 'Reality' Together: BBC News*, Constable, London.

Schudson, M. (1996) 'The sociology of news production revisited', in *Mass Media and Society*, 2nd edn, Curran, J. & Gurevitch, M. (eds), Arnold, Sydney, NSW.

Steemers, J. (1998) 'On the threshold of the "digital age": prospects for public service broadcasting', in Steemers, J. (ed.), *Changing Channels: The Prospects for Television in a Digital World*, University of Luton Press, Luton.

Tracey, M. (1998) *The Decline and Fall of Public Service Broadcasting*, Oxford University Press, Oxford.

Van Leeuwin, T. (1989) 'Changed times, changed tunes: music and the ideology of the news', in Tulloch, J. & Turner, G. (eds), *Australian television: Programs, pleasures and politics*, Allen and Unwin, Sydney, NSW.

CHAPTER 14

Alternative radio and television in South Dakota: A place study of public service electronic media in the US

Warren Bareiss

Noncommercial radio and television[1]

Introduction: scope and context

The invitation to write this chapter was straightforward. I was asked to contribute an essay on 'subscription broadcasting' in the US; that is, radio and television services which depend on audiences' financial contributions to survive. In the US, these stations are characterized as 'public radio/television' and 'community radio.' Many scholars have already written extensively on these subjects, so I decided to both broaden and narrow my focus in ways that have not typically been addressed in communication texts. By broadening, my intention was to address other forms of electronic, mass media that are similar to public and community broadcasting in their noncommercial ethos – for example, college radio – but which are usually passed over in texts and journals. In narrowing my scope, I decided to examine media in a single state so that I could delve into more detail than would be possible in a national survey. For convenience, I chose the rural, Midwestern state of South Dakota where I teach and reside (Figure 14.1).

That's where my troubles began. Initially, I had no idea that a sparsely populated farming state would have such a plethora of non-commercial media venues available to its residents. Just when I thought I had covered everything, I would find out about yet another form of media that I had not considered. More reading, phone calls, and writing followed in a series of chapter revisions. As such, this chapter represents something of a personal journey into the fringes of mass media.

'Fringes' is an important concept here, because, by far, the dominant form of radio and television in the US is based on the free-market approach – private ownership of stations and services supported by commercial sponsorship, with minimal forms of government control. A major justification for this system is that marketplace competition – in theory – will produce programming which reflects the desire of most audience members. Following this line of thought, viewers 'vote' for programs via ratings. Such an approach seems highly democratic, but critics often charge that the result is far from egalitarian. According to these critics, the primary motive of media industries is financial profit, and media content is driven by the need to, in effect, 'sell' consumers to sponsors via programming (Schiller 1989).

For decades, however, a different model of radio and television has operated along the borders of mainstream media. In this model – which, for lack of a better term, I will call 'the alternative model' – financial gain is not a major goal beyond costs involved in structural maintenance and day-to-day operations. Rather, the primary object is a vaguely defined notion of communal well-being which has been operationalized in a number of ways. For instance, communal well-being might involve broadcasting from the perspective of labor rather than management (Godfried 1997), promoting political perspectives which have few venues in mainstream broadcasting (Eliasoph 1988), and using mass media to build coalitions among women and minorities (Bredin 1991; Butalia 1993).

While these examples imply somewhat divergent agendas, they are all united by the basic assumption that social equity at the local, national, regional, and global levels requires that mass media be accessible to marginalized groups rather than just to telecommunication corporations and their sponsors. As such, these alternatives to the dominant model tend to be noncommercial, at least in principle, so that the free-flow of ideas are shielded from marketplace dictates.[2] Also, they tend to promote more 'front-end' access wherein the public is invited to share in program production and the overall decision-making process. The alternative model is thus informed – in widely varying degrees – by an appreciation for the nonprofessional touch, a recognition that professional expertise need not act as a barrier to public discourse.

Although they operate along the outskirts of mainstream media, with only a tiny fraction of the possible audience tuning in, alternative forms of radio and television abound in the US. I have already mentioned public broadcasting, community radio, and college radio. Other services include local cable-access television, various national cable channels, and Internet sites, the latter multiplying exponentially in ways that directly and self-consciously undermine the dominant corporate structures of mass media in the US.

Each of the following sections in this chapter examines one or more forms of alternative media as they are accessible to people in South Dakota. While it might seem strange to choose a single state for analysis – a low-populated state at that (700,000 residents) – this chapter provides a specific, grounded perspective permitting me to venture into individual media organizations while also suggesting the range of variations available among alternative media in other states. As such, connections will continually be made between the specifics of alternative media in South Dakota and trends within the US alternative media scene more generally.

Figure 14.1: South Dakota (shaded area)

South Dakota Public Broadcasting (SDPB)

Organizational structure

The best-known form of noncommercial broadcasting within South Dakota – and the US in general – is public broadcasting. Public television and radio in the US officially began when Congress passed the Public Broadcasting Act of 1967, although the roots of public broadcasting reach back much further to various forms of experimental radio and television (Engelman 1996). Loosely based on the BBC model, public broadcasting was founded on the principle that commercial broadcasting was ideologically and economically prevented from fully serving the public's interest with regard to educational and local programming as well as experimental forms of production.

The Public Broadcasting Act established the Corporation for Public Broadcasting (CPB) which disburses federally allocated funds to public stations and networks. The CPB, in turn, established the Public Broadcasting Service (PBS) to distribute programming among a loosely organized network of television stations and National Public Radio (NPR) to produce and distribute radio programs to its affiliates. Nationally, there are 348 PBS affiliates and almost 600 NPR affiliates.

Public broadcasting licensees can be divided into three categories. University licences are held by university regents, community licences are held by local governing boards, and state licences are held by state governments. Whereas university and community stations are

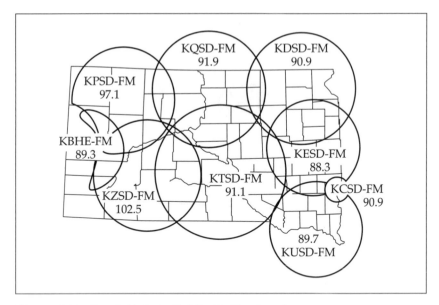

Figure 14.2: South Dakota Public Radio signal ranges

independent of one another, state licensees form intrastate networks wherein individual stations all broadcast the same material from a single operating source. In all three cases, the program schedule is determined by the licensees, featuring a mix of locally originated and nationally syndicated programming. All public stations are non-profit, non-commercial organizations with a strong mandate to broadcast programming of an educational nature.

South Dakota Public Broadcasting (SDBP) is based on the state-network system (Figures 14.2 and 14.3). The state governor appoints a seven-member board that oversees radio and the television services, each of which are managed on a day-to-day basis by another seven-member SDPB management team.[3] South Dakota Public Television (SDPTV) consists of eight stations reaching over 90 percent of the state. South Dakota Public Radio (SDPR) covers almost the entire state via nine stations whose signals are boosted by translators in more remote areas. Most SDPTV and SDPR programming originates in the town of Vermillion in the southeastern part of the state. SDPB is closely tied to the University of South Dakota, also located in Vermillion.

SDPB budget

SDPB's annual budget is US$5.7 million, of which the state provides 62 percent and the CPB provides 16 percent. The remainder is raised by an independent organization called 'Friends of South Dakota Public Broadcasting.' Friends of SDPB organizes on-air fund drives wherein

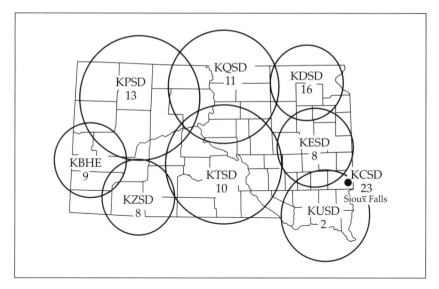

Figure 14.3: South Dakota Public Television signal ranges

viewers are urged to become 'members' of SDPB; for US$35, members receive a monthly schedule and, presumably, satisfaction in taking a direct part in the organization. Friends of SDPB also raises money via 'underwriting' – a form of promotion in which businesses pay for brief mentions of their products and services at the opening and closing of programs.

As with public broadcasting in general, SDPB has come under intense governmental scrutiny over the past decade, following a national trend toward deregulation and budget tightening. Federal and state legislators increasingly expect public broadcasters to raise more of their own money and thereby require less tax support. As a result, CPB and state funds for SDPB have not been growing despite inflation rates, and in some years have been drastically cut, but not eliminated (Brokaw 1996).

As tax funds dwindle, public broadcasters rely increasingly upon business underwriting, which to many critics, means that public broadcasting has become little more than a highbrow commercial service (Hoynes 1994). During the 1980s, federal underwriting guidelines were loosened to permit 'enhanced underwriting', including corporate logos, slogans, and descriptions of business services, thus making underwriting seem a lot like commercials. SDPB underwriters include major corporations with operations in South Dakota as well as smaller businesses and foundations located throughout the state.

According to many media critics, public broadcasting's increasing reliance upon money from businesses has a chilling effect on the types of programming featured on public radio and television. Bullert (1997), for instance, convincingly argues that reliance on business funds causes public television to shy away from controversial issues and to program 'safe', albeit mundane shows.

223

Radio programming

SDPR strips most of the same programming from Monday through Friday, with a different set of regular programs on the weekends. About one-third of the schedule is produced by SDPR. In-house productions include *SD Forum* (a mix of news and public affairs), two jazz shows, new age music, a story reading program, and a weekly series showcasing South Dakota musicians. Short news and arts features are also heard throughout the day. By far, however, the bulk of local programming consists of classical music heard weekdays from 9am to 12pm, from 1pm to 4pm, and during the late-night/early morning hours every day – over 70 hours per week.

SDPB's reliance upon classical music (and, to a lesser extent, jazz) to fill its broadcast day is common among public radio stations, giving public radio something of an elitist reputation. On the other hand, the classical/jazz format at least partially satisfies public radio's complex agenda. First, it is vaguely educational. Secondly, classical music is ideologically safe, since long-dead composers generate little controversy. Thirdly, the classical/jazz format appeals to upscale listeners who contribute to public broadcasting and who are also the target audience of specialized businesses that underwrite public broadcasting.

Besides numerous classical and jazz features, SDPR broadcasts several other syndicated programs from NPR and Public Radio International (PRI) – a second public radio program distributor founded in 1982.[4] Two of these programs – NPR's *Morning Edition* and *All Things Considered* – are among the most highly acclaimed radio news programs in the US (Looker 1995). Other syndicated programs include the popular homespun humor of *A Prairie Home Companion*, a new-age music series called *Hearts of Space*, and the Irish music of *Thistle and Shamrock* – SDPR's only international music feature.

Except for five minutes of *National Native News* heard Monday through Friday, SDPR broadcasts no regularly scheduled programs regarding Native American culture, although Native Americans make up 7 percent of South Dakota's population. Nor are there any programs with a special interest to other racial or ethnic groups or for women. Indeed, one of the major criticisms of public broadcasting in general has been an absence of programming for, about, and by minorities (Lashley 1992).

Television programming

As is typical with state licensees, a large portion of SDPTV's program schedule is reserved specifically for educational purposes – reminiscent of the pre-CPB era in which 'non-commercial television' largely meant 'educational television' (Engelman 1996). From 2am to 7am, instructional programming is broadcast through which students earn credit. Video courses include civics, photography, sociology, and anthropology. Only one of these instructional programs is produced by SDPTV; the rest are imported from other program providers.

From 7am to 5.30pm on weekdays, SDPTV broadcasts nothing but programming for small children, all of which is syndicated from PBS and other program suppliers – no fewer than 21 different series. While high-quality, educational children's programming is rare on US television, over 52 hours per week seem excessive to some critics (see, for example, Ledbetter 1997: 231–2). Indeed, children's programming on public television seems to serve much the same function as classical music and jazz on public radio, filling the daily schedule with innocuous, arguably educational programming that few people would object to.

SDPTV's evening schedule consists mostly of syndicated programming from PBS and other sources. PBS affiliates are expected to carry specific network feeds during prime time (7pm–10pm), making it rather difficult for SDPTV to program more locally produced shows during those hours. This obligation has caused some conflict between SDPTV and PBS on occasions when SDPTV broadcasts in-house programming during prime time (Van Maanen 1999).

Among PBS programs on SDPTV broadcast are *The NewsHour with Jim Lehrer* and numerous mini-series and specials. While most PBS programming seen on SDPTV is produced in the non-controversial mold so common in public broadcasting, two notable exceptions are *Frontline* and *P.O.V.* Both are hard-hitting, documentary series specializing in the exploration of sensitive issues such as homosexuality, the US military, and US foreign policy. It is doubtful, however, that either program would be broadcast by SDPTV had they not been virtually required by PBS, since programming concerning race and sexuality generate many complaints from South Dakota's conservative viewers (Doll 1999).

SDPTV also acquires programs from sources other than PBS. Several of these shows comprise SDPTV's Saturday-night line-up. These programs include 1950s and 1960s variety shows formerly seen on commercial networks (e.g. *The Lawrence Welk Show*), plus several British sitcoms such as *Are You Being Served?* and *Keeping Up Appearances*. Of all the criticisms levied against public broadcasting, none is applied with more venom than those which attack these endless reruns. Why, critics ask, does the alternative to commercial television broadcast ancient commercial fare? (Ledbetter 1997: 12–13.) In fact, *Keeping Up Appearances* and *Are You Being Served?* are also seen commercially on direct-broadcast-satellite television. One should keep in mind, however, that British programming and old reruns are often shows with the most viewer loyalty. In other words, they are money makers, and public broadcasters must walk a fine line between ideals and financial solvency.

Although local programming is highly touted in SDPTV's promotional literature, the network actually produces very few programs. In the entire month of September 1999, less than 16 hours of programming were locally produced. Even so, SDPTV managers are quick to point out that SDPTV produces more hours of local television than do most other PBS affiliates (Doll 1999).

Much of SDPB's in-house programming consists of round table discussions with calls from audience members. For example, *GardenLine* offers tips from home garden experts. More in-depth public affairs programming include *South Dakota Focus* and *Buffalo Nation Journal*. The latter is the only regular program on SDPTV of special interest to a racial minority group – in this case, Native Americans.

SDPB – between a rock and a hard place

SDPB must deal with competing and contradictory demands made by a diversity of funding sources. State government's mandate that SDPB must be educational and nonpolitical (Brokaw 1996) ensures a preponderance of instructional and children's programming. SDPB's reliance upon business contributions discourages themes that underwriters find distasteful or dangerous to their public image. Finally, SDPB must appease a wide range of viewers holding diverse opinions of what public broadcasting should be. In short, because of conflicting economic and political constraints, SDPB is not in a position to take risks (Figure 14.4).

On the other hand, it is easy to criticize public broadcasting 'in a vacuum.' Scholarly critical standards are high and difficult to meet, and if we were to examine commercial broadcasters with the same criteria, in the aggregate, commercial broadcasters would fail miserably. Commercial broadcast news is often shallow and brief, advertisements fill the broadcast hours, and most programming serves little public interest beyond entertainment. Seen in this light, SDPB surpasses much of what is available from commercial broadcasters. No commercial broadcaster in South Dakota, for instance, provides the depth of national and world news coverage presented on NPR's news services. And while SDPB dedicates little time to items of particular appeal to minorities or to criticism of dominant cultural institutions, most local commercial broadcasters provide far less. For these reasons, and despite scathing analyses, critics in the popular and scholarly press generally conclude that public broadcasters such as SDPB ultimately provide an important service to their communities – despite many limitations (Day 1995).

Minnesota Public Radio

Besides SDPR, South Dakota has one other public radio station: KRSD in Sioux Falls. KRSD's offices are on the campus of Augustana College, having been invited to take up residence by the college in the 1980s. Although it might seem out of place, KRSD is actually an affiliate of Minnesota Public Radio (MPR), the most financially successful of all state-based public broadcasting systems. (Minnesota shares South Dakota's eastern border.)

MPR has a total of 29 affiliates in Minnesota and neighboring states. These affiliates are grouped into three sets: some stations program all

Figure 14.4: SDPB *Programming Guide*
Note traditional Independence Day iconography.
Source: South Dakota Public Broadcasting.

news, while others – such as KRSD – program mostly classical music. The third set of affiliates programs a mix of news and classical.

MPR's financial success is in part due to its for-profit ventures which raise capital for its non-profit noncommercial network. MPR aggressively publishes a mail-order catalog of upscale products such as classical music CDs, videotapes of British television, and various trendy items such as gargoyle bookends and expensive chess sets. MPR also operates a for-profit radio network, and is a successful fund-raiser with regard to its non-profit stations; in its most recent fund-raiser, the network raised over US$900,000 from listeners in just five days (Hetland 1999). Other sources of MPR funding include the CPB and underwriting from some of the country's largest corporations, such as Cargill – a massive food-producing conglomeration.

227

As with public radio in general, MPR stations have been accused of programming elitist radio fare, particularly their all-classical format. And again, critics argue that MPR provides little programming of special interests to minorities, but instead relies upon programming popular among upper-class, white audiences and major corporations. On the other hand, it is worth noting once more that, at least in the case of MPR's news services, there is virtually nothing of comparable comprehensiveness in commercial radio.

Community radio in South Dakota

'The voice of the Lakota Nation'

A close relation to US public radio is known as 'community radio'. Like public radio, community stations are non-profit organizations which depend on various combinations of CPB funds, underwriting, grants, and listener contributions. However, whereas public radio is a highly polished, professional operation in which individual stations form national and statewide networks, community radio stations are only loosely federated, with minimal numbers of paid staff augmented by volunteer programmers. Volunteers play a central role in community radio, representing the voices of the community and foster – in principle, at least – a synergistic relationship between stations and their listeners. Often, independent community boards hold community stations' broadcast licences, and thus, ultimate responsibility for programming and management.

Community radio began with KPFA in Berkeley, California in 1949 (Lewis and Booth 1990). The station was the inspiration of Lewis Hill who believed that commercially sponsored radio content was extremely limited due to the timid nature of advertisers fearful of having their products associated with controversial issues. KPFA was among the first stations to appeal to listeners for financial contributions, and its programming featured a wide array of left-wing (as well as some conservative) content (Stebbins 1969).[5] KPFA management later established three other stations, thus forming Pacifica Radio which today distributes national news programs.[6]

The counter-culture movement of the 1960s motivated the creation of many more non-Pacifica community stations across the country, each of which was driven by faith in grassroots self-initiative as well as suspicion of increasingly global forms of capitalism (Barlow 1988). In 1975, 25 community radio stations formed the National Federation of Community Broadcasters (NFCB) to lobby for stations' interests and to distribute information among member stations.

South Dakota has four stations that could be characterized as 'community radio,' although only three are NFCB members.[7] Each of these four stations is located on one of the eight Indian reservations in the state (Figure 14.5). Community radio is particularly important to Native Americans on remote reservations, and since 1971, Indian rights advocates

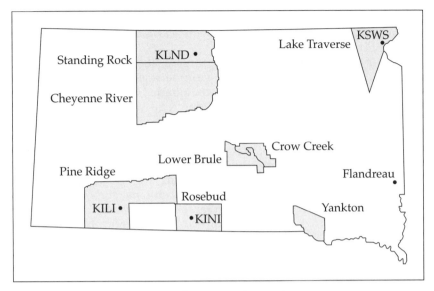

Figure 14.5: Reservations and community stations

have developed community radio as an integral means of preserving oral and musical traditions while promoting a feeling of unity within and across tribal boundaries (Rupert 1983; Keith 1995).

KILI

Of the four reservation stations, KILI (pronounced KEE-lee) is the old-est, having broadcast from the Pine Ridge Reservation since 1983. KILI is supervised by a seven-member board of directors which holds KILI's licence and is independent of the Sioux tribal governmental structure.

Like many community stations, KILI employs five full-time, paid staff members. The number of paid staff is significant, because non-commercial radio stations must employ five full-time employees in order to be eligible for CPB funding. In the case of KILI, CPB funds amount to about 30 percent of the station's annual, US$300,000 budget. Besides paid staff, 25 volunteer staff handle most of the programming as well as some administrative duties.

Along with receiving CPB funds, KILI raises money in a variety of ways: 30 percent of the station's budget is provided by local business underwriting. Also, an unusual funding event occurs once per year, when WLIB – a predominantly African American radio station in New York – broadcasts KILI programming all day; significantly, that occa-sion falls on Columbus Day, and the joint project is a reminder of mutually oppressed conditions among African Americans and Native Americans. KILI's remaining funds are provided by contributions from listeners and from others beyond the station's listening range who believe in the station's goals; fund raising beyond the station's broadcast range began in the mid-1980s when federal cutbacks almost forced the station to close down (Barlow 1998).

KILI is assisted by a fund-raising organization called Allies of the Lakota which also helps raise money for the reservation's health clinic. Together, the clinic and the station are 'founded in the belief that community control of health care, education, and communications is the key to bettering the lives of our people and ending the cycle of *poverty*' as the Allies' web page explains (www.lakotamal.com/allies).

As part of its community-strengthening mission, KILI broadcasts over one hundred public service announcements per day in both English and Lakota. Most of the station's programs are also Lakota-oriented and feature a diverse collection of music (traditional and contemporary Native music as well as mainstream fare), local news, and talk. Nationally syndicated programming is acquired from American Indian Radio on Satellite (AIROS) which nationally distributes radio programs produced by over 30 Indian nations.

For the past nine years, KILI has been managed by a non-Native, and this situation has led to occasional conflict at the station. Some listeners believe that the station should be managed by a Native American, in keeping with KILI's tribal emphasis (Peniska 1998). This conflict was particularly acute in 1992, when it, along with other disagreements concerning the firing of some station personnel, led to a long-running protest outside the station (Casey 1999). Internal strife such as this is fairly common in community radio where clear lines of authority are muddled amidst the egalitarian organizational spirit (Bareiss 1997; Hochheimer 1993).

KLND

KILI is closely associated with the newest of the four reservation-based, community stations in South Dakota – KLND broadcasting from Little Eagle on the Standing Rock Reservation. KLND has much the same organizational structure as KILI, except that KLND receives direct funding from the Standing Rock tribe totaling about US$20,000 for equipment, maintenance, and other operational costs.

Generation Media, Inc. supervises KLND's general development. The eight-member board consists of enrolled members of the Lakota tribe whose primary qualification, according to station manager, Dennis Neumann, is a strong interest in media as agents for social change (Neumann 1999).

As with KILI, Neumann is a non-Native, and this factor has led to an ongoing, low-level tension at the station; however, a much bigger problem facing KLND, according to Neumann, is educating people on how to have open, on-air discussions without evolving into chaotic discourse and defamatory content. The reservation has no history of broadcasting prior to KLND, so the rules have to be learned from scratch – all the more difficult when non-professionals are on both sides of the microphone.

KSWS

In the northeastern part of the state, KSWS is located on the Lake Traverse Reservation. Again, KSWS has five full-time, paid employees. Only four volunteers work at KSWS, strongly suggesting that direct community access to programming is very limited.

Indeed, KSWS is much more of a professional operation than either KILI or KLND, with longer blocks of programming and fewer volunteer disc jockeys. As federal funding for community radio becomes tighter, some noncommercial stations are moving in this direction and becoming more like professional, commercial stations in their management and programming strategies (Stavitsky 1994: 24–5). This means that the number of programs is reduced, with less variation in order to maintain a consistent sound throughout the day. Listeners are expected to stay with a station longer if the overall sound is consistent and, therefore, contribute more money during fund-raising periods (Stavitsky 1994). This strategy has led to particularly bitter feuds within community radio, with some insiders charging that community radio's dynamic energy and direct community involvement are sacrificed as such stations move further toward commercial and public radio broadcasting models (Campbell 1999).

KINI

Further south, on the Rosebud Reservation, KINI is a community station with a strong religious emphasis. Owned and operated by the Rosebud Educational Society of St. Francis, KINI has five full-time, paid staff members and only two volunteer disc jockeys. As with KSWS, KILI has a tight format: country music during the weekday, soft rock in the evening, and rock at night. Weekends are dominated by religious programming and oldies. Programming blocks are often interrupted with news from the Associated Press, weather, sports, and other regularly scheduled syndicated segments typical of mainstream radio. AIROS programs are not heard at all on KINI, and rap music is strictly forbidden.

KINI's religious programming includes Lutheran and Catholic services on Sundays, morning prayers every weekday, and religious music throughout the block music shows. This abundance of Christian programming, again, distinguishes KINI from other Native stations and is more typical of the many religious stations heard across the United States.

Generalizations about religious radio in the US are difficult to make, due to a wide variation among stations (Gross 2000: 116). Some stations are owned and operated by individual denominations, while others are shared by numerous religious groups. Some religious programmers purchase time on commercial stations and depend upon listener contributions, while others are noncommercial enterprises. Many religious stations broadcast within the 88.1 to 91.5 FM channel range reserved for noncommercial, educational purposes, although KINI broadcasts at 96.1 FM.

KINI does not receive funds from the CPB. Except for about US$13,000 in underwriting, KINI's US$170,000 annual budget is provided entirely by the Rosebud Educational Society, which in turn, raises funds from a variety of sources. Because of its religious affiliation, and since no funds are provided directly from listeners, KINI is not a community station in the most commonly used sense of the term.[8] Even so, KINI's commitment to community welfare and its non-profit, non-commercial status certainly place the station on the outer fringes of community radio, with strong leanings toward religious broadcasting.

A communal mandate

The four Native American community stations in South Dakota comprise a range of configurations found in community radio across the country, with KILI at one end of the spectrum, representing the most typical form of community radio, to the more mainstream sounds of KSWS and the mainstream/religious programming of KLND at the other end. Besides the fact that all four stations are non-commercial operations, the fundamental quality that unites them all is a sense of social purpose – a primary commitment to their local communities rather than to financial profit. These community stations are first and foremost place-centered, with a mandate to help residents in their listening areas via cultural programming (to promote pride and self-respect) and encouragement for listeners suffering from chronic problems faced on the reservation such as poverty, alcoholism, and drug addiction. Although most community stations in the US are not Native stations, they all share the same non-profit commitment to the social well-being of marginalized groups within their listening areas (Barlow 1988).

College radio

'Broadcasting from the basement of . . .'

The fourth major noncommercial media presence in the US is college radio. College radio licensees in the US range from small colleges, broadcasting at just ten watts, to major universities whose signals reach upwards of 60 miles. Ostensibly, college radio is a training ground for students interested in learning broadcasting first-hand, but in reality, college radio has little to do with the 'real world' of commercial radio. Most often, college stations are run by volunteer or part-time, paid student committees with minimal faculty supervision. Programming is usually produced by student volunteer deejays who play music heard nowhere else on the radio dial – independent music labels, 'alternative' music, various splinter rock genres, and so forth. Five college stations broadcast in South Dakota (Figure 14.6).

Of the public/community/college radio triumvirate, college radio has the longest history. From the early days of broadcasting, colleges

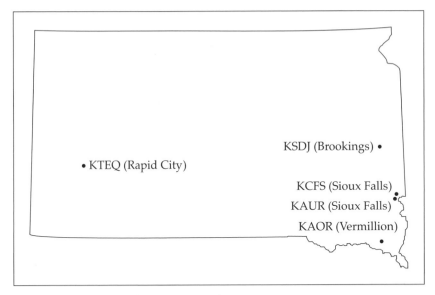

Figure 14.6: College/university radio stations

and universities operated radio stations, experimenting with radio waves at first, and later broadcasting lessons over the air (Gross 2000). The University of South Dakota (USD) in Vermillion, for example, operated a station as early as 1922.

By the late 1920s and early 1930s, however, the airwaves became crowded by commercial stations, and federal regulators – whose policies were already shaped by the commercial broadcasting model – relegated college stations to shared frequencies where they were forced to broadcast at odd times. As a result, early college radio all but faded from the airwaves (McChesney 1994).

College radio received a boost in 1945 when the Federal Communications Commission (FCC) reserved 20 FM channels for noncommercial use, largely at the behest of educational broadcasters (Avery 1988). Three years later, the FCC authorized ten-watt stations with a signal reach of less than five miles. Due to their low cost, these stations proliferated among colleges and universities. In 1978, the FCC urged '10-watters' to increase their power to 100 watts so that they could join NPR; many stations did increase their power, but few of those bothered to become NPR affiliates, preferring to remain student-run operations (Gross 2000).

An alternative mission

KSDJ, broadcasting from South Dakota State University in Brookings is a typical college station in its structure, its sound, and its carefully constructed, self-reflexive identity. KSDJ began operation in 1993 and

233

broadcasts at 90.7 FM, reaching a radius of about 15 miles. Its budget is just over US$10,000 per year, about 90 percent of which is paid by mandatory student university fees (which fund many other campus organizations). A tiny fraction of income is provided from underwriting which costs an amazingly low one dollar per spot.

KSDJ programmers are all students who program two-hour shifts of specialty shows such as 'techno,' 'alternative folk,' 'loud rock,' and more traditional genres of jazz and country. All programming is produced live, in-house from 7.30am until 2am on weekdays and from 10am until 2am on weekends. The station does not broadcast during winter and spring breaks.

Similar college stations broadcast from the campuses of the University of South Dakota in Vermillion (KAOR), the School of Mining Technology in Rapid City (KTEQ), and Augustana College (KAUR) in Sioux Falls. Again, these stations are more or less independent from academic programs, featuring volunteer deejays who program a variety of specialty shows.

The term 'alternative' is often bandied about among college stations to describe not only the programming but also the identity of the station. Although impossible to clearly define, 'alternative' has a definite anti-corporate ring to it, denoting the fact that college stations specialize in music produced by obscure bands and tiny recording companies. KAUR is particularly assertive in this regard; a sign posted in the control room warns programmers never to play top-40 songs, even if the songs were popular many years ago. Deejays violating this rule run the risk of losing their shows. Also, KAOR's web page links to other websites which are particularly bitter in their censure of the corporate music business (Figure 14.7).

Upon close examination, however, one can see that the anti-corporate sentiments implied by 'alternative' usually extend no further than the music industry itself. Virtually no overt connection is made between the grip that major corporations have on musical expression and the control that the same industrial structure has on a multitude of other inter-related phenomena such as environmental destruction and political oppression – unless those connections are made specifically in the music. Largely isolated from their off-campus communities and lacking the ethnic, racial, and ideological imperatives of community radio, college stations' approach to cultural resistance can thus seem shallow – alternative rhetoric without sociological awareness.

Be that as it may, college radio's rough-edged programming and in-your-face deejays do provide a distinctly different perspective than is heard on other stations. Their programming is usually far more vibrant and inquisitive than anything heard on either commercial radio or public radio.

Finally, it should be noted that not all college stations are driven entirely by an 'alternative' ethos. KCFS at the University of Sioux Falls, for instance, is also classifiable as a religious station because it primarily programs contemporary Christian music – usually in various alternative genres, however. Friday and Saturday nights on KCFS are

Figure 14.7: Alternative sentiments
Source: www.antigrammy.org

dedicated to alternative music more generally. KCFS' Sunday schedule is a mix of church services and Latino shows – the only Spanish-language programming heard on any non-commercial venue in the state. Sundays are also programmed by volunteers, lending a community radio atmosphere to the station on those days.

Community access cable television

Almost every city and large town in South Dakota receives cable television. As is true across the US, cable companies compete for local monopolies which are called 'franchises'. Usually, franchises involve the reservation of one or two channels for community use, and sometimes, cable companies even offer to provide equipment and training to community producers.

During the early 1970s, community access television (also known as 'public access television') reflected the counter-cultural mood of the nation. Like community radio, cable access was believed to have significant democratic potential, since reserved channels were open venues for all points of view. Unfortunately, public access television gained a reputation for self-indulgent, sometimes obscene, programming, and in some cases programming consisted of hate mongering from racist and other extremist groups. Ultimately, public-access television failed to gain a popular foothold, remaining instead, an obscure, isolated form of communication, although it does still thrive in some towns and cities where a supportive infrastructure can sustain it (Engelman 1996; Kellner 1998).

South Dakota's community access channels vary widely. Often, these channels are nothing more than a series of rotating screens with typed-in information regarding community events. In other cases, community access channels are more substantial services run by the local school system wherein students and faculty produce numerous low-budget programs. Still others record city and county government meetings and run them at various times in the following weeks. All community access stations in South Dakota are under the administration of some sort of governmental institution such as a school board.

An example of a school-managed cable channel is Owl TV in Sioux Falls through which the Sioux Valley School District has furnished cable programming since 1974. Owl operates on an annual budget of just US$50,000 which covers a teacher's salary, books, a van, and some equipment. The cable link is provided by Sioux Valley Cable which reaches all of Sioux Falls and many surrounding towns. Programming features school plays, non-profit organizational events, and some instructional shows. In all, some one hundred programs are produced annually with the most minimal equipment imaginable. Students often participate as production crew members.

A somewhat different configuration is found in Rapid City, where two channels are managed by the city council. Channel 16 is reserved for school use and began operation in 1999. Channel 2 is operated by the fire department. During the day, the signal is scrambled and used for training programs among the various fire houses. In the evening, city council and county commissioner meetings are shown live and re-run every night. Also, the police department has a regular series on Channel 2 regarding neighborhood news, and some programming is supplied by the Air Force. (An Air Force base is located near Rapid City.)

Considering the promising start of public-access television during the 1970s, the current state of community access television in South Dakota and most other US states is rather disappointing. Skeletal funding budgets and institutional barriers prohibit direct public participation, and community access channels remain an under-utilized service in most communities – especially those offering nothing more than a revolving bulletin board. Although some opportunities to produce shows do exist on a limited basis – for example, in high school production classes – the notion of participatory democracy via television production remains largely unfulfilled. Still, one could argue that replays of local government meetings at least suggest a democratic mandate by opening public meetings to those who cannot attend.

Cable, DBS and the Internet

Other alternative radio and television services are also available in South Dakota, although they don't fit neatly into the public/community/college/cable-access model typically discussed in academic literature.

Noncommercial cable and DBS stations

Besides community access channels, cable systems and direct-broadcast satellite (DBS) systems carry several other noncommercial channels. Most obviously, pay (or 'premium') movie and sports channels are commercial-free, but lacking an explicit public-service mission, such channels are not alternative media as described in this chapter. A few other, non-premium channels are worth mentioning, however. While they are virtually inaccessible to public participation (beyond call-in shows), these channels are noncommercial, and serve the public via educational and experimental programming. They are included in many basic cable packages at no extra cost. C-SPAN I and C-SPAN II, for example, cover press conferences, Congressional hearings and various types of conferences. PBS-YOU programs several telecourses in fields such as mathematics, business, and film history. LINKS shows documentaries and dramas from around the world – very rare commodities on US television, with the exception of British programming. And Turner Classic Movies shows old American films, often re-mastered and rarely seen elsewhere on US television.

Internet programming

A plethora of alternative audio and video services are becoming available over the Internet. Many public and community stations simulcast via their web pages, sometimes offering services available only on-line. SDPB, for instance, maintains an archive of audio programs on-line and will soon offer an on-line venue for amateur videographers from South Dakota.

Other forms of alternative media available on the Internet are proliferating almost daily. For instance, since July 1999, California-based Live365.com has 'broadcast' hundreds of radio 'channels' programmed entirely by amateurs from their homes; although Live365 is financially supported by banner advertisements, the radio stations do not include advertising at this time. Without doubt, the Internet surpasses all forms of electronic media discussed in this chapter with regard to public accessibility in program production; however, the public-service dimension of websites varies widely. (One can only wonder, for instance, what public benefit an audio course in conversational Klingon can possibly offer.)

Conclusion

Unresolved issues

As we have seen, alternative radio and television in South Dakota comprise an extensive, diverse, and unorganized array of public service possibilities. Arguably the most striking feature of these media is their sheer ubiquity. Virtually every mile of South Dakota is touched in some way by an alternative radio or television service. In many locations, residents receive multiple public service stations and channels. What's more, this vast array suggests a veritable cornucopia of similar media forms available across the US.

Even so, it must be remembered that all of these media forms combined attract only a tiny fraction of the radio/television audience which watches and listens to mainstream, commercial services. This marginality is arguably the most significant unifying factor among all of these services. Whereas, commercial media address audiences as consumers first and secondarily as rational citizens in order to turn a profit and stay in business, alternative media function under a different set of principles. From NPR and PBS at the national level, to the most understaffed community-access channels at the local level, alternative media embody two interrelated assumptions. First, audience members are expected to be highly selective in their media use, deliberately choosing media for intellectual enrichment and/or for meaningful forms of community participation. Secondly, alternative media in principle belong to the people and should be used as tools *for* the people – a fundamental principle in federal legislation regarding all forms of broadcasting and yet never fully realized in actuality (see Zechowski 1998).

Despite the public service ethos of alternative radio and television, we must be careful not to romanticize such media. Positions along the periphery are fraught with all sorts of complicated choices and misplaced energies. As we have seen with SDPB, an elitist tendency can work its way into the effort when compromises are made with well-meaning government authorities, *de-facto* sponsors, and even dominant voices among the audience. Also, iconoclasm can take hold, preventing essential connections from being forged between the community and noncommercial media, as we have seen with college radio. Thirdly, without a clearly defined ideological purpose (or better yet, an interconnected set of purposes), alternative media can get mired in bitter infighting as often happens with community radio. Fourthly, filters prohibiting full public accessibility hamper the democratic spirit and ultimate flowering of noncommercial media, as we have witnessed in the case of community access cable and public broadcasting. Finally, alternative media can be terribly self-indulgent – a problem that plagues community and college radio and is particularly evident on the Internet.

Tensions within alternative media

In his groundbreaking analysis of public and community radio, Barlow (1988) theorizes that noncommercial radio can be divided into two general

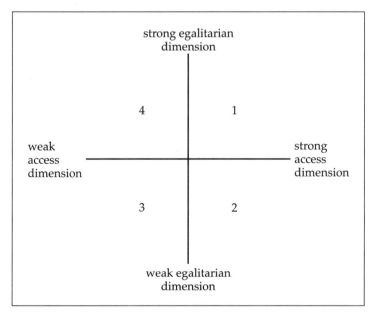

Figure 14.8: Alternative media accessibility and egalitarian sentiments

categories: Stations that are primarily 'of' their communities, and stations that are primarily 'for' their communities. Radio stations 'of' the community rely heavily upon volunteers, whose rough-edged programs represent the beliefs, experiences, and values of various segments of the listening audience. Most community stations would fall into this category. Stations 'for' the community, on the other hand, provide a more polished sound produced by professional station staff or relayed through syndication. Public radio stations primarily fall into this category. By and large, Barlow's model is based upon the degree to which noncommercial radio stations are accessible to nonprofessional program producers, with community radio being more accessible than public radio.

A new dimension could be added to Barlow's model that will help us to better understand the alternative media examined in this chapter. I will call this the 'egalitarian dimension', meaning a deliberate stance by which alternative media are used to promote perspectives that are marginalized by mainstream media in the hopes of fostering a more equitable society. As with Barlow's 'of' and 'for' notions, the egalitarian dimension is an idealized, heuristic device with no pure, real-world instances of a fully egalitarian exemplar. Instead, we may conceive of the egalitarian dimension as a continuum which, when combined with Barlow's model is represented in Figure 14.8.

Figure 14.8 illustrates four ways that alternative media can be classified according to their respective degrees of accessibility and egalitarian sentiments. Community radio station KILI, for example, would fit into

Quadrant 1 because of its heavy reliance upon volunteer programmers and its mission of promoting Native American perspectives and cultures. Community access television in South Dakota, however, would fall into Quadrant 3 due to its relative absence of both public participation and egalitarian agendas. South Dakota's college radio stations would fit into Quadrant 2, whereas SDPB would fall somewhere between Quadrants 3 and 4.

Degrees of egalitarian sentiments and public accessibility are always unstable among alternative media, causing a perpetual tension within individual settings. For instance, we have seen how community stations KILI and KLND experience ongoing conflicts regarding whether the station manager should be a Native American. And college radio seems poised for a more egalitarian approach to broadcasting, yet programmers seem to lack ideological awareness which would take them beyond fashionable alternative rhetoric. These tensions will probably never be fully resolved within any alternative media setting. Nor need they be, since conflicting views regarding the identities of alternative media suggest a vitality required for such organizations to survive. In other words, internal conflict demonstrates the fact that people of diverse opinions are interested enough to invest something of themselves and to actively participate in alternative media. In contrast, alternative media where little or no tension exists – notably, South Dakota's community access channels – are virtually dead, serving little, if any public function.

Notes

1 Thanks to the following people for their assistance in preparing this chapter: Russ Bailey, Otto Doll, Terry Harris, Carol Robertson, Larry Rohrer, and Michelle Van Maanen of SDPB; Mike Kills His Enemy and Dennis Neumann of KLND; Tom Casey of KILI; Bernard Whiting of KINI; Michael LaBelle of KSWS; Cara Hetland of KRSD; Kirk Danielson and Chris Miller of KSDJ; Hannah Ford of KAUR; Mark Tim of KCFS; Linda Clarke of the Rapid City School District, Capt. Mark Kirchgesler of the Rapid City Fire Dept. Also, thanks to South Dakota State University for release time during which this chapter was researched and written.

2 This notion is often associated with Jurgen Habermas' (1962) model of the 'public sphere'.

3 Power could feasibly be abused by such an arrangement if the governor appointed board members who were sure to carry out his/her specific political agenda. At the national level, this same possibility exists in Presidential power to appoint CPB members. Indeed, a case of power abuse in this regard allegedly occurred during the Nixon Administration in the mid-1970s (Lashley 1992).

4 PRI was initially called American Public Radio. Its name was changed in 1994.

5 Godfried (1997) writes that Chicago Federation of Labor station WCFL was the first listener-supported station, having first began broadcasting in 1926.

6 The other Pacifica stations are KPFK in Los Angeles, WBAI in New York City, and KPFT in Houston.
7 The three S.D. NFCB members are KILI, KSWS, and KLND.
8 KINI's station manager does classify the station as 'community radio', thus illustrating the vagueness of the terminology amongst non-commercial broadcasters (pers. interview, Whiting: 1999).

References

Avery, R.K. (1998) 'College and university stations', in Godfrey, D.G. & Leigh, F.A. (eds), *Historical dictionary of American radio*, Greenwood Press, Westport, Conn.

Bareiss, W. (1998) 'Public space, private face: audience construction at a noncommercial radio station', *Critical Studies in Mass Communication*, 15: 405–22.

Barlow, W. (1988) 'Community radio in the U.S.: the struggle for a democratic medium', *Media, Culture and Society*, 10: 81–105.

Bredin, M. (1991) 'Feminist cultural politics: women in community radio in Canada', *Resources for Feminist Research*, 20: 36–41.

Brokaw, C. (1996) 'Janklow backs funding for public TV, radio', *Argus Leader* (12 September) D4.

Bullert, B.J. (1997) *Public Television; Politics and the Battle Over Documentary Film*, Rutgers University Press, New Brunswick, NJ.

Butalia, U. (1993) 'Women and alternative media', in Lewis, P. (ed.), *Alternative Media; Linking the Global and Local*, Unesco Publishing.

Campbell, D. (1999) 'Radio rage', *Guardian* (9 August): 4.

Casey, T. (1999) Personal Interview (19 November), Mr. Casey is General Manager of KILI.

Day, J. (1995) *The Vanishing Vision; The Inside Story of Public Television*, University of California Press, Berkeley.

Doll, O. (1999) Personal Interview.

Eliosaph, N. (1988) 'Routines and the making of oppositional news', *Critical Studies in Mass Communication*, 5: 313–34.

Engelman, R. (1996) *Public Radio and Television in America*, Sage, Thousand Oaks.

Godfried, N. (1997) *WCFL; Chicago's voice of labor, 1926–78*, University of Illinois Press, Urbana.

Gross, L.S. (2000) *Telecommunications: An introduction to Electronic Media*, McGraw-Hill, Boston.

Habermas, J. (1962, transl. 1989) *The Structural Transformation of the Public Sphere: An Inquiry into a Category of Bourgeois Society*, The MIT Press, Cambridge, MA.

Hochheimer, J.L. (1993) 'Organizing democratic radio: issues in praxis', *Media, Culture and Society*, 15: 473–86.

Hoynes, W. (1994) *Public Television for Sale: Media, the Market, and the Public Sphere*, Westview Press, Boulder.

Keith, M. (1995) *Signals in the Air: Native Broadcasting in America*, Praeger, Westport, Conn.

Kellner, D. (1998) 'Public access television,' in Newcomb, H. (ed.), *Encyclopedia of Television*, Chicago, Fitzroy Dearborn Publishers: 1310–11.

Lashley, M. (1992) *Public Television: Panacea, Pork Barrel, or Public Trust?*, Greenwood Press, New York.

Ledbetter, J. (1997) *Made Possible by . . . The Death of Public Broadcasting in the United States*, London, Verso.

Lewis, P.M. & Booth, J. (1990) *The Invisible Medium: Public, Commercial and Community Radio*, Howard University Press, Washington, DC.

Looker, T. (1995) *The Sound and the Story: NPR and the Art of Radio*, Houghton Mifflin, Boston.

McChesney, R.W. (1994) *Telecommunications, Mass Media, & Democracy; The Battle for the Control of U.S. Broadcasting, 1928–1935*, Oxford University Press, New York.

Neumann, D. (1999) Personal Interview (November).

Peniska, K.F. (1998) 'KILI radio riding the airwaves for 15 years strong', *Indian Country Today* (30 March): B1.

Rupert, R. (1983) 'Native broadcasting in Canada', *Anthropologica*, 25: 53–61.

Schiller, H. (1989) *Culture, Inc.: The Corporate Takeover of Public Expression*, Oxford University Press, New York.

Stavitsky, A. (1994) 'The changing conceptions of localism in U.S. public radio', *Journal of Broadcasting and Electronic Media*, 38: 19–33.

Stebbins, G.R. (1969) 'Listener-sponsored radio: the Pacifica stations', dissertation, Ohio State University.

Van Maanen, M. (1999) Personal Interview (September).

Whiting, B. (1999) Personal Interview (November).

Zechowski, S. (1998) 'Public interest, research and necessity', in Newcomb, H. (ed.), *Encyclopedia of Television*, Fitzroy Dearborn Publishers, Chicago: 1311–13.

CHAPTER 15

Participatory community radios building civil society in post-war El Salvador

Diana Agosta

The argument of this chapter is that the participatory community radios of post-war El Salvador are crucial to the formation of a functional, inclusive civil society for the first time in this country's history. The radios help create civil society by creating public spaces and an inclusive public sphere, which had previously been severely constrained by limited transportation and communication infrastructure, an underdeveloped educational system, and broad repression of public organizing and expression. The radios help create a vibrant civil society in the ways that all media do – by providing visibility and publicity to the autonomous organizations that people create to express their needs and creativity; a space for debate of important issues, they strengthen a sector which can be a counterbalance to the power of the institutions of the state. But these radios are particularly effective because they are participatory in several ways: in their ownership and control, in their programming, in their collaborations with other organizations, and in their relationships with their audiences. In fact, the radios refer to themselves as 'participatory' radios rather than as 'community' radios. So in addition to providing visibility for what are now called civil society organizations, they also create a place for interaction and connection between these organizations and their constituencies through a two-way flow of information between radio programmers and audiences. In turn this helps to construct and maintain community memory and a sense of shared identity.

This paper is a work in progress, based on a year of ethnographic fieldwork in El Salvador in 1997 and 1998, during which I lived with three different communities (two rural and one urban) and worked with the three radios to document their programming, staff, and interaction with their audiences, in the context of their communities and other significant issues.

Inclusive public sphere

Especially for the rural communities, space for public interaction has been extremely limited. The radios help create civil society by creating

243

public spaces which extend existing communication and social networks, providing the conditions for an inclusive public sphere to develop. The development of this space for expression, debate and interaction has been inhibited or obstructed in the past by an underdeveloped transportation and communication infrastructure, a limited educational system, and by repression and lack of democratic processes, especially for the poor (and middle-class) rural and urban majorities.

In the countryside people are isolated not so much by distances, which are not great in a country that barely reaches 150 miles from east to west (70 north to south), but by inadequate transportation and communications systems. The road system in El Salvador was mostly developed to service the coffee industry (the main export crop on which the Salvadoran economy has been dependent for most of this century), bringing this crop from where it is grown in the north-western and south-eastern mountains to southern ports. So while most east–west and north–south highways are paved, many major roads even to department capitals are not. Trucks, certain kinds of buses, or four wheel drive cars are needed for most rural transport. Travelling even short distances can take a long time – the first handful of kilometres from the department capital to the town in Chalatenango where I stayed regularly took 30–45 minutes. And while there is an extensive and relatively inexpensive bus system which serves most areas where there are roads, only a handful of buses may pass each day, and even these are beyond the means of many rural residents. I knew many people who regularly walked two or three hours to visit family or a patron saint festival. Lack of transportation meant meetings or public gatherings beyond each small town's borders were occasional, not regular events.

Most rural towns had no household phones, only a phone company office offering service during daytime hours (as long as rain or other impediments didn't knock out the lines). In the city, more people had phones, or access to pay phones on the street. Still, projections for 1997 for San Salvador were for only 8.58 phones for every 100 inhabitants (Lungo and Oporto 1994).[1]

The major national television and radio stations reach into most regions, even the highly mountainous regions near the borders, thanks to a network of repeating towers, and border areas also receive commercial and government radio and TV signals from the neighbouring countries of Honduras, Guatemala and Nicaragua. Since the end of the war, local commercial media have sprung up as well, mostly in the larger department capitals. But these are more conceived of as purely commercial enterprises and provide minimal news or coverage of local activities.

Newspapers and print media are scarce in the countryside, limited by the weak economy and scanty transportation system as much as the low literacy rates. The returned refugee communities which started the community radios were unusual, since a major effort was made in the refugee camps to increase adult literacy, and claims of 70–90 percent functional adult literacy on their return were common. But the overall picture in these regions gives a sense of what an accomplishment, even if transitory as some claim, this was: literacy over the region of Morazán averaged 52.8 percent but ranged from 85–100 percent illiteracy near the Honduran border to 32.9 percent in the departmental capital, Gotera (Censo Nacionales 1995b: 96–7; Fundación Segundo Montes 1997: 21). For the department of Chalatenango, literacy rates were 63 percent overall but only 49 percent for women (over five) and less than 6 percent of the population had finished ninth grade (Censo Nacionales 1995a: 108).

Together these factors mean that the vibrant public spaces and places for interaction, such as cafés, meetings, plazas, or their media equivalents – newspapers, magazines, call-in radio shows – had little to support their existence. Even the network of agricultural and craft markets essentially disappeared during the war, moving to the larger towns and department capitals, victims to the fear of attack in the countryside.

The lack of a tradition of free expression or democratic governance also has contributed to the weak public sphere. For some, there is a continuing fear of any civic or organized involvement, the legacy of the repression which intensified in the decade preceding the war, and continued throughout it, so that anyone could be picked up by one of the several armed forces, paramilitary groups (or in certain situations, the guerrilla forces) and attending meetings, even prayer groups, was suspect. An explosion of criminality after the peace accords were signed meant that people still rarely ventured out after dark, even after the war. But perhaps more significant in terms of the development of civil society is the weak democratic tradition of the country. The barriers to the full exercise of democracy have historically been high in El Salvador, as in many parts of Latin America: lack of civilian control over the armed forces, many obstacles to free speech and association, overwhelming pressures from external forces pursuing their own political and economic interests. Historically Central American states have been able to repress growth of both political and cultural elements of civil society (Biekart 1999: 24–8). In El Salvador, civil society could not emerge until the 1992 peace accords implemented basic reforms, through UN, internal and international pressures. One part of civil society is the emergence and dynamism of all the activities and organizations that people create to fill their needs and desires, autonomous of the state. But the other part is what is indicated by 'civil', the roles that citizens, as legitimate members of the constituency of the state, play in structuring and constraining the state through voting, public meetings and demonstrations, and other expressions of opinion. This is still weak in El Salvador and consequently 'civil society' is not an abstract concept there: a real civil society means having an effective voting bloc of elected officials who will hear and act on your issues, not having your organization's office broken into, or not receiving (credible) death threats when advocating positions which may not particularly benefit elite sectors.

This democratic transition, and the struggle to create a civil society, still faces obstacles. For example, while the death squads and repression of the war years has mostly disappeared, attacks on civil society organizations have been increasing. I recently received a report from a solidarity organization whose first paragraph reads:

Since the beginning of 1999, non-governmental organizations (NGOs) and labor unions have faced continuous violence and threats. In the past 10 months roughly 20 organizations have suffered one or more of the following: kidnappings of activists in which no ransom was demanded, break-ins stealing valuable equipment (in one case a data base was erased and the computers left in the office), death threats and shootings. (Centro de Intercambio y Solidaridad 1999)

These attacks were not on political organizations, but on an organization that trains mental health workers, a national doctor's association, government workers' union, a women's organization, a gay/lesbian/transsexual organization, a consumer advocacy group – a wide range of groups.

The radios themselves have had to fight for their existence. While most of the urban participatory radios were able to gain legal operating licences one way or another, when the rural community-based radios filed for licences they were either turned down or the state refused to act on their requests. The radios continued to operate, risking huge fines and closure, and in fact in December 1995 the National Civilian Police was sent to seize the equipment of all eleven rural radios. But the radios maintained that they were not operating illegally, but a-legally, since existing broadcasting law did not take into account non-profit radios with social and cultural, not commercial, goals. It took over five years of intense lobbying, international support, and persistence in offering their local radio services to gain legal status for most of the rural participatory radios.

All this adds up to the fact that it has been and remains a sustained struggle to establish and maintain the basic conditions, the infrastructure and democratic space for a public sphere to develop; because of these inadequacies, the community radios, particularly in the countryside, play a critical role in providing the space for a civil society to develop. People involved in the community radios within El Salvador repeatedly differentiated between the guerrilla radios which operated during the civil war (Radio Venceremos and Radio Farabundo Martí) and the post-war community radios. The former radios were part of a social movement, they told me, and their function, in addition to being a reliable source of information about the war itself, was to 'conscientizar' (help people become conscious of their true interests) and build support for the guerrilla war effort. When the guerrilla radios were legalized as part of the peace accords, they unlinked from their constituencies and became essentially commercial radios. But the post-war community radios are meant to be open to all sides, to help build democracy. While they articulate and advocate for their communities, above all they help build this new thing called civil society – a society which for the first time in their history includes the country's broad majority populations, and in which these populations can organize and speak for themselves and be heard. Mario Maida, the co-director of one urban radio, explained that the participatory radios' purpose is, 'to give spaces to the entities, to those associations and organisations, to citizens so that they can express . . . what we are living in this country'; their programmes are 'not programmes of debate, but of encounter, with information about civil society, what it does'.[2] The radios see their role not as part of a movement, which is seen as an oppositional force acting outside of accepted means, but to help build a new, inclusive society, which allows social action on the wide range of issues that the public initiates, and within which conflicts can be resolved. Attempts to prevent this new dynamic of activity are seen not only as attacks against the particular issue, but as attacks on the whole project of building a 'civil' society.

It seemed that everyone I met in El Salvador who was involved with the radios or with the new organizations used the term 'civil society' to refer to the sense of building a new society, creating a new network of organizations serving the range of people's needs, a new set of political rules encompassing 'transparency' and popular participation, and a flowering of cultural expression. Helping civil society emerge and flourish was seen as one of the core purposes of community radio. But in the academic world, the term has been rightly criticized for its vagueness. In this section I carve a pragmatic definition of civil society, based on both the debate in scholarly literature and its use in the Salvadoran context.

One key element of this notion of civil society is its character as an arena of association which is internally diverse and conflictive. One standard definition describes civil society broadly as 'an intermediate associational realm between the state and family populated by organizations which are separate from the state, enjoy autonomy in relation to the state, and are formed voluntarily by members of society to protect or extend their interests or values' (White, cited Biekart 1999: 32–3). There are disagreements in the literature about the relationship of the state and political society to civil society (most agree that civil society is autonomous from the state but linked to it through political society, the political parties, lobbyists, etc.) and the relationship to the market, or economic society (here it seems the tendency is to include this within civil society in some way). What is interesting is that in the Salvadoran context, the distinctions or relationships between civil society and economic life have less to do with the nature of the interactions (political, economic, cultural) than the relation of the agents or actors to dominant power holders. Carlos Ayala (the director of the Jesuit University radio and a major theorist of the community radios in El Salvador) says civil society includes 'women and men who do not form part of established power, that is, neither of economic power, political power, military power, religious power, nor of the power of the large media of social communication' (Ayala 1997: 43). For example, community radios in El Salvador include as part of their constituency small, locally owned businesses, but not large national conglomerates, subsidiaries of transnationals, or businesses which are part of the power structure. For Mario Maida (a co-director of one of the urban participatory radios), the radios are constructing a new form of communication which is opening spaces for the formerly marginalized populations.[3] This could be seen as extending the public sphere beyond the elite, but their focus on the formerly marginalized and exclusion of the dominant political or economic powers makes it seem more precise to say that they are creating an alternative national public sphere (Fraser 1992).

Beyond visibility: building participation in civil society through radio

How are the 16 participatory community radios part of the 'civil society' movement? Why these radios, and not media in general, or other locations for communication such as newspapers, TV, journals, cafes, the Internet? Certainly other media and public spaces are involved, but these urban and rural radios are crucial, in my view, not only for practical reasons – they reach larger numbers of people because they are broadcast, and because of high illiteracy rates – but also because they are participatory. What does this mean?

These radios are participatory because they were created by and are controlled by the communities they serve. The post-war rural community radios were at first begun as a response to the loss of the two guerrilla stations. They were created by several communities – Segundo Montes in Morazán, around Guarjila in Chalatenango, Santa Marta in Cabañas, Nuevo Gualcho in Usulután – made up of large groups of returned refugees, who organized as communities while they were in the refugee camps and returned together to rebuild their towns and regions in El Salvador. Their self-governing *asambleas* (now being integrated into the municipal government system of the country) created local or regional radio stations, and the *junta directivas* or boards of directors of the radios include representatives of the community's self-governments, as well as representatives from significant local organizations such as women's and youth groups, and local development organizations. They are participatory because they belong to their communities, who through their town meetings and representatives on the radio's board of directors control the radios' budgets, staff, and policies.

These radios generally have small core staffs of four to five people who are paid a small *stimulo* (about half the national minimum wage – a typical family would need two or three minimum wage-earners even in the countryside) with groups of volunteers ranging from two to twenty who help with programming and other work. (Often the director is the only person from outside the community – from San Salvador or in some cases, solidarity volunteers who now live permanently in the country, from Mexico, North America or Europe.) Staff tend to be young, literate, energized, committed, and like the popular teachers, the staff is highly respected and seen as potential local leaders. At the same time, as leaders they're often expected to live to higher standards than everyone else – accusations of drinking can be cause for removal from the station, because the radios are seen as representing their founding communities to the world.

Secondly, the radios are to some extent participatory in their programming. Most music is culled from the Latin American commercial market, especially influenced by Mexico. But the selection is based on local tastes – the Mexican-based *ranchero* or country music that adults identify with; Spanish language rock, mostly from Spain, Argentina, Mexico and some border rap/reggae/techno that many youth prefer; some English language rock (usually there's a quota on this, keeping it to a minimum – while several commercial Salvadoran stations play only English language pop or classic rock). They also play Latin American pop or *romantica* (as well as bolero and other older forms) as well as Mexican pop, some Caribbean salsa and *merengue*. And there's also *musica popular* – the folk-based social protest music of Latin America, based on the *nueva cancion* or *nueva trova* which began in Cuba, and expanded to Argentina, Chile and beyond since the 1970s, plus music from Nicaragua and El Salvador itself, especially during the war years. Some of the stations feature their own recordings of local bands, which mostly fit in this category. What makes the music programmes participatory is that a large part of them are chosen directly by the audience and introduced with *saludos* (dedications) sometimes in the form of poems, for friends, birthdays, lovers, Mother's Day, graduations, or any other important events in people's lives.

While music may take up the most air time, information programmes are considered more important by the audiences; they really listen to these, versus keeping them as background (according to the survey and focus groups I did). Some stations write and broadcast their own versions of local, national and international news, choosing the stories to fit local relevance, and 'translating' the language to the ways country people talk. More common are local news programmes, which usually mean longer reports and interviews with local leaders, or about local events. For example, one of the stations has a daily, half-hour news programme, five days a week. In a month, over half of the programmes centred around activities and events of organizations which were part of the community, six focused on other local organizations, four on national or international organizations, one on local government and one on an individual. Topics ranged from post-war reconstruction programmes to agricultural development, education, women's issues, and local culture or history; two included political opinion.[4]

But *avisos* (announcements) are the main thing people listen for. They include announcements of events, opportunities, dangers, all short items contributed by both individuals and local organizations. There are no local newspapers or bulletin boards – the only other way of reaching the population is by going door to door or driving around with a truck and a loudspeaker. The *avisos* for one day in December for one station included: a meeting in the departmental capital for people with family members in the US; announcements of two different *fiestas patronales*, or town patron-saint festivals; someone looking for lost licence plates; someone calling on someone else to pay a debt; the opening of a new cattle market in the community; the vigil commemorating the El Mozote massacre, one of the major tragedies of the war which involved family members of many in the community; eye examinations available at the rehabilitation centre; a concert at the cultural centre; a trip to a religious shrine sponsored by the local pastoral group to raise funds for the community's new church; a second announcement about the vigil commemorating the massacre. Over the course of the month, local events and organizations predominated. There were 25 announcements from local organizations, six from local government, seven from individuals and four from national organizations.[5] In this way the radios are seen to be participatory; the announcements are supplied by the audience itself, they represent the audience using the radio as their own communication media. Through these announcements and the local news programmes, a sense of local activity, the existence and dynamism of all these different organizations is produced in a concrete and cumulative way. Knowing about these activities makes participation possible; this programme helps create civil society in an ongoing way.

Another way the radios are participatory, and that they create the interactive dynamic of civil society, is through their collaborations with 'civil society' organizations. They make programmes with local and national organizations; these may be short information spots, or socio-dramas used to educate audiences; they may be taped programmes supplied by national or international sources and simply introduced or contextualized by the *locutor* or on-air radio staff. For example, a programme targeted at women and women's issues made in San Salvador by a UNESCO office was played by almost all the radios in the year of my research; other examples are an environmental series made by a Latin American community radio training centre, and a history of the war based on Radio Venceremos' broadcaster's memoir. Some are produced at the stations: one radio produces a weekly programme on sustainable, ecological agricultural techniques, co-ordinated with a workshop programme of a local organization. Other examples are educational spots about cholera and about health services offered by the local health clinic. One station – the urban case study in my research – explicitly focuses on 'civil society' organizations, with an interview programme at noon everyday. Frequent guests on this programme later developed their own weekly programmes produced collaboratively with radio staff; these included a human rights centre, consumer advocacy organization, and a environmental action group. (The most participatory programme on this station, by the way, the one receiving non-stop phone calls during its entire broadcast, was one focusing on Doom/Death metal music – I'm still trying to figure this out!)

Finally, the radios are participatory because they are seen as accessible by audiences. In surveys and audience focus groups I held, the possibility of using the radio for their own messages was always ranked as one of the most important things about these radios, even if most had not used this potential yet, except for the celebratory *saludos*. Of course, the local and national commercial stations do announcements and dedications but these are not perceived as open or accessible, especially for a rural audience. The cost of transportation and lack of phone service alone, never mind the reception they would expect from station staff, are significant obstacles. And the local radios are trusted – the focus groups said commercial radios lie, but the community radios are ours, they tell the truth.

None of this programming or collaboration is ground breaking in the world of community radio practice – announcements, local news, song dedications, collaborative production, socio-dramas, close association with, and decision-making power by audiences. But in the context of the former lack of any kind of public spaces or public sphere for the populations these radios serve, the weak communications infrastructure and meagre resources available, the rural and urban participatory radios are very influential. They create visibility for the wide range of organizations which have emerged since the war. By their presence together on the radio, these organizations create a sense that their efforts are linked, are together part of something. The collaboration and participation of listeners creates a sense of a shared public sphere – (the civic sense of civil society) as well as a sense of a shared vision (the solidarity of a social movement). 'We're learning to be citizens – it's new in Central America, it's not new, since the French Revolution . . . towards democracy, not just elections, but towards a participatory democracy, more active, more real, to recuperate the term.'

Notes

1 My fieldwork took place before (or just as) the government-run phone system was being privatized, a system in which lucrative international call profits were used to subsidize local phone rates and upgrade lines, switching and other infrastructure.
2 Interviews with Mario Maida, 30 January 1998, 4 February 1998.
3 Idem.
4 Fieldnotes, December 1997.
5 Idem.

References

Ayala, Ramirez Carlos (1997) 'La comunicacion alternativa: opción de la sociedad civil', in *Comunicación Alternativa y sociedad civil*, Konrad-Adenauer-Stiftung, (based on José Ignacio López Vigil, 'Buenas ondas de la sociedad Civil', en *Chasqui*, no. 53, CIESPAL, abril, 1996, Quito, Ecuador.)
Biekart, Kees (1999) *The Politics of Civil Society Building*, Antenna Press, Amsterdam.
Censo Nacionales (1995a) V de Población y IV de Vivienda 1992. Tomo IV, Departamento de Chalatenango. Republica de El Salvador, Ministerio de Economia, Direccion General de Estado y Censos. San Salvador.
Censo Nacionales (1995b) V de Población y IV de Vivienda (1992), Tomo XIII, Departamento de Morazán. Republica de El Salvador, Ministerio de Economia, Direccion General de Estado y Censos. San Salvador.
Centro de Intercambio y Solidaridad (1999) 'Action Alert' (19 November).
Fraser, Nancy (1992) 'Rethinking the public sphere', in Calhoun, C. (ed.), *Habermas and the Public Sphere*, MIT Press, Cambridge, MA.

Fundación Segundo Montes (1997) Estudio Socio-Economico de la Comunidad Segundo Montes y sus perspectivas. Resultado de la investigación Sept – Dic. Unidad de Investigación para el desarollo. San Salvador.

Lungo, Mario, and Francisco Oporto (1994) *San Salvador, Estadisticas Basicas*, FLACSO/Proyecto, El Salvador.

Maida, M. (1998) Personal Interviews.

Index